Relaxation Techniques

For Churchill Livingstone

Commissioning editor: Mary Law
Project editor: Dinah Thom
Project manager: Valerie Burgess
Project controller: Nicola S. Haig/Pat Miller
Indexer: Liz Granger
Copy editor: Teresa Brady
Design direction: Judith Wright
Sales promotion executive: Hilary Brown

Relaxation Techniques

A Practical Handbook for the Health Care Professional

Rosemary A. Payne BSc(psychology) MCSP

Private Practitioner and Tutor in Relaxtion Techniques, Cardiff

Photographs by

Keith Bellamy MSc AIMI ABIPP ARPS RMIP

Deputy Director, Department of Medical Illustration, and Audiovisual Services,
University of Wales, College of Medicine

CHURCHILL LIVINGSTONE
EDINBURGH, HONG KONG, LONDON, MADRID, MELBOURNE, NEW YORK AND TOKYO
1995

CHURCHILL LIVINGSTONE
Medical Division of Longman Group Limited

Distributed in the United States of America by Churchill
Livingstone Inc., 650 Avenue of the Americas, New York,
N.Y. 10011, and by associated companies, branches and
representatives throughout the world.

First published 1995

ISBN 0-443-04933-5

British Library Cataloguing in Publication Data
A catalogue record for this book is available from the British
Library.

Library of Congress Cataloging in Publication Data
Payne, Rosemary.
    Relaxation techniques: a Practical handbook for the health care
professional/Rosemary A. Payne.
        p.   cm.
    Includes bibliographical references and index.
    ISBN 0-443-04933-5
    1. Relaxation.   I. Title.
    [DNLM: 1. Relaxation Techniques.   WB 545 P346r 1995]
RA785.P39   1995
613.7/9--dc20
DNLM/DLC
for Library of Congress   94-33408

Produced through Longman Malaysia, TCP

Contents

1995

Preface   VII

SECTION 1: Introduction

1. Theoretical background   3

2. General aspects of relaxation training   13

3. Stress   19

SECTION 2: Physical methods of relaxation

4. Progressive relaxation   29

5. Progressive relaxation training   37

6. A tense-release script   43

7. Passive muscular relaxation   53

8. Applied relaxation   61

9. Behavioural relaxation training   69

10. The Mitchell method   77

11. The Alexander technique   85

12. Differential relaxation   95

13. Stretchings   99

14. Physical exercise   109

15. Breathing   115

SECTION 3: Mental approaches to relaxation

16. Self-awareness   127

17. Imagery   133

18. Goal-directed visualization   143

19. Autogenic training   155

20. Meditation   161

21. The relaxation response   171

SECTION 4: Miscellaneous topics

22. 'On-the-spot' techniques   177

23. Relaxation in pregnancy and childbirth   183

24. Assessment and research   187

25. Drawing the threads together   195

Appendix and References   203

Index   213

Preface

A few years ago, when giving a talk on relaxation techniques, I was asked by a social worker if the techniques I was describing could all be found in one publication. I said I knew of no book which contained them all. Since then, other health care professionals have, on different occasions, put similar questions to me. Is there a book which focuses on the practical side of relaxation training? Can the detail of the methods be found under one cover?

Many books mention relaxation techniques but tend not to present them in any depth, that is, unless the entire work is devoted to a single method. It seemed that there was a gap which needed to be filled.

It is estimated that 80% of modern diseases have their origins in stress (Powell & Enright 1990) and that stress-related illness accounts for at least 75% of GP consultations (Looker & Gregson 1989). As concern about the safety, efficacy and cost of psychotropic drugs grows (Sibbald *et al* 1993), there is increasing interest in non-drug treatments, of which relaxation training is an example.

The book is addressed to health care professionals such as nurses, occupational therapists, physiotherapists, speech therapists and social workers; GPs and psychologists also may find it useful. It can equally be used by lay people since it is written in a non-jargon style.

Factors of practicality have governed the selection of methods. Thus, techniques which require expensive equipment or specialized expertise are not included, while the methods chosen are those which lend themselves to presentation in small group settings.

The book begins with a review of some of the theory surrounding stress and relaxation. This is followed by a chapter on general procedure which is applicable to all methods. Chapter 3 discusses stress, beginning with a further passage of theory and moving on to consider a variety of practical coping skills. The following 18 chapters each deal with a specific technique; 12 chapters are, broadly speaking, concerned with physical or 'muscular' techniques and six deal with 'mental' or psychological methods. There follows a chapter concerning 'on-the-spot' techniques for dealing with stressful situations, using skills drawn from earlier lessons. Relaxation in the antenatal context is the subject of Chapter 23, and is included because of the prominent role that relaxation plays in the field of obstetrics. Assessment is addressed in Chapter 24, and the final chapter takes a look at a few topics not so far discussed: the relation between the approaches themselves, some ways in which they can be combined, and a brief reference to approaches which are not included. Physical and psychiatric disorders are not within the scope of this work.

Techniques whose main purpose is to promote relaxation are termed primary. The 'muscular' methods belong in this category, as does autogenic training. Where relaxation is not the main purpose, the technique can be seen as secondary: visualization, meditation and the Alexander technique fall into this category. Other approaches which enhance relaxation may be still further removed. These include cognitive techniques such as uncovering irrational assumptions and modifying automatic thoughts. Here, relaxation can be seen as a side-effect rather than a goal (Fanning 1988).

It is not intended that health care professionals should, on the strength of reading this book, consider themselves teachers of autogenics and the Alexander technique. These two methods are included to indicate their contribution to the field; they are described for interest and for the applicability of their central ideas. For example, images of warmth and heaviness (autogenics) are relaxing in any context, as also is postural advice (Alexander technique). Such concepts have universal value.

Indications of the effectiveness of the techniques are included but the book does not set out to review the evidence from the scientific literature. Other works do that, for example Lichstein (1988). Pitfalls associated with some methods are listed at the end of the relevant chapters.

The word 'relaxation' is used in two ways here as it is in other works: first in a general sense where it signifies a global state of rest; and second, as a technique such as progressive relaxation. It is difficult to aviod both meanings in a book of this sort. Efforts are however made, throughout the work, to distinguish the meanings wherever ambiguity arises.

The author is aware of the implications of gender-weighted language. She is also aware of the cumbersome phrasing that can result from a determination to avoid sexist forms of speech. In an attempt to avoid both traps and for the sake of clarity, it has been decided to refer throughout the book to the trainer as female. The trainee is referred to as male in Chapters 2–15 and as female in Chapters 16–25.

The words 'trainer' and 'instructor' are both used, the choice being largely determined by the nature of the method: for example, in autogenics, progressive relaxation and behavioural relaxation training the word 'trainer' is often used, while in imagery, meditation, Alexander technique and Mitchell's approach, the word 'instructor' seems more appropriate. The word 'therapist' is also used where it seems fitting.

A number of people have helped in the making of this book. One important contributor is Mr Keith Bellamy, whose photographs have done so much to make the book what it is, not forgetting Miss Sarah McDermott, who acted as the model. I would also like to mention those who have read chapters and to whom I am indebted for their helpful suggestions. Ms Alexandra Hough, Mr Ian Hughes, Miss Wendy Mair, Mrs Margaret Polden and Dr Jim Robinson have all been kind enough to do this, and Dr Christopher Rowland Payne undertook to read the whole manuscript. Thanks also go to Dr Michael Adams, Miss Joyce Gibbs, Dr Olga Gregson, Miss Brenda MacLachland, Ms Pat Miller, Mrs Alison Ough, Mr Stuart Skyte, Mrs Dinah Thom, Miss June Tiley and Dr Elizabeth Valentine. Finally, a word of appreciation for the members of all the groups with whom I have worked. Without them, this book would never have been written.

Cardiff 1994   R.A.P.

Introduction

SECTION CONTENTS

1. Theoretical background 3

2. General aspects of relaxation training 13

3. Stress 19

CHAPTER CONTENTS

Physiological theories 4

Psychological theories 7

The 'specific effects' hypothesis and unitary theories 9

Stress management 10

Types of relaxation technique 10
 'Deep' and 'brief' relaxation 11
 Physical and mental techniques 11

1

Theoretical background

It could be said that relaxation is doing nothing; yet, many people say they find it difficult to relax. Doing nothing, it seems, is not as easy as it sounds, and the existence of a wealth of relaxation techniques appears to endorse this view.

'Relaxation' is often used with reference to muscles, where it signifies release of tension and the lengthening of muscle fibres, as opposed to the shortening which accompanies muscular tension, or contraction. Such a definition could be applied to the methods described in the earlier chapters of this book. However, since relaxation has a mental, as well as a physical, dimension, this definition is too restricted for our purposes.

A more comprehensive view comes from Sweeney (1978) who defines relaxation as 'a positively perceived state or response in which a person feels relief of tension or strain'. This includes psychological aspects of the relaxation experience, such as the pleasant sensation and absence of stressful or uncomfortable thoughts.

Thus, the word 'relaxed' is used to refer either to lax muscles or to peaceful thoughts. It is assumed that a link exists between them since an apparently general state of relaxation can be induced by using either physiological or psychological methods.

Relaxation can be said to have three aims (Titlebaum 1988):

1. As a preventive measure, to protect body organs from unnecessary wear, and in particular, the organs involved in stress-related disease (Selye 1956, 1974).

2. As a treatment, to help relieve stress in conditions such as essential hypertension (Patel & Marmot 1988), tension headache (Spinhoven et al 1992), insomnia (Lichstein 1983), asthma (Henry et al 1993), immune deficiency (Antoni et al 1991), panic (Ost 1988) and many others.

3. As a coping skill, to calm the mind and allow thinking to become clearer and more effective. Stress can impair people mentally; relaxation can help to restore clarity of thought. It has been found that positive information in memory becomes more accessible when a person is relaxed (Peveler & Johnston 1986).

Mechanisms thought to be responsible for bringing about the state of relaxation have been explored, giving rise to a number of theories. Some of these emphasize physiological aspects, such as autonomic activity and muscle tension, while others focus on psychological elements such as attitudes towards the self. The major theories are briefly described below.

PHYSIOLOGICAL THEORIES

Body systems associated with the states of stress and relaxation, include:

- the autonomic nervous system,
- the endocrine system, and
- the skeletal musculature.

The autonomic nervous system

Physiological arousal is governed by the autonomic nervous system. This has two branches: the sympathetic, which increases arousal when the organism is under threat, and the parasympathetic, which restores the body to a resting state. Their actions are involuntary and designed to enable the organism to survive (Fig. 1.1).

In a situation of challenge or excitement the sympathetic nervous system increases the activity of the heart and redistributes blood from the viscera to the voluntary muscles. Blood pressure and respiratory rate are increased; sensory awareness is heightened, and there is a mechanism for

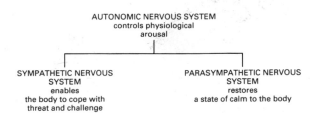

Figure 1.1 The autonomic nervous system.

losing excess heat. These factors enable the individual to make a physical response. The changes are collectively known as the 'fight–flight response', which is characterised by an increase in:

- heart rate
- blood pressure
- blood coagulation rate
- blood flow to voluntary muscles
- glucose content of the blood
- respiratory rate
- acuity of the senses
- sweat gland activity.

and a decrease of:

- activity in the digestive tract.

In the absence of challenge or excitement, these actions are reversed: the sympathetic nervous system loses its dominance and the parasympathetic assumes control. The actions of these systems are shown in greater detail in Figures 1.2 and 1.3.

Some of the changes which occur as a result of sympathetic stimulation produce noticeable symptoms such as, for example, an increased respiratory rate, palpitations and cold sweat. Such manifestations underline the association between the emotions and the internal organs. Negative emotional states, such as fear and anger particularly, are accompanied by the physiological changes associated with sympathetic activity. When the changes are pronounced and occur frequently, the organs concerned can become fatigued; which has given rise to the concept of psychosomatic illness (p. 23). The relaxation response method of Benson, aims to counteract

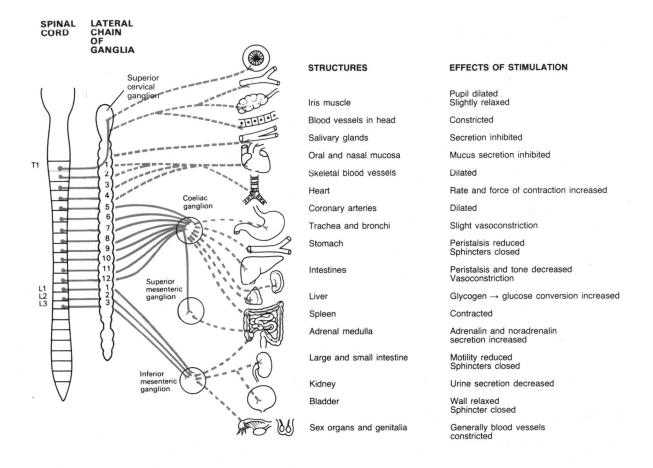

Figure 1.2 The sympathetic outflow, the main structures supplied, and the effects of stimulation. Solid lines —— preganglionic fibres; broken lines – – – postganglionic fibres. (From Wilson 1990 with permission.)

the effects of sympathetic activity by promoting the action of the parasympathetic nervous system (Ch. 21), thereby exploiting the reciprocal nature of the two parts of the autonomic nervous system.

However, activity of the parasympathetic system is not always benign (Poppen 1988). Asthma is exacerbated by bronchial constriction and gastric ulcers by acid secretion. Both bronchial constriction and acid secretion are associated with parasympathetic dominance, yet the conditions of asthma and gastric ulcer are relieved by relaxation and aggravated by stress. The theory is not consistent regarding these conditions.

The endocrine system

Closely associated with the autonomic nervous system is the endocrine system and, in particular, the adrenal glands. These release hormones which modify the action of the internal organs in response to environmental stimuli. Situated above the kidneys (Fig. 1.4), the adrenal glands consists of cortex and medulla (Fig.1.5).

The medulla produces the catecholamines noradrenaline and adrenaline, whose release is controlled by the sympathetic nervous system. Noradrenaline is thought to produce changes associated with aggression and fighting behaviour. The hormone increases alertness and creates, on the whole, a pleasant feeling of arousal.

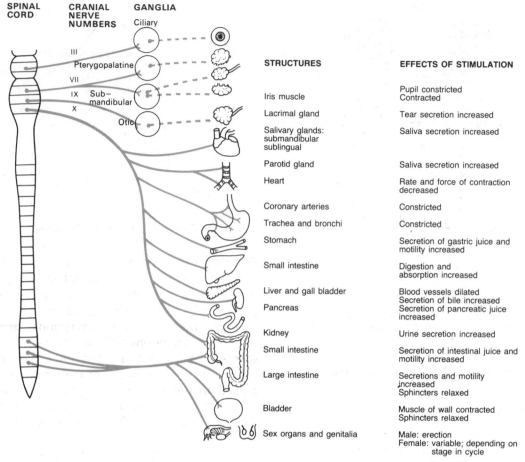

SPINAL CORD **CRANIAL NERVE NUMBERS** **GANGLIA**

Ciliary

III
Pterygopalatine
VII
IX Sub-mandibular
X
Otic

STRUCTURES	EFFECTS OF STIMULATION
Iris muscle	Pupil constricted Contracted
Lacrimal gland	Tear secretion increased
Salivary glands: submandibular sublingual	Saliva secretion increased
Parotid gland	Saliva secretion increased
Heart	Rate and force of contraction decreased
Coronary arteries	Constricted
Trachea and bronchi	Constricted
Stomach	Secretion of gastric juice and motility increased
Small intestine	Digestion and absorption increased
Liver and gall bladder	Blood vessels dilated Secretion of bile increased
Pancreas	Secretion of pancreatic juice increased
Kidney	Urine secretion increased
Small intestine	Secretion of intestinal juice and motility increased
Large intestine	Secretions and motility increased Sphincters relaxed
Bladder	Muscle of wall contracted Sphincters relaxed
Sex organs and genitalia	Male: erection Female: variable; depending on stage in cycle

Figure 1.3 The parasympathetic outflow, the main structures supplied and the effects of stimulation. Solid lines ——, preganglionic fibres; broken lines – – –, postganglionic fibres. (From Wilson 1990 with permission.)

Adrenaline is associated with anxiety and flight behaviour; blood supply to the leg is increased, feelings of threat are experienced and mental abilities are reduced (Cox 1978, Looker & Gregson 1989). Both hormones are produced under conditions of challenge, but their relative dominance seems to be influenced by the prevailing emotion. Thus, a person faced with a challenge which he perceives to be enjoyable, will tend to produce more noradrenaline than adrenaline, while a person who views the same challenge as a threat, will tend to produce more adrenaline than noradrenaline.

The adrenal cortex produces glucocorticoids, the most important of which is cortisol whose function it is to maintain the fuel supply to the muscles. In this way it promotes the action of the catecholamines. There is also evidence suggesting that normal levels of cortisol enhance the immune system (Looker & Gregson 1989, Jefferies 1991). High levels of cortisol, such as those created by prolonged stress or by pharmacological doses, are however, associated with a suppressed immune system.

Under challenge, all the above hormones are released. When the situation of challenge passes, and the stress response is no longer needed, the parasympathetic nervous system produces the chemical transmitter acetylcholine which brings about the reciprocal state, i.e. relaxation. The organs

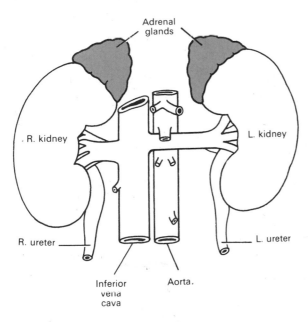

Figure 1.4 The positions of the adrenal glands and some of their associated structures. (From Wilson 1990 with permission.)

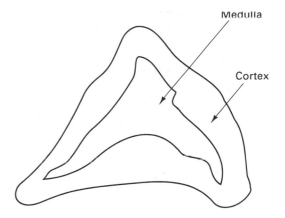

Figure 1.5 Cross-section of an adrenal gland.

which were previously activated are now at rest.

The Skeletal musculature

Jacobson (1938) proposed that the release of tension in the skeletal musculature had the effect of calming the mind. The neuromuscular system is thus seen as a mediator in the relief of stress and anxiety. Jacobson's method, progressive relaxation, consists of tense–release techniques designed to cultivate awareness of muscular sensations. This awareness allows the individual to develop the skill of consciously releasing tension (Ch. 4).

PSYCHOLOGICAL THEORIES

Three types of psychological theory concerning relaxation are discussed in this section:

- cognitive,
- behaviour, and
- cognitive–behaviour.

Cognitive theories

'Our thoughts define our universe' writes Piero Ferrucci in *What We May Be* (1982). The way we view what happens to us determines how we feel about it. This idea epitomizes the cognitive approach which sees feeling as a function of thought. Interpretations, perceptions, assumptions and conclusions will all give rise to particular feelings, which in their turn govern our behaviour. Our experience of stress and anxiety is related to the way we interpret events in our lives: we may for example, appraise situations in ways which make them appear unncessarily threatening.

Ellis (1962, 1976), a psychotherapist, attributes much anxiety to the irrational responses made by individuals, and cites the following example:

If person X puts me off, it must mean she doesn't like me, and if she doesn't like me it's probably because I'm unlikeable.

In this example the individual is basing his view of himself on one isolated event. Ellis also indicates that such a person tends to think in terms of absolutes, for example: 'I must be liked by everyone, otherwise I'll feel worthless'. An individual locked into this pattern of thinking is doomed to disappointment and anxiety because of the impossible standards he has set for himself.

The aim of treatment is for the individual to identify his irrational beliefs, to challenge them, and to consider more rational alternatives.

Beck (1984), a contemporary psychiatrist, also sees anxiety (and depression) as stemming from wrong thinking. To Beck, the distress is created by faulty thinking patterns which allow the individual to have a distorted view of events. For example:

- An individual blames himself whenever something goes wrong although he is not responsible.
- He feels he is unemployable after one job rejection.
- He blows up a minor mistake into a catastrophe: accidentally scratching his car, he sees it as irredeemably damaged.

Such a person tends to magnify his weaknesses and to see his minor mistakes as disasters; he dwells on his failures and dismisses his achievements. The first step in therapy is to identify the automatic thoughts that make up the faulty thinking patterns. This is done by keeping a diary of anxiety-related events together with the thoughts and fantasies which accompany them. These thoughts are then tested against reality by asking what evidence there is to justify them. Are there alternative explanations? Does it matter if what he fears happens? If the automatic thoughts do not stand up to reality testing, he will need to modify them. Some thought patterns may need to become more positive and less negative, but the principal aim is to help the individual adopt a more realistic view of himself, his world and his future (Beck 1976).

Recognition of the value of Beck's cognitive therapy is increasing. Its effects have been compared with pharmacological treatments, behaviour therapy, supportive nondirective therapy and anxiety management, and found to be either superior or of equal efficacy (Beck et al 1979, Durham & Turvey 1987, Blackburn & Davidson 1990).

Both Ellis and Beck see the individual as having control over his thoughts, and thus having the power to modify his feelings and his behaviour if he wants to. Their models are respectively concerned with challenging irrational thoughts and questioning faulty thinking patterns. Such approaches belong to the area of cognitive restructuring, i.e. the combatting of 'self-defeating thought patterns by reordering the client's perceptions, values and attitudes' (Lichstein 1988).

Although their theories are similar in many ways, the styles of therapy differ; Ellis adopting a confrontational approach while Beck is more collaborative (Neimeyer 1985).

While cognitive theory is referred to several times in this book, the theories of Beck and Ellis are particularly relevant to the chapter on goal-directed visualization (Ch. 18).

Also influential in this field, is Kelly (1955, 1969), whose theory of personal constructs offers a different approach. To Kelly, interpretations are not irrational or illogical, so much as the product of the way each individual construes the world. If the individual has problems, Kelly helps him work out alternative ways of looking at the world, and he does this by attempting to enter the individual's frame of reference (Neimeyer 1985). His approach is thus, essentially explorative.

While sharing the view that the interpretation of events can be as important as the events themselves, Kelly has rejected the label 'cognitive theorist'. Such a label has, in the past, implied that cognitions and emotions could be studied separately, while to Kelly, they are components of a single psychological entity. The climate has, however, changed in recent years, as cognitive theorists in general have come to see emotion and cognition as 'intricately and intimately intertwined' (Strongman 1987).

Cognitive methods may be seen to include most approaches involving the mind. Thus, self-talk and mental distancing are cognitive, as are other techniques which aim to restructure cognitions. Some of these however, are less amenable to scientific investigation than the structured approach of Beck.

Behaviour theory

Behaviour theory by contrast, is concerned with observable actions. Discounting what goes on in the mind, it sees behaviour as conditioned by environmental events. Such events are seen as leading the individual to act in predictable ways. In the case of classical conditioning, behaviour is governed by associations, for example, Pavlov's dog learned to salivate at the sound of a bell because the bell was linked with the smell of food. In the case of operant conditioning, behaviour is shaped by a system of reward and punishment. For example, a rat presses a lever on learning that lever-pressing delivers food, but avoids pressing a lever that delivers electric shocks (Skinner 1938).

Since these theories were first propounded, behaviour theory has developed in ways which take it away from its original reductionist models. However, it still retains its central principle that observable behaviour is more worthy of investigation than behaviour which is only inferred, i.e. mental processes.

Behavioural approaches include muscular relaxation, distraction, graded exposure and social skills training. Muscular relaxation is described in the early chapters of this book; distraction consists of activity which diverts the attention; graded exposure offers a step-by-step approach towards mastery over a feared object or situation, and social skills training concerns interpersonal communication and covers verbal and nonverbal behaviour. Assertiveness techniques, developed in the 1970s by Alberti & Emmons, are a central component of social skills training. These writers define the concept as behaviour where people are acting in their best interests without experiencing undue anxiety and without denying the rights of others (Alberti & Emmons 1982). Topics included in assertiveness training are:

- exercising personal rights
- setting personal priorities
- expressing views
- making requests
- refusing requests
- countering manipulative behaviour in others
- allowing oneself to make mistakes.

Behaviour styles can range from aggressive to submissive, but the style of choice in most situations is the assertive one. Knowing when and how to use it is one of the social skills.

It can be seen from the above items that assertiveness training contains a strong cognitive element. There is a certain overlap between cognitive and behavioural methods, and this has led some researchers to combine the two approaches.

Cognitive–behaviour theory

Meichenbaum & Cameron (1974) were early proponents of the integration of cognitive and behavioural techniques. Their aim was to promote behavioural change through the restructuring of conscious thoughts, an approach which was further developed by Meichenbaum (1977). Behaviour was seen as largely governed by the 'self-talk' in which we engage. This is the internal dialogue we conduct with ourselves in order to interpret the world. If the self-talk is positive, the outcome of a given task tends to be viewed in positive terms; if the self-talk is negative, the outcome tends to be viewed in negative terms. Positive self-talk leads to goal achievement and increased confidence; negative self-talk to feelings of defeat. The approach was designed to give the individual a feeling of greater control over his life and a protection against unnecessary stress.

In this, and in a later approach (Meichenbaum & Cameron 1983), three phases are planned. Phase 1 is educative and aimed at developing awareness of thoughts, feelings, sensations and behaviours; the individual identifies his self-talk. In phase two he restructures his self-talk, converting responses from negative to positive, while other coping skills such as problem solving, relaxation, assertiveness and distraction are learned and practised. Finally, in phase three, these new responses are applied to events through mental rehearsal, role play and graded exposure. The method is designed to bring about an inoculation against stress. It has been found to be effective in a wide range of anxiety states (Davis et al 1988).

Cognitive–behavioural principles underlie some of the stress-relieving strategies in Chapter 3; they also feature in some of the goal-directed visualizations in Chapter 18.

THE 'SPECIFIC EFFECTS' HYPOTHESIS AND UNITARY THEORIES

Anxiety can express itself in any of three modes: the somatic (physiological), the cognitive (mental) and the behavioural (observable actions). The 'specific effects' hypothesis (Davidson & Schwartz 1976) states that a treatment which operates in the presenting mode of the anxiety will be more effective than one which operates in a different mode; in other words, benefit can be derived from matching the treatment to the problem. For example, tension headache will be more likely to respond to a somatic approach such as releasing muscle tension than to a cognitive one such as correcting faulty thinking patterns. Thus training in one mode is inappropriate if anxiety manifests itself in another. Table 1.1 groups relaxation methods according to the presenting mode of anxiety. It is only a rough classification since some approaches, e.g. autogenics, operate in more than one mode. Even the preeminently somatic method of progressive relaxation contains cognitive elements, by virtue of the attention that is focused on muscle sensations (Ch. 4).

In contrast, unitary theories propose a single, generalized relaxation effect resulting from any one method. Benson's 'relaxation response' (Benson et al 1974) is based on the hypothesis that all relaxation techniques elicit a single, common, generalized response (Ch. 21). Jacobson's progressive relaxation method is also based on a unitary theory, in that the release of muscle tension is seen as creating a general state of relaxation (Ch. 4).

The gulf between the 'specific-effects' and 'generalized' theories narrowed somewhat when it was proposed that the specific effects them-selves might be superimposed on a general relaxation response, i.e. that any relaxation technique creates a general effect, on which is superimposed a specific pattern of changes elicited by the particular technique employed (Schwart et al 1978). The mechanism however, is far from being fully understood (Lichstein 1988).

STRESS MANAGEMENT

Relaxation training is often viewed as one component of a more comprehensive package, variously referred to as stress management, anxiety management or stress inoculation (Keable 1989, Powell & Enright 1990). What however, is stress management? There is no precise definition because it is not a specific treatment and there is no one standard method. It is a general approach which offers coping skills.

However, the varying methods do contain common threads, delineated by Lichstein (1988). There is always some element of each of the following:

- Cognitive restructuring: modifying conscious thought patterns in order to promote more sucessful behaviours.
- Relaxation for reducing physiological arousal.
- Social skills and assertiveness training to enhance interpersonal activity.
- Self-monitoring. This consists of recognizing the items which cause stress, recording their occurrence and noting the level of stress which they generate. Self-monitoring encourages an individual to take a more objective view of himself as well as charting his progress. It has been found that the very fact of monitoring increases the likelihood of desired behaviour occurring and decreases the likelihood of undesired behaviour occurring, in a phenomenon known as the 'reactivity of monitoring' (Hiebert & Fox 1981).

TABLE 1.1 Modes of anxiety and appropriate relaxation methods according to the 'specific effects hypothesis' (Davidson & Schwartz 1976)

Somatic	Progressive relaxation Applied relaxation Mitchell's relaxation Breathing
Cognitive	Cognitive restructuring Imagery Self-statements Meditation
Behavioural	Behavioural relaxation training Social skills
Cognitive and somatic	Autogenics

TYPES OF RELAXATION TECHNIQUE

Thus, relaxation is only one component of stress management. The present work focuses on that component, setting out a variety of methods and techniques. These techniques are drawn from recognized sources and are presented here in slightly paraphrased versions of the originals. Wherever possible, a short evaluation of the method is included.

The range is not comprehensive: methods which require specialized training such as hypnosis and advanced autogenics, or elaborate apparatus such as biofeedback, are left out. In general, choice has been governed by factors of practicality. The criteria for inclusion are that methods should:

- be easily learned and applied
- not require specialized expertise on the part of the trainer
- not require elaborate equipment
- be convenient for use with small groups
- be suitable for all ages.

'Deep' and 'brief' relaxation

Lichstein (1988) distinguishes between methods which create 'deep relaxation' and those which create 'brief relaxation'. Deep relaxation refers to procedures which induce an effect of large magnitude, and which are carried out in a calm environment with the trainee lying down, e.g. progressive relaxation, autogenic training, meditation. Brief relaxation refers to techniques (often contracted versions of the above) which produce immediate effects and can be used when the individual is faced with stressful events; the object here is the rapid release of excess tension. Thus, whereas deep relaxation refers to a full process of total-body relaxation, brief relaxation applies these procedures in everyday life.

Physical and mental techniques

Most methods, whether deep or brief fall roughly into one of the two broad categories: physical and psychological. The physical methods presented in this book are:

- Jacobson's progressive muscular relaxation (1938)
- Bernstein & Borkovec's modified version (1973)
- Everly & Rosenfeld's passive relaxation (1981)
- Madders' release-only (1981)
- Öst's applied relaxation (1987)
- Poppen's behavioural relaxation training (1988)
- the mitchell method (1987)
- the Alexander technique (1932)
- differential relaxation
- stretchings
- exercise
- breathing methods.

The psychological methods are:

- self-awareness
- imagery
- goal-directed visualization
- autogenic training (1969)
- meditation
- Benson's relaxation response (1976).

FURTHER READING

Physiological and psychological background
Blackburn I, Davidson K M 1990 Cognitive therapy for depression and anxiety: a practitioner's guide. Blackwell Scientific Publications, Oxford
Hawton K, Salkovskis P M, Kirk J, Clark D M (eds) 1989 Cognitive behaviour therapy for psychiatric problems. Oxford Medical, Oxford
Wilson K J W 1990 Ross and Wilson anatomy and physiology in health and illness, 7th edn. Churchill Livingstone, Edinburgh

Stress management
Keable D 1989 The management of anxiety: a manual for therapists. Churchill Livingstone, Edinburgh
Powell T J, Enright S J 1990 Anxiety and stress management. Routledge, London

CHAPTER CONTENTS

Aspects of procedure 13
  Setting 13
  Establishing confidentiality 13
  Position 13
  Introducing the method to participants 14
  Delivery 15
  Termination 15
  Homework 15
  Number of sessions 16
  The trainer/instructor/therapist 16
  Supervisory back-up 16
  Pitfalls 16
  Autonomy of the individual 16

Working with groups 16
  Organization 17
  Falling asleep 18

2

General aspects of relaxation training

Aspects of relaxation training which apply to all approaches are discussed here and include setting, confidentiality, position, introductory remarks, delivery, termination, number of sessions, homework, the therapist, supervisory back-up and pitfalls. Working with groups is then considered.

ASPECTS OF PROCEDURE

Setting

Most authorities advise a quiet, warm setting free from disturbance. However others favour one that bears more resemblance to the normal environment, on the grounds that the relaxation skills learned will be more readily transferred to real life, and also that too heavy a silence is artificial, or even anxiety-inducing. For this reason a background which includes faint external sounds may be deliberately sought.

Establishing confidentiality

In the case of group work, confidentiality must be established at the outset and reestablished each time a new member joins. Confidentiality in this context, means that nothing mentioned by a member during a session is referred to, by any other member, outside the session.

Position

For deep relaxation lying is preferable to sitting,

13

since a totally supported body will more readily lose its tension. However, some people, for different reasons, do not like lying. In defence of sitting, it can be argued that the skill of relaxing transfers to everyday situations more effectively if it is taught in a position in which stress is more likely to occur, i.e. sitting rather than lying. Another drawback of the lying position is a tendency on the part of the trainee to fall asleep (p. 18). Thus it can be seen that both positions have value and may be used on different occasions during tuition.

Various starting positions will be mentioned in later chapters. Mitchell (p. 78) lists three: lying supine, lean-forward-sitting with the arms and head supported on a high surface, and sitting upright (1987). Jacobson (1938) mentions two: lying and sitting (p. 30); Bernstein & Borkovec (1973) favour a reclining chair or an easy chair with a footstool (p. 39), as also does Poppen (1988) (p. 70).

Many groups meet in public buildings, such as schools or church halls, where the floors are wooden or tiled. These are hard, but a length of foam or a beach mattress provides a suitably softer surface and can be supplied at very little cost by the participant himself. Women will find trousers more comfortable than a skirt for most of the exercises.

Whether the eyes are open or closed is determined by the nature of the approach and the preference of the trainee.

Introducing the method to participants

An introduction which describes the method and justifies its use is advocated by proponents of all relaxation approaches. It has the advantage of:

- increasing interest and motivation
- allaying fears of the unknown

Lichstein (1988) believes that participants want to know two things above all others: that the approach is well-established, and that it works. In addition, for the benefit of any trainees who fear that they are going to be hypnotized, Hendler & Redd (1986) suggest adding a disclaimer to reassure participants that such is not the purpose.

It can also reduce the possibility of unintentional trance induction.

A sample introduction might be:

This relaxation procedure is one that has been practised for x [number of] years. It has been studied by researchers and found to be effective. You will feel very relaxed and calm as a result. It is not the same as hypnosis and you will not lose consciousness at any point.

The trainer would then proceed to describe the particular method she wished to teach. The concept of muscle action, if appropriate, could be included, as in the example below.

Muscle action

When a muscle contracts, its fibres shorten making the muscle fat. On relaxing, the muscle returns to a resting state in which the fibres are by comparison long and thin. A contracting muscle feels hard to the touch. You can illustrate this by taking your thumb across the palm of your hand and, using the fingers of the other hand, feel the muscle below the thumb getting hard. Now, relax the thumb, and feel the muscle below it become soft.

This exercise demonstrates that the relaxation, as well as the contraction of skeletal muscles is controlled by the will.

The two introductory passages above need only be stated once; however one of the two following passages may be used every time a session begins. These are used to help create the mood for relaxation by gently leading the trainee into a calm frame of mind. The first approach is called 'sinking' and the second 'imaginary bubble'. It is not necessary to use both.

Sinking

Make yourself as comfortable as you can . . . become aware of the surface underneath you . . . let your body settle into it . . . notice how it supports you . . . notice the points of contact between you and the floor: your head . . . shoulders . . . spine . . . ribs . . . hips . . . heels . . . elbows . . . forearms and hands . . . feel your body sinking into the surface you are lying on . . . feel your body getting heavier as the tension ebbs away . . . feel at peace . . . Take one good breath and as you let it out, feel it carrying all your tensions away . . . then let your breathing settle into a gentle rhythm . . .

Imaginary bubble

As you lie or sit, reflect on the idea that you are going to give the next half-hour to yourself. No telephone can ring for you; no doorbell disturb you; no-one will call your name. You may hear sounds around you: voices, horns, sirens, bangs and revs . . . think of them as being outside your world. With these thoughts in mind, draw an imaginary circle around yourself, about three feet from the centre. Create an imaginary bubble . . . think of the interior as *your* space . . . your own private space. Feel how safe it is . . . safe to get in touch with yourself. Turn your thoughts inwards.

Delivery

Any relaxation procedure calls for a tone of voice that is quiet and calm. That does not imply that it should be hypnotic. Bernstein & Borkovec suggest that the tone should be conversational to begin with, but that the volume and pace of speech should be gradually reduced as the session wears on. They advise a 'Smooth and quiet, perhaps even monotonous, but not purposely hypnotic' tone (Bernstein & Borkovec 1973).

The pauses between instructions should always be long to give the trainees time to carry out the action or to evoke the image. Dots in the text indicate these pauses.

The 'live' voice is more effective at inducing relaxation than the taped voice (Paul & Trimble 1970, Beiman et al 1978, Hillenberg & Collins 1982). Tapes are not recommended for teaching (Lichstein 1988). They may however, have value; for example, a trainee might learn initially from the live voice, then continue at home with a tape (preferably one containing the trainer's voice) until he knows the technique (Borkovec & Sides 1979). A disadvantage of tapes is that the individual may become dependent on them and unable to relax without them. Any advantage that tapes have in controlling the verbal aspect of the instruction is more relevant to research than to therapy.

Termination

All deep relaxation procedures should be brought to a gradual end, allowing the participant to make a slow return to the alert state. A variety of methods are described throughout this book. Some practitioners use a counting process; others, a simple sentence such as: 'When you feel ready, please open your eyes and sit up'. Some teachers recommend bending and stretching the limbs, while others advise sitting quietly for a few minutes. Most of the relaxation approaches mentioned in this book carry their own form of termination. The following is a sample procedure:

I am going to bring this relaxation session to an end . . . I'd like you gradually to become aware of the room . . . feel the floor/chair underneath you . . . open your eyes . . . give your limbs a few gentle stretches . . . have the feeling that you are alert and ready to carry on with your life . . .

Homework

Emphasis is placed on homework in every method of relaxation training. Relaxation is a skill, and like any other skill benefits from practice. This point needs bringing out as trainees do not always appreciate the need to practice. Investigating this topic in 1983, Hillenberg & Collins found significant levels of noncompliance in the home practice component of their study; a finding with implications for both therapy and research.

The frequency and duration of homework are conventionally set at two periods a day, each lasting 15 minutes (Bernstein & Borkovec 1973). Whether or not this should be carried out soon after meals has been debated, the above researchers pointing to the benefits of postprandial low arousal. Others however, favour avoidance of that time: Benson (1976) suggests that the process of digestion interferes with the physiological changes associated with meditation (Ch. 21). Lichstein (1988) advises trainees to experiment and find the times that best suit them.

When the tuition course has come to an end, trainees are urged to continue with some less frequent form of practising in order to extend the benefit derived from the training.

Number of sessions

It is possible to learn most methods in about six sessions, assuming that attention is given to home practice. Transcendental meditation can be taught in six, and progressive relaxation in five to ten sessions (Lichstein 1988). Many relaxation courses however, cover several methods, and may do more than simply teach relaxation. They may include group discussion, topic (see p. 23), mutual support and other concerns, thus extending the duration beyond six sessions.

The trainer/instructor/therapist

On the thorny question of training, Luthe (1970), referring to autogenics, insists that only medically qualified practitioners are equipped to teach. Lichstein (1988) views this position as untenable, believing that health care professionals have much to offer, provided they use their judgement and recognize the limits of their training. He feels that the interests of society are best served by allowing and even encouraging such individuals to teach relaxation methods.

The requirements for therapists who wish to teach relaxation methods include:

1. basic training as a health care professional
2. professional experience with the type of group with whom they are working
3. arrangements for supervision on a regular basis (see below)
4. recognition that relaxation therapy is not a panacea, while it can be a powerful tool.

A therapist is further advised to take three measures (Lichstein 1988):

1. to study beforehand the method she plans to use
2. to experience the method herself, as a trainee
3. to practise the method on friends, relatives or colleagues in order to build up a skillful presentation.

Supervisory back-up

Our own suppressed emotional experiences can be stirred by listening to other people recounting theirs. Both individual and group work can trigger emotional reactions in the therapist. Old wounds, opened in this way, may be difficult to handle and should be discussed with a colleague of greater experience. Contact with a more experienced colleague is useful for resolving other problems which may arise in a group, as well as for protecting the therapist from emotional fatigue and the possibility of 'burn-out' (a state of exhausted empathy).

Finding a supervisor is the responsibility of the therapist.

Pitfalls

Relaxation training includes techniques which can have powerful effects. It therefore needs to be handled responsibly and with due regard to the attendant pitfalls. These are discussed in the relevant chapters. It is essential, before taking up any method, to become aware of its pitfalls.

Autonomy of the individual

A central feature of relaxation training is that the individual is seen as a self-determining organism. Throughout all procedures he remains aware and free of control by outside forces. The state of relaxation he achieves is of his own making. Relaxation training is firmly rooted in this principle.

WORKING WITH GROUPS

The material in the succeeding chapters may be used with individuals or with groups of people. As group work is a subject on its own, a short summary will be relevant. Groups, in this context, may be of three kinds.

Led. Here a leader offers a previously prepared programme. Although it is presented in a systematic way, the leader displays flexibility when appropriate.

Facilitated. Responsibility for the group is taken by a particular individual who at the same time, imposes no strict format. The facilitator helps to steer the group in the way the members have decided it shall go but she avoids telling them what to do. Her role is to suggest possibilities. If problems arise however, she is responsible for dealing with them.

Self-help. There is no designated leader or facilitator. The style is informal but the members are usually highly committed, attending as they do for mutual help and support. Relevant information is collected for circulation among them and their experiences are shared. A role of acting facilitator is often rotated.

Lichstein (1988) considers that the group format is an effective way of delivering relaxation. The led group particularly lends itself to this function since an entire course can be worked out in advance. Relaxation training also occurs in facilitated and self-help groups; however, since the facilitators may not have had relevant training and experience, extra care should be taken in observing the pitfalls.

Organization

Starting a group is one matter, but keeping it going can be more difficult. In order to build up and maintain group bonding, certain points need attention.

1. *Establishing and maintaining confidentiality.* The need for confidentiality was mentioned above. It is repeated here as it cannot be overstated.

2. *Course programme.* A knowledge of what to expect enables members to make plans. Dates should be supplied in advance together with, in the case of a formal course, a syllabus.

Some classes offer relaxation alone; others begin each session with a topic related to the needs of the participants (p. 23), before moving into the area of relaxation itself.

3. *Client choice.* The sense of belonging to the group is enhanced if members are given some choice in the way it is run. How much choice depends on the nature of the group: in the formal led group, less choice than in the informal self-help group may be appropriate. However, choice can still be introduced into the formal group by finding out from the members at the outset why they joined and what they hope to get out of the meetings. This strategy helps the instructor to meet their needs and provides the participants with a more rewarding experience.

A system of paper slips can be used to collect the written answers. The alternative is to ask members directly. However, many people find it threatening to have to voice their private thoughts in front of strangers; such an approach may also be nonproductive if it draws false replies. In the author's experience, people prefer not to be asked such questions in a group context, but respond more favourably to the paper slip system (Payne 1989).

4. *Ice-breakers.* These are strategies for relaxing the atmosphere. Their essential characteristic is that the members physically participate. Some are for use in pairs while others involve the whole group. An example of the first is when one member of each pair tells the other about something pleasant that happened in the previous week; then they switch over. Another example of working in pairs is when person A talks to person B for two minutes telling him who she is and what she does. Then B talks to A.

Whole group activities are particularly useful for learning people's names. Remocker & Storch (1992) suggest a game in which each member wears a name tag. The aim is to collect everyone's name in the shortest time.

5. *Discussion.* This is an essential ingredient of any kind of group work. It provides the opportunity for members

- to express their point of view
- to exchange information and share experiences with fellow members
- to have items clarified.

It also serves to hold the group together. Powell & Enright (1990) refer to the strategy of 'circular questions' as a method of promoting interaction. This entails drawing one participant into conversation with another, for example: 'Mr Brown, you've been in this situation. What would you say to Mrs Williams who is going through the same experience?'

Although the discussion period has value, participants should not feel under any obligation to take part. The voluntary principle which states that pressure should never be exerted on individuals, must be upheld (Heron 1977).

6. *Handouts.* Printed material setting out the points made in the session acts as an aide-memoire for participants (Ley & Spelman 1967). Handouts should relate to the topic currently being discussed: the information loses its relevance if it is produced a week later.

7. *Sharing the time.* Inevitably, some people talk more than others. Trainers are glad to have 'talkers' in the group: they liven it up. At the same time, it is part of the trainer's responsibility to see that the quiet ones have an opportunity to speak. Thus, the trainer may feel that she sometimes has to intervene. A tactful way of doing it is the following: 'I don't want to dismiss what you are saying, but I wonder what X thinks about it?'

8. *Friction–dispelling techniques.* Occasionally, friction arises; a member may consistently disagree with the way the group is run. Calmly facing such a person and asking how she would like things changed, then putting it to the rest of the group, often resolves the matter.

Falling asleep

There is a tendency in group work for some members to fall asleep during the session.

This is discouraged by most therapists. Bernstein & Borkovec (1973) take the view that it interferes with the learning of a skill and suggest strategies for preventing or dealing with it:

- regularly asking for signals (e.g. the lifted index finger to confirm that the individual is relaxed)
- directing the voice towards the sleeping trainee
- avoiding the early afternoon for teaching sessions.

Keable (1989) suggests informing participants at the outset that they will be awakened with a light tap if they fall asleep. Others suggest that people who are inclined to fall asleep should sit in a chair rather than lie down, since making people less comfortable reduces their tendency to fall asleep (Lichstein 1988). Kokoszka (1992) refers to the effectiveness of focusing attention on a monotonous stimulus, e.g. counting breaths, for keeping people awake.

Thus, falling asleep tends to be seen in negative terms. Fanning (1988) however, takes the view that if people have come purely for respite from stress, they should be allowed to sleep. Snoring is more difficult to justify as it may disturb the other participants.

CHAPTER CONTENTS

Theories of stress 19

Symptoms of stress 21

Measuring of stress 21

Sources of stress 21
Stress in the environment 21
Stress in the individual 22

Stress-related topics as a component of relaxation training 23
Some ideas for reducing stress 24

3

Stress

THEORIES OF STRESS

The concept of stress in relation to the living organism was studied by Selye (1956). His work showed that when a body is subjected to a challenging stimulus, a characteristic response occurs. Selye identified three stages (Fig. 3.1):

- alarm
- resistance
- exhaustion.

Exposure to the stimulus results in the release of hormones and chemicals whose purpose is to create appropriate physiological changes. This is the alarm reaction. It is cancelled as soon as the stressor is withdrawn. If exposure to the stressor persists, the body will adapt by developing a

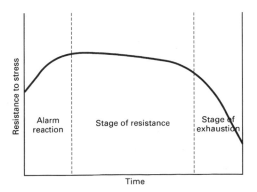

Figure 3.1 The 'general adaptation syndrome'. (Adapted from Cox T 1978. Stress. With permission from Macmillan, London.)

resistance which serves it well at the time. Such resistance however, takes a toll of the organism's resources and the stage will not last indefinitely. As body resources become depleted, a stage of exhaustion takes over. Together these stages make up the 'general adaptation syndrome'. (Selye 1956).

Selye, whose concern was for physiological aspects, viewed stress as the nonspecific response of the body to any demand made on it. (By nonspecific, he meant that the same response would occur irrespective of the nature of the stimulus.) Twenty years later, the psychologists Cox & Mackay (1976) defined stress as 'a perceptual phenomenon arising from a comparison between the demand on the person and his ability to cope. An imbalance . . . gives rise to the experience of stress and to the stress response'. The emphasis here is on the individual's perceptions, on the subjective nature of stress and on its psychological dimension. Selye in 1956, had ignored the role of psychological processes (Cox 1978).

Cox & Mackay's model introduces the idea of perceived coping powers as a factor governing the resulting stress. If an individual perceives his ability to cope as weak, and sees environmental demands as heavy, the level of stress he experiences will be high. If his self-perceived coping powers are strong, then those same demands may be readily tolerated and the level of stress experienced will be comparatively low. The environmental demands may, however, be too low, so low that stress arises from boredom. When the individual's perception of environmental demand is matched by his perceived coping ability, a state of balance can be said to exist.

It is clearly desirable for the individual to operate in situations where demands and coping skills are balanced. Establishing and maintaining that balance may involve regulating his exposure to the stressor. Alternatively he could reduce his anxiety levels and increase his coping ability.

This is a model which allows for variation among individuals as well as for changing perceptions over time in the same person. The ideas enshrined in it have led to the concept of the 'human performance curve' which is based on

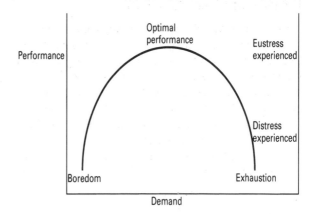

Figure 3.2 Human performance curve. (Adapted from Cox T 1978. Stress. With permission from Macmillan, London.)

the relationship between demands placed on the individual and his coping ability (Fig. 3.2). Moderate levels of demand are associated with efficient performance. When demands are perceived as too heavy, the overtaxed individual begins to experience fatigue; when they are too low, boredom results from understimulation. Distress is experienced in both events (Looker & Gregson 1989).

At the top of the curve is the zone of high performance. Here the individual is operating at levels of demand which match his coping skills. Daily variation may result in one slightly outweighing the other, for example, sometimes he feels that he has more capacity than he is being called upon to use, which gives him a feeling of confidence and control; other times he may feel that environmental demands are mildly drawing on untapped inner resources, creating the rewarding experience of being pleasantly stretched. These feelings are collectively referred to as 'eustress' or 'good' stress.

Lower down the curve, on either side, the individual's experience gradually becomes more negative as the curve runs through transition zones of moderate stress and ultimately, into zones of deep distress.

Thus, while distress erodes his quality of life, eustress enhances it. Working at levels of arousal that feel comfortable promotes not only the efficiency of the individual's output, but also his mental well-being.

SYMPTOMS OF STRESS

Stress is associated with physiological symptoms, characteristic of sympathetic nervous system activity. These symptoms relate to the fight/flight response (p. 4) and are summarized below, together with the psychological symptoms of stress, both the subjective (how a person feels) and the behavioural (how a person acts), although there is some overlap in these areas.

The symptoms vary among individuals because of the differing sensitivities of organs to the experience of stress.

Physiological symptoms

As mentioned in Chapter 1, these comprise:

- raised heart rate
- increased blood pressure
- sweating
- raised blood coagulation rate
- increased ventilation
- raised blood glucose level.

Subjective symptoms

These include:

- tiredness and/or difficulty in sleeping
- muscle tension particularly in neck and shoulder muscles
- indigestion, constipation, diarrhoea
- palpitations
- headache
- difficulty in concentrating and a tendency to worry
- impatience; feeling irritable and easily roused to anger.

Behavioural symptoms

Behavioural symptoms include:

- increased consumption of alcohol, tobacco, food, etc.
- loss of appetite or excessive eating
- restlessness
- loss of sexual interest
- a tendency to experience accidents.

MEASURING STRESS

A Physiological assessment of stress would include measurements of heart rate, blood pressure, respiratory rate and skin conductance. Psychological as well as physiological attempts have been made to measure stress. One which has had particular influence is the Social Readjustment Rating Scale of Holmes & Rahe (1967). These researchers compiled a table of life events ranging from minor violations of the law to the death of a spouse, rating each one in terms of the mental readjustment it demanded (Table 3.1). Scoring over 300 in one year was associated with a high risk of developing a stress-related illness. There are however, difficulties with this kind of approach. First, an event can have a different meaning for individuals; moving house for example, can be a pleasant form of stress if you choose to move, but a source of deep distress if you are forced to do so. Second, some people adjust more readily to change than others, as may be seen in their varying reactions to events such as retirement.

This rating scale has been much modified by subsequent researchers who have devised versions which seek to overcome some of these criticisms.

SOURCES OF STRESS

Stress can arise from a multitude of sources. Broadly speaking, these sources can be categorized as those in the environment and those within the individual (Powell & Enright 1990).

Stress in the environment

The work environment

Conditions may be such that the levels of noise are excessively high; it may be too hot or too cold; the atmosphere may be polluted by tobacco smoke or exhaust fumes.

The individual may be suffering from work overload in the form of unrealistic deadlines, long hours or a feeling that the job is beyond his competence. On the other hand, the job may lack stimulation causing him to feel bored; or it may lack opportunity for him to demonstrate his ability.

Table 3.1 The social readjustment rating scale. (Reprinted from Holmes T H & Rahe R H 1967 Journal of Psychosomatic Research 11: 213–218, with kind permission from Elsevier Science)

Rank	Life event	Mean value
1	Death of spouse	100
2	Divorce	73
3	Marital separation	65
4	Jail term	63
5	Death of close family member	63
6	Personal injury or illness	53
7	Marriage	50
8	Fired at work	47
9	Marital reconciliation	45
10	Retirement	45
11	Change in health of family member	44
12	Pregnancy	40
13	Sex difficulties	39
14	Gain of new family member	39
15	Business readjustment	39
16	Change in financial state	38
17	Death of close friend	37
18	Change to different line of work	36
19	Change in number of arguments with spouse	35
20	Mortgage over $10 000	31
21	Foreclosure of mortgage or loan	30
22	Change in responsibilities at work	29
23	Son or daughter leaving home	29
24	Trouble with in-laws	29
25	Outstanding personal achievement	28
26	Wife begins or stops work	26
27	Begin or end school	26
28	Change in living conditions	25
29	Revision of personal habits	24
30	Trouble with boss	23
31	Change in work hours or conditions	20
32	Change in residence	20
33	Change in schools	20
34	Change in recreation	19
35	Change in church activities	19
36	Change in social activities	18
37	Mortgage or loan less than $10 000	17
38	Change in sleeping habits	16
39	Change in number of family get-togethers	15
40	Change in eating habits	15
41	Vacation	13
42	Christmas	12
43	Minor violations of the law	11

There may be uncertainty as to the boundaries of his responsibility and the work objectives may be inadequately defined. Relationships with colleagues and superiors may be strained. He may be obliged to move to other departments or to other geographical locations; he may be declared redundant or be forced to retire before he wants to (Powell & Enright 1990).

The social environment

Social support has been shown to moderate the effect of negative life events. Where there is an absence of supportive relationships and the individual is unable to share his burdens, he experiences their full impact (Ganster & Victor 1988).

Stress in the individual

Personality types

Friedman & Rosenman (1974) described a personality type particularly associated with coronary heart disease. This type was characterized by a tendency for the individual to:

- drive himself to achieve goals one after another
- have a spirit of fierce competitiveness
- create a programme filled with deadlines
- perform activities as fast as possible
- be excessively alert
- have a constant need to be recognized.

Individuals who displayed these tendencies were referred to as 'Type A' personalities, while those with the opposite characteristics were described as 'Type B'. Type B individuals were found to be almost immune to coronary heart disease. Type A characteristics are seen as negative insofar as they may lead to stress-related illness. However, they also lead to high achievement which is to be valued. Cooper (1981) suggests emphasizing the need to *manage* Type A behaviour rather than extinguish it. This may mean slowing down, resetting goals, regularly taking five minutes off and recording the occasions when this is performed. It may also mean seeking alternative ways of gaining rewards.

Kobasa (1982) described what he called the 'hardy' personality. Such a person was seen as being relatively resistant to stress by virtue of possessing three qualities: a sense of control over his life, a feeling of being committed to his work, hobby or family, and a sense of challenge in which change was viewed as an opportunity to develop himself rather than a threat to his equilibrium. Individuals who do not possess these qualities are more likely to suffer from stress than those who do.

Other stressors of internal origin

Beck (1984) refers to stressors of internal origin, such as the tendency to interpret events in a consistently negative way. Ellis (1962) points to the maladaptive effect of holding unrealistic belief systems, for instance believing one has to be right every time in order to be a worthwhile person (p. 7). Other maladaptative styles include:

• Having unclear goals; a lot of effort can be wasted if people do not know where they are going.

• Failing to make decisions; unmade decisions can so preoccupy the individual that he cannot get on with his life. The unresolved matter continues to claim his attention and eventually wears him out.

• Bottling up emotions; anxiety and anger are examples of emotions that people often keep to themselves, allowing the feelings to grow out of proportion.

• Having low self-esteem; a feeling that one lacks the rights that are accorded to others. Such a person may allow himself to be overruled on every side.

STRESS-RELATED TOPICS AS A COMPONENT OF RELAXATION TRAINING

When offering relaxation training sessions to a group of people, the health care professional may wish to include certain topics and a discussion. The topics will relate to those conditions from which group members are suffering and may include some of the following:

• Anxiety, panic.
• Depression.
• Substance dependency, e.g. tobacco, alcohol, tranquillizers.
• Life crises, e.g. bereavement.
• Life changes, e.g. menopause.
• Eating disorders, e.g. bulimia, anorexia.
• Insomnia.
• Hyperventilation.
• Stress-related physical disorders. Stress has been associated with a number of medical conditions such as bronchial asthma, essential hypertension, peptic ulcer, ulcerative colitis, neurodermatitis, rheumatoid arthritis and thyrotoxicosis. These conditions have been described as psychosomatic illnesses. The concept of psychosomatic illness has, however, been extended in recent years, from the original few illnesses for which the term was coined to include many more, as it has come to be realized that psychosocial elements are present in the aetiology of a wide variety of medical conditions (Robinson 1994).

(Relaxation should not be seen as a substitute for medical help. However, insofar as stress is an acknowledged component of any particular condition, health care professionals may find themselves being asked to help alleviate it.)

It is assumed that the instructor has knowledge concerning the problems from which her group members are suffering, and is in a position to provide material about the topic. This can in turn lead into a discussion. The relaxation method subsequently offered can where possible, be linked to it, for example: slow breathing can be offered in the case of hyperventilation (p. 119), smoking cessation imagery for people quitting smoking (p. 148), and eye and tongue exercises in cases of insomnia (p. 34).

In a study investigating the components of stress management, Powell (1987) reports that information and group support were rated the most helpful components of the treatment package. The present author however, found that participants rated relaxation as the most helpful element, in a small study conducted on self-referred members of a led group featuring information concerning a topic, discussion and relaxation (Payne 1989).

The topic can revolve around coping skills, such as assertiveness as well as causes of stress. Other examples of coping skills are given in the list below, which could also provide starting points for discussion.

Some ideas for reducing stress

1. Getting as much control over the stressor as circumstances allow. While accepting the restrictions of the situation, there may be areas of freedom which can be developed.

2. If control is not possible or expedient, a person can change the way he thinks about the stressor: for example, instead of being irritated by traffic queues, he could see the time as an opportunity to play music tapes.

3. Training oneself to predict stressful situations in order to weaken their impact.

4. Being task-oriented and not letting emotions take over. Emotions fuddle the mind and interfere with problem solving. If the emotion is strong, it can first be acknowledged, then separated from the issue which can then be judged dispassionately.

5. Avoidance of blaming; the latter tends to arouse anger. A more constructive attitude is to see mistakes as the result of a series of events which simply happened.

6. Dealing with anger. Some anger may serve a useful purpose; much anger however, is purely destructive. The energy that goes into its arousal could often be more profitably spent in solving the problem. Ways in which anger can be controlled include:
- Reinterpreting the stimulus in a more positive light; many situations contain ambiguities which allow reinterpretations to be made.
- Being realistic in his expectations of other people.
- Modifying his internal dialogue to include self-statements such as 'I am easygoing' or 'I keep my cool'.
- Focusing on the issue rather than the personality.

7. Giving oneself permission to make a mistake. It is part of being human to make mistakes occasionally.

8. Distancing oneself. If circumstances seem to be overwhelming, one can try stepping back mentally to get a more objective view (p. 139 and p. 146). It is sometimes useful to visualize another person coping with the same problem.

9. Introducing humour at suitable moments. When a person smiles and laughs the relaxation response takes over (p. 198).

10. Managing time efficiently. Priorities need to be established and time allotted to tasks proportionately. If time is short, inessentials can be cut out and tasks delegated. It is sometimes possible to say 'No' to demands that would further restrict the available time.

11. Having someone to confide in.

12. Rewarding himself if he has done a job well.

13. Living in the present. This means savouring the moment; enjoying the journey as well as the arrival. A lot of stress arises from regret for the past and fear of the future.

14. Establishing good relationships. The support derived from both intimate relationships and the wider social network acts as a buffer to protect the individual from the full effects of stressful events (Ganster & Victor 1988). Relationships, however, whether at work or at home, demand time and attention.

15. Taking exercise (Ch. 14).

Table 3.2 sets out some stress-evoking factors alongside appropriate coping strategies.

Table 3.2 Stress-evoking factors and related coping strategies

Stress-evoking factor	Coping strategies
Faulty belief system	Cognitive restructuring
Unclear goals	Goal setting
Unmade decisions	Decision making
Low self-esteem	Building positive self-image
Bottling up feelings	Confiding, assertiveness
Deadlines and time constraints	Restructuring time
Deteriorating relationships	Enhancing personal interaction

FURTHER READING

Burnard P 1991 Coping with stress in the health professions: a practical guide. Chapman and Hall, London

Fisher S, Reason J (eds) 1988 A handbook of life stress, cognition and health. John Wiley, Chichester

Fletcher B 1991 Work, stress, disease and life expectancy. John Wiley, Chichester

Looker T, Gregson O 1989 Stresswise: a practical guide for dealing with stress. Hodder and Stoughton, London

Robinson J O 1994 Personal communication

Physical methods of relaxation

SECTION CONTENTS

4. Progressive relaxation 29

5. Progressive relaxation training 37

6. A tenserelease script 43

7. Passive muscular relaxation 53

8. Applied relaxation 61

9. Behavioural relaxation training 69

10. Physiological relaxation: the Mitchell method 77

11. The Alexander technique 85

12. Differential relaxation 95

13. Stretchings 99

14. Physical exercise 109

15. Breathing 115

CHAPTER CONTENTS

The work of Edmund Jacobson 29

Presenting progressive relaxation 30
  Conditions 30
  Introducing the method 30
  Procedure 31
  'Diminishing tensions' 33
  Eye movements 33
  Speech movements 34

Further work of Jacobson's 35
  Differential relaxation 35
  Self-operations control 35

Evaluation of progressive relaxation 35

Pitfalls of muscular relaxation 36

4

Progressive relaxation

THE WORK OF EDMUND JACOBSON

To many people, relaxation training means learning techniques such as 'tense–release', i.e. the tightening and letting-go of specific muscle groups. Tense–release is an active process in the sense that the individual is working his muscles. Some muscle relaxation methods however, are concerned only with the 'release' part of the sequence, and these could be described as passive muscular approaches.

This chapter introduces the work of Edmund Jacobson, a pioneer in this field. His work lays the foundation of both the tense–release and the passive approaches, which are described here and in Chapters 5–8.

Working as a physiologist-physician in the 1930s, Jacobson was investigating the startle reaction that follows a sudden loud noise. He noticed that when subjects had been taught to relax their muscles, they made no start. Thus, the state of the muscle influenced the magnitude of the reflex. He invented a technique for measuring the electrical activity in muscles and nerves which became known as electromyography (EMG), and which allowed him to study aspects of mind–body interaction. As a result, he found that thinking was related to muscle state and that mental images, particularly those associated with movement, were accompanied by small but detectable levels of activity in the muscles concerned.

This integrated activity between the mind and the muscles led him to view the brain centres and the voluntary muscles as working together 'in one effort circuit' (Jacobson 1970); a neuromuscular circuit since it was composed of both neural and muscular tissue. He proposed that a relaxed musculature could lead to the quietening of thoughts and the reduction of sympathetic activity, and saw his task as finding a way of inducing the skeletal muscles to lose their tension.

Muscle activity is accompanied by sensations so faint that we do not normally notice them. To promote awareness of tension, Jacobson emphasized the need to concentrate on those sensations, cultivating what he called 'learned awareness'. Once tension had been recognized, it would be easier to release it. If relaxation were then achieved, however, how deep would it be?

It is traditionally held that healthy muscle, even during rest, is in a state of sustained, slight contraction. This is called muscle tone. Jacobson's EMG studies (1938) did not however, support this notion. He found that voluntary muscle could achieve a state of complete relaxation during rest. He consequently formed the view that the aim of relaxation training should be to eliminate all tension; and relaxation could only be called complete if it proceeded 'to the zero point of tonus for the part or parts involved' (Jacobson 1938). Any tension that remained while resting a muscle was called 'residual', and it was this residual tension that Jacobson sought to eliminate in deep relaxation. 'Doing away with residual tension is . . . the essential feature of the present method' (Jacobson 1976).

Defining relaxation as the cessation of activity in the skeletal (voluntary) muscles, Jacobson devised a technique which he called progressive relaxation. It consisted of systematically working through the major skeletal muscle groups, creating and releasing tension. As a result, the trainee learned how to recognize muscle tension. Only one muscle action was carried out in each session and it was repeated twice. The rest of the time was spent releasing tension. Jacobson (1938) insisted that his method be regarded as a skill to be learned. Unlike most other approaches, he discouraged the use of suggestion. Trainers were urged to avoid planting ideas of the kind: 'Your limbs are heavy/limp/relaxed' or even 'Notice how your limbs are feeling heavy/limp/relaxed'.

Jacobson wanted the learner to make his own discoveries.

PRESENTING PROGRESSIVE RELAXATION

Conditions

Ideal conditions for presenting progressive relaxation include the following.

- A room that is quiet.
- Somewhere to lie down. A large room with a wooden floor is suitable for a group. Trainees may be asked to bring a beach mattress or the equivalent to lie on, and a small pillow for the head. Lying is the position of choice; however, it is possible to learn progressive relaxation in the sitting position.

Introducing the method

Before starting the training proper, the basis of the method must be introduced. With the trainees seated, the trainer describes the rationale of progressive relaxation on the following lines:

Knowing how to rest the body enables body energy to be used more efficiently. It can also help to protect us from illness. This is a method of relaxing that involves the muscles. By creating and releasing tension you will learn to tune into subtle feelings in the muscles, to recognize different levels of tension and to release that tension.

Muscle tension is believed to be closely associated with your state of mind: it is believed that muscles which are unnecessarily tense reflect their tension in the mind. If that muscle tension can be released, you will feel mentally calmer.

Your internal organs will also benefit in that pulse rate and blood pressure will be lowered while you are relaxing.

The method we are using is called progressive relaxation. It is not possible to learn it in one lesson. However, every bit as important as the lessons is the practice that you put in, between them. Like any skill, the more you practise it, the more proficient you will become, and the more you will benefit from its effects, in this case, relaxation.

The muscle action to be taught is then demonstrated, after which trainees are asked to lie down, face upwards, with arms resting on either side of the body, legs uncrossed. The eyes are open to begin with, but after three or four minutes, trainees are asked to close them and to spend a few minutes quietly unwinding.

Procedure

First session: wrist bending backwards

A first session would take the following form. The trainee is asked to extend the left wrist (bend it back) and to hold it in that position for one minute (Fig. 4.1). He then releases the tension, letting it go all at once, and continues to relax it for three minutes while he releases any residual tension. This action is then repeated twice. The instruction might run as follows:

Would you please bend the left hand back at the wrist. Do this steadily without seesawing . . . and avoid raising the forearm . . . continue to hold the hand back for a full minute, noticing the different sensations you get from doing it.

Using Jacobson's technique, it is not suggested to the trainee what these sensations might be; the idea is that the trainee should discover them for himself. However, in this case they would include tension in the working muscles, situated along the top of the forearm, together with some sensations of strain in the wrist joint and skin-stretching in the palm. Of these, it is the muscle sensations that the trainee should learn to focus on.

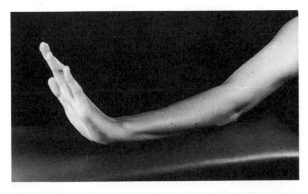

Figure 4.1 Wrist-bending backwards.

As you continue to bend your wrist back, distinguish between the various feelings you are experiencing . . . pick out particularly those related to the muscles . . . concentrate on the sensation of tenseness . . . keeping the action sustained until the minute is up . . .

And now, discontinue the action . . . allow the hand to fall by its own weight. Let it flop down. Avoid lowering it or in any way controlling its descent.

Although you have let go as completely as you could, there may still be some tension there. Give it plenty of time to disappear . . . give it at least three minutes . . .

Now, bend the wrist back a second time . . . feel the effort . . . if you are finding difficulty in sorting out the feelings in the arm, allow the hand to fall down and try the following: with your right hand, pick up the left hand and gently press it back as if it didn't belong to you . . . continue to press for about half a minute. Make sure the right hand does all the work. The feelings you're getting are coming from the wrist and from the palm. With your left hand still bent back, take away your right hand and as you do, transfer the power to your left arm. You are now using muscles in the left forearm to hold the left wrist back. Notice the new feelings you are getting now . . . these are the feelings you are asked to concentrate on . . . continue to hold the wrist back for about a minute . . .

Now, cease the action and allow the hand to fall down, letting all the tension go . . . letting the muscle go negative . . . continue in that direction for the next three minutes . . .

The trainee is not asked to 'relax', which Jacobson felt might create tensions on its own account, but to 'discontinue', 'cease to bend' or 'go negative'. Relaxation occurs on its own as the learner releases tension.

One further repetition is carried out before the trainee adopts a state of continuous rest for the remainder of the hour when the session comes to an end.

Second session: wrist-bending forwards

At the following session a new action is introduced: wrist flexion (bending forwards). This action follows the same pattern as the previous one except that the wrist is bent forwards instead of backwards (Fig. 4.2).

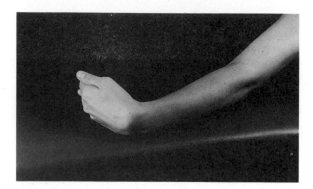

Figure 4.2 Wrist-bending forwards.

I'd like you to bend the left hand forward at the wrist . . . hold the position steadily . . . locate the
feeling of tenseness (the underside of the forearm) . . . and . . . (when the minute is up) . . . discontinue the action . . . let the hand fall back . . . continue letting go any remaining tension over the next few minutes . . .

Two repetitions are carried out, after which the trainee rests. That marks the end of session number two.

Third and subsequent sessions

The third session does not contain any tensing component. Instead, the time is entirely devoted to releasing tension. Subsequent sessions are spent addressing other actions (90 in all) and may cover many weeks. The protocol is outlined below and laid out in full in Table 4.1.

Table 4.1 Progressive relaxation: schedule of items. The participant is supine for these procedures. Adapted from Jacobson (1964)

Arms	Extend wrist (bend hand back)
	Flex wrist (bend hand forward)
	Relax only
	Flex (bend) elbow
	Extend elbow (straighten arm)
	Relax only
	Stiffen whole arm
Legs	Dorsiflex foot (bend foot up at ankle joint)
	Plantarflex foot (bend foot down at ankle joint)
	Relax only
	Extend (straighten) knee from a bent position
	Flex (bend) knee dragging foot along floor
	Relax only
	Flex hip (raise bent knee towards chest)
	Extend hip (press thigh down into floor)
	Relax only
	Stiffen entire leg
Trunk	Contract (pull in) abdomen
	Extend spine (arch back slightly)
	Relax only
	Observe the action of breathing
	Brace shoulders back
	Relax only
	Flex shoulderjoint (bring bent arm across chest)
	Repeat with other arm
	Relax only
	Raise (hunch) shoulders
Neck	Press head back into pillow/headrest
	Raise head off pillow
	Relax only
	Bend head to right
	Bend head to left
	Relax only
Eye area	Raise eyebrows
	Frown
	Relax only
	Close eyes tightly
	Look left with eyes closed
	Relax only
	Look right with eyes closed
	Look up with eyes closed
	Relax only
	Look down with eyes closed
	Look forward with eyes closed
	Relax only
Visual imagination	Imagine a pen moving slowly, then fast
	Imagine a train passing, a person walking by
	Relax eyes
	Imagine a bird flying and stationary
	Imagine a ball rolling, the Houses of Parliament
	Relax eyes
	Imagine a horse grazing, a reel of cotton
	Imagine the Prime Minister
	Relax eyes
Jaw, voice, and auditory imagination	Close jaws firmly
	Open jaws
	Relax only
	Bare teeth
	Pout
	Relax only
	Press tongue against teeth
	Pull tongue backwards
	Relax only
	Count aloud up to 10
	Count half as loudly up to 10
	Relax only
	Count softly up to 10
	Count under your breath up to 10
	Relax only
	Imagine you are counting
	Imagine you are reciting the alphabet
	Relax only
	Imagine saying:
	your name three times
	your address three times
	the Prime Minister's name three times

Arms. Seven items for each arm; tensing and releasing of arm and hand muscles.

Legs. 10 items for each leg; tensing and releasing of thigh, leg and foot muscles.

Trunk. 10 items; tensing and releasing of back, abdomen and shoulder muscles.

Neck. 6 items; tensing and relaxing of muscles around the neck.

Eye area. 12 items; tensing and relaxing the muscles of the forehead and the eyes.

Visualization. 9 items; imagining different objects, moving and stationary.

Speech area. 19 items; tensing and relaxing muscles associated with speech; counting and reciting, first in a normal voice, then gradually getting fainter.

Only one or two new actions are introduced at each period of tuition, and the whole programme takes more than 50 sessions. In addition, an hour a day is devoted to home practice.

'Diminishing tensions'

Jacobson avoided using the word 'exercise' to describe the actions, since exercise, designed as it is to strengthen muscles, implies increasing effort. The wrist bending (and other actions) in progressive relaxation are concerned only with demonstrating the different sensations that arise in activated muscle tissue, and therefore require, on the contrary, an ever-decreasing intensity of contraction to fulfil their purpose. To help the trainee become sensitized to low levels of tension, Jacobson devised a technique called 'diminishing tensions'.

This is introduced as the learner becomes proficient in recognizing the sensation of tension. Returning to the action of wrist bending, the trainee would be instructed in the following way:

Bend your wrist back but this time using only half as much effort as you did the first time. Hold it back for about a minute, noticing the sensations you're getting from the muscle . . . and at the end of the minute . . . cease holding it back. Go negative . . . feel the tension leaving . . . allow plenty of time for the remaining tension to disappear . . . allow three minutes . . . then bend the wrist back again, this time tensing the muscle half as much as last time . . . hold it for about a minute, tuning in to the sensations . . . then release the tension . . . release it further . . . and further still . . . allow three

minutes . . . now, raise the wrist the smallest amount possible . . . hold it there . . . for one minute . . . discontinue . . . allow three minutes . . . and finally, make the action just a thought . . . hold the idea . . . go negative . . .

These progressively diminishing tensions train the individual to recognize differing levels, thus increasing his control over the voluntary musculature.

Jacobson's assigning of every third session to passive relaxation is evidence of the relatively low value he gave to the contraction phase, using it simply as a means of cultivating sensitivity to the tension sensation. Many of his successors have, by contrast, attached great importance to the contraction, claiming that it leads to a deepening of the subsequent relaxation. Jacobson argued that the reverse may be the case, namely, that tensions which build up during the contraction phase would continue to persist for some time, thus hindering relaxation. In untrained subjects he showed that muscle tension continues to remain elevated for up to several minutes following a contraction, even when the subject is cooperating with appeals to 'go negative' (Jacobson 1934). Thus, deliberate muscle tensing may, in the short term at least, prevent the individual relaxing.

The issue of tense–release versus a release-only approach has not been satisfactorily resolved. It has been common in clinical practice to favour tense–release. However, the results of a recent study (Lucic et al 1991) supported the view that initial tensing is detrimental to relaxation, and this finding may have strengthened interest in passive approaches.

Eye movements

The procedures for the eye and forehead and for the area of the speech muscles differ somewhat from those of the trunk and limbs. Consequently they are presented in detail.

Although Jacobson (1938) indicated that only one or two actions should be carried out in each session, it is customary today to work through all the eye actions in a single session. Plenty of time should still be allowed for 'going negative'.

Jacobson's studies had demonstrated the effectiveness of progressive relaxation in reducing muscle tension. He had also been able to show that a relaxed musculature had a calming effect on the mind (Jacobson 1938). Muscle relaxation could thus be seen as a mental relaxant. But Jacobson went further: he claimed that in deep relaxation, thought itself disappeared. In the totally relaxed body, the mind would be a blank.

The eye muscles were considered by him to be particularly closely related to thought, since thinking created mental images which were accompanied by a sense of tension around the eyes. Releasing tension from the eyes, Jacobson believed, had the effect of cancelling those images.

The following sequences are adapted from Jacobson (1970). Time should be allowed between the items for the trainee to absorb the message:

With your eyes open, raise your eyebrows . . . feel the tension . . . and release the tension . . . frown . . . feel the tension . . . and release it . . . shut your eyes tightly . . . feel the tension . . . and let it go . . . with your eyes still closed, spend a few minutes releasing tension in this part of your face . . .

Moving on to the eyes themselves (they are still closed) . . . without moving your head, turn your eyes upwards as if you were looking at the ceiling. As you do so, notice the sensation you get in the eye region . . . next, turn your eyes downwards as if you were looking at your feet, again taking note of the feelings around the eyes . . . repeat that several times, until you become familiar with the sensation in the eye muscles . . . then discontinue, going negative for a minute or so . . . still with your eyes closed, turn your eyes to the left for a few moments . . . now to the right . . . repeat this a few times to experience the transient sensations in the muscles . . . then, cease the action . . . do nothing for a few minutes . . .

Would you now, still with your eyes closed, *imagine* you are looking at the ceiling and the floor; do not actively look up and down, but simply think of looking up and down . . . notice the feelings (that is, the same sensations as when you deliberately turned your eyes up and down, although to a much lesser degree) . . . when you have identified the feeling, let your eye muscles go negative . . . notice what happens to the images . . . rest for a few minutes . . .

Now, imagine that you see the wall on your left . . . and the wall on your right . . . imagine seeing one after the other, noticing that slight tensions accompany the images . . . now, let your eyes go . . . and notice what happens to the images . . .

Similar effects can be created by imagining objects from everyday life:

Imagine a car passing . . . or a ball bouncing up and down . . . notice the sensation that accompanies the image . . . then let the eye muscles go negative and notice what happens to the images . . .

Multiply 16 by 82 in your head . . . when you have got the answer, notice how the eyes felt during the task . . . then, rest the eyes and notice what happens to the figures . . .

If the eyes are completely relaxed, the image disappears and the thought dies (Jacobson 1964). The individual however, has made no effort to stop the thought process. He is asked only to release tension, 'letting other effects come as they may' (Jacobson 1976). Whether thought does in fact disappear in a totally relaxed body has not been scientifically established. Jacobson (1938) was however, able to produce clinical evidence of the success of ocular relaxation in overcoming insomnia.

Speech movements

The speech muscles are also closely related to thought. Thinking with the use of words causes minute flickers of tension in the muscles of the tongue and jaw. Conversely, when these muscles are relaxed, thinking with the use of words is no longer possible (Jacobson 1970).

The following script begins with tensing of the speech muscles and ends with sequences of counting using 'diminishing tensions'. As with the eye actions, it is customary today to present the whole group in one session. As a rough guide, 5–10 seconds can be allowed for each action and 30–40 seconds for 'going negative'. Each action is repeated once.

Close the jaws firmly, noticing the sensations you get from the action . . . hold it . . . and . . . discontinue . . . let your jaw drop . . . feel the tension leaving you . . . and continuing to leave you . . . then repeat the action . . .

Next, bare your teeth . . . feel the tension in the cheeks . . . hold it for a few seconds . . . and release the tension . . .

Make a tight 'O' with your lips . . . hold it, while you register tension in the lips . . . and . . . cancel the action . . .

Press your tongue against your teeth . . . feel the pressure . . . and release it . . .

Now, pull the tongue back towards the throat. Feel the muscles drawing it back and note the sensations you get from this action . . . and . . . release it . . . let it go negative . . .

Tune in to the presence of residual tension in any of the muscles associated with speech and let that tension recede . . . and go on receding . . .

(Allow several minutes for the last phase.)

A counting sequence follows, using diminishing tensions.

Count aloud slowly from one to ten, picking up the sensations you get from the muscles in the mouth, throat, face and chest. Repeat it a few times . . . then stop counting . . . allow time for the tension to recede . . .

Now, count again, half as loudly . . . noticing the reduced amount of tension in the speech muscles . . . release that tension . . . next time, count softly . . . notice the tension . . . and let it go . . . and now, under your breath . . . still concentrating on the feelings you get in the mouth, jaw and throat . . . rest a moment . . . and now, simply imagine the counting . . . here perhaps you can detect a flickering in the speech muscles . . . finally, cease to count altogether . . .

When the speech muscles ceased to be involved, Jacobson (1938, 1964, 1976) claimed that it was no longer possible to think in verbal terms.

FURTHER WORK OF JACOBSON'S

Differential relaxation

Jacobson (1938) also investigated the degree of tension necessary for carrying out a particular activity. He drew a distinction between those muscles actually performing the activity and those muscles not involved in it. The first group

needed the minimum level of tension consistent with performing the task; the second group could be totally relaxed or as relaxed as possible. This differential in the degree of tension required was studied by Jacobson for the purpose of reducing both the excessive effort often used by the first group and the unnecessary effort often used by the second. Differential relaxation is discussed in more detail in Chapter 12.

Self-operations control

In addition to progressive relaxation, Jacobson (1964) developed a method of instruction which he called 'self-operations control'. The principles of recognizing and eliminating tension are the same as those of progressive relaxation. The emphasis however, is placed on self-direction: the individual controls his muscle tension throughout the events of daily life, learning 'to go on and off . . . as different occasions may require' (Jacobson 1964). He learns to monitor all sensations of tension, simultaneously and automatically, and to release those that are not desired, in a continuing process (McGuigan 1984). The result is a decreased consumption of energy, whose effect extends to other body systems such as the autonomic nervous system, where sympathetic activity is reduced. Thought processes are also believed to benefit from the tension-decreasing effect (McGuigan 1981).

This method, however, takes as long to learn as Jacobson's original technique.

EVALUATION OF PROGRESSIVE RELAXATION

Jacobson used electromyography, a technique which he invented, to measure muscle tension. By this means he showed that progressive relaxation had a direct effect on the release of tension in the skeletal musculature. The more practised the trainee, the greater the effect. He also showed that progressive relaxation had an indirect effect on anxiety levels, and that, via brain mediation, it promoted parasympathetic dominance (Jacobson 1938).

Subsequent research on the effectiveness of progressive relaxation and comparison with other relaxation approaches has not however, produced consistent results, although much of this later work suffers because of the superficial training in progressive relaxation given to the subjects (Borkovec & Sides 1979, Lehrer 1982).

Jacobson, who was a pioneer in this unexplored area, carried out research which was meticulous by the standards of his day. However, despite careful attention to method, his work, by present day standards, suffers from certain shortcomings. One of these is subject self-selection (subjects volunteering to take part). Jacobson drew on his close associates and private patients for subjects, whereas modern standards would demand random selection.

A second methodological deficiency is the relative absence of statistical analysis. Jacobson seldom tested for significance, i.e. conducted analyses to estimate the probability that the results he obtained did not arise by chance (Lichstein 1988). It was not conventional to use probability statistics in his day (Lehrer 1982). In spite of this however, his results often reached levels of statistical significance (Blanchard & Young 1973).

Progressive relaxation in one form or another, is widely used in the clinical field for reducing mental tension. Based on a substantial amount of evidence, it is believed that the mind becomes calmer as a result of relaxing the musculature. Not all research findings however, support this view, and there are studies which show little or no correlation between anxiety level and muscle tension. It would seem that any influence exerted by the musculature on mental activity is part of an interactive process as yet not fully understood (Lichstein 1988).

The major disadvantage of Jacobson's original technique is its length, with accompanying problems of time and money. These problems have inevitably led to a plethora of modifications, one of which is described in the following chapter.

PITFALLS OF MUSCULAR RELAXATION

See Chapter 6 (p. 50).

FURTHER READING

Jacobson E 1938 Progressive relaxation, 2nd edn. University of Chicago Press, Chicago
Jacobson E 1976 You must relax. Souvenir Press, London
McGuigan F J 1984 Progressive relaxation: origins, principles and clinical applications. In: Woolfolk R L, Lehrer P M (eds) Principles and practice of stress management. Guilford Press, New York.

CHAPTER CONTENTS

Differences between progressive relaxation and progressive relaxation training 38

The PRT procedure 39
The first session 39
Practice 41
Summarized versions 41
Relaxation through recall 41

Evaluation of progressive relaxation training 41

Pitfalls of progressive relaxation training 41

5

Progressive relaxation training

Although Jacobson's method (Ch. 4) was found to reduce both pulse rate and blood pressure, it was time-consuming and unlikely to have wide appeal as it stood. Some form of abbreviation was needed. The first major attempt at shortening the format was made by Wolpe (1958), who reduced the training to six sessions and later reduced it further to one. Countless other modifications have followed of which Bernstein & Borkovec's (1973) is one of the best known.

Named 'progressive relaxation training' (PRT) by its authors, the approach is defined as learning to relax specific muscle groups while paying attention to the feelings associated with both the tensed and relaxed states. Its aims are (Bernstein & Given 1984):

1. to achieve a state of deep relaxation in increasingly shorter periods
2. to control excess tension in stress-inducing situations.

The trainee works through the sequential tensing and releasing of 16 muscle groups. These are reduced to seven in the next stage and to four in a subsequent stage. The tension component is then withdrawn, in what is called 'relaxation through recall', and the final stage consists of a mental summary in the form of a count from one to ten. Proficiency at each level depends on the skill obtained in the previous stage. The tense–release element of PRT is described in this chapter (p. 39). Relaxation through recall is presented in Chapter 7 (p. 54). Two additional components are described in later chapters: 'conditioned relaxation' in Chapter 8, (p. 65) and 'differential relaxation' in Chapter 12 (p. 95).

Differences between progressive relaxation and progressive relaxation training

Although PRT is founded on Jacobson's principles of recognizing and eliminating tension, there are important differences between the two approaches (Table 5.1).

The contraction phase

One of these differences is the prominence given to the tensing component in the modified version. Bernstein & Borkovec (1973) describe an effect whereby the strength of the contraction determines the depth of the succeeding relaxation, in the manner of a pendulum which, when lifted high on one side, swings back to the same height on the other side. Thus, the stronger the initial contraction, the more effective the subsequent relaxation. Jacobson (1938, 1970) does not share this view. He sees the contraction phase simply as a means of cultivating the individual's sensitivity to the presence of muscle tension. He never intended it as a means of 'producing' relaxation (Lehrer et al 1988).

The strength of the contraction is not specified by Jacobson, except in such terms as 'Do not stiffen your arm to the point of extreme effort, but only in moderation' (Jacobson 1964); and the command to 'tense', even at greatest magnitude is taken to convey only a comfortable level, since the object is merely to enable the individual to identify the sensation of tension. To Jacobson, the lower the level of the contraction, the more useful it was. Bernstein & Borkovec, in contrast, use phrases such as 'tight fist' and refer to 'trembling neck muscles', suggesting a high level of tension. Wolpe & Lazarus (1966), similarly, in their version, urge clients to clench the fist 'tighter and tighter'.

Use of suggestion

Both Jacobson (1938) and Bernstein & Borkovec (1973) discuss suggestion.

Addressing trainees who fear they might be put into a trance state, Bernstein & Borkovec point out the difference between hypnosis and relaxation. In hypnosis, maximum use is made of direct suggestion such as: 'Now your arm is limp'. Direct suggestion, so crucial in hypnosis, is not appropriate in relaxation.

PRT does, however, use indirect suggestion, such as 'Notice how your muscles are feeling more and more relaxed' and 'Let a feeling of relaxation flow through your limbs', in order to

Table 5.1 Differences between Jacobson's progressive relaxation method and Bernstein & Borkovec's progressive relaxation training

	Progressive relaxation	Progressive relaxation training
Position of relaxation	Lying or sitting	Reclining
Total number of muscle groups worked	48	16
Number of new muscle groups worked in one session	1 or 2	All groups
Emphasis of technique	Releasing tension	'Producing' relaxation through tense–release cycles
Perceived value of the contraction	To alert the individual to the tension sensation	To deepen each relaxation component by providing a 'running start'; a strong contraction leads to a deep relaxation
Part played by suggestion	None: technique is purely a muscular skill	Indirect suggestion is used to enhance the effect
Use of tapes	Not used	Advised against
Number of sessions needed	50 +	About 6

deepen the sense of relaxation. Voice modulations to reinforce the distinction between tension and relaxation are also encouraged: crisp tones during the tensing component and soothing tones during the relaxation component.

To Jacobson however, even indirect suggestion is unacceptable. He sees progressive relaxation exclusively as a muscular skill, the mastery of which is impeded by any kind of suggestion.

Relevant to this discussion is the work of Paul (1969) who has shown relaxation training to be more effective than hypnosis at reducing muscle tension.

THE PRT PROCEDURE

The first session

In Bernstein & Borkovec's approach, training is governed by a fixed procedure.

1. The rationale of the technique is presented to the trainee, and the items involving the 16 muscle groups are then described and demonstrated. (See Introductory remarks section below.)

2. For the procedure itself the trainee is seated in a reclining chair. If this is not available, the trainee can sit in a chair with a high back and arms.

3. The procedure starts with the trainee being asked to focus attention on a given muscle group. (See Item one section below.)

4. A signal, such as the word 'Now', indicates that the group is to be tensed.

5. The contraction is carried out all at once, not gradually.

6. Tension is maintained for 5–7 seconds during which the instructor asks the trainee to focus on the sensations of muscle contraction.

7. On a predetermined cue such as the word 'Release', 'Relax' or 'Let go', the muscle group is relaxed (again, all at once).

8. As the muscle group relaxes, the trainee is asked to notice the feelings that accompany the relaxation while the trainer maintains a patter which is indirectly suggestive of relaxation.

9. This continues for the duration of the relaxation period which is 30–40 seconds.

10. All 16 muscle groups are worked in the first training session.

Introductory remarks to trainees

The method you are going to learn is called 'progressive relaxation training' and it consists of tensing and releasing muscle groups throughout the body. The object is to produce relaxation and this occurs after the tension is released. A firm contraction can lead to a deep relaxation, rather like a pendulum swinging high on both sides. You will be asked to concentrate on the feelings that accompany the tension and the relaxation; feelings that up to now, you may have taken for granted. There are 16 muscle groups to be tensed and released and it takes 20–30 minutes to complete the whole schedule. First, I'll run through the items, demonstrating them and giving you a chance to try them out.

The trainer demonstrates the following items:

1. Making a fist with the dominant hand without involving the upper arm.
2. Pushing the elbow of the same arm down against the arm of the chair (activating the biceps), while keeping the hand relaxed.
3. & 4. The nondominant arm is worked separately.
5. Raising the eyebrows.
6. Screwing up the eyes and wrinkling the nose.
7. Clenching the teeth and pulling back the corners of the mouth.
8. Pulling the chin down and pressing the head back against a support, tensing the neck muscles.
9. Drawing the shoulders back.
10. Tightening the abdominal muscles (making the stomach hard).
11. Tensing the thigh of the dominant leg by contracting the knee flexors and extensors together.
12. Pointing the dominant foot down (plantarflexion).
13. Pulling the dominant foot up towards the face (dorsiflexion).
14. & 15. & 16. The nondominant leg is worked separately.

The trainer continues:

When we begin, I'll first describe each item but please do not tense the part until I give you the cue word 'Now'. Similarly, let it go only when I give you the cue word 'Relax'. Let it go completely. Now, please close your eyes.

Item one

The first item involves the muscles of the right hand and forearm; the hand is drawn into a fist (Fig. 5.1):

We'll start with the right hand and forearm. I'm going to ask you to tense the muscles in the right hand and lower arm, by drawing up your hand into a tight fist . . . Now . . . clench the hand . . . keep it tight . . . feel the tension in the muscles as you pull hard . . . and . . . Relax . . . let go immediately and as the fingers uncurl, notice the feelings you now have in the muscles of the hand . . . focus on the sensations you are getting in the muscles of the forearm also, as they lose their tension . . . feel relaxation flowing into the area as the muscles get more and more deeply relaxed . . . completely relaxed . . . notice the way your muscles feel now, compared to how they felt when tensed.

All items are performed a second time, after which there is an extended relaxation phase lasting a full minute. Trainees can be asked to raise the little finger of the right hand to indicate that they are fully relaxed before the next item is introduced.

Item two and subsequent items

Item two involves the muscles of the right upper arm: the bent elbow is pressed down into the arm of the chair (Fig. 5.2).

Let the hand and forearm go on relaxing while you transfer your attention to the muscles in the right upper arm (biceps). I'd like you now to press your elbow down against the arm of the chair. Do this without involving the muscles of the hand and forearm . . . Now . . . feel the tension in your upper arm as the elbow presses down . . . and . . . Relax . . . let it go completely . . . focus your attention on the relaxing muscles . . . feel the tension flowing out . . . enjoy the pleasant feelings of the muscles unwinding . . . experience the feeling of deep relaxation and of comfort . . . then notice if the upper arm feels as relaxed as the lower arm . . . if it does, then signal with your little finger.

The above items give an idea of the nature of PRT, and in the first session the remaining 14 items are also worked through.

Ending the session

At the end, the trainer terminates.

I am going to bring the session to an end by counting backwards from four to one . . . four . . . start to move your legs and feet . . . three . . . bend and stretch your arms and hands . . . two . . . move your head slowly . . . and . . . one . . . open your eyes, noticing how

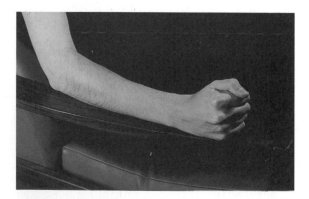

Figure 5.1 Making a fist.

Figure 5.2 Pressing elbow down into arm of chair.

peaceful and relaxed you feel . . . as if you'd just woken from a short sleep.

Practice

Two daily practice sessions of 15–20 minutes each are considered essential, the trainee picking moments when he is not under any pressure.

Summarized versions

When the trainee has learned the above procedure, it can be regrouped in a summarized form, enabling him to cover the process in a shorter time:

1. Right arm items combined.
2. Left arm items combined.
3. Face and head movements worked together.
4. Neck and shoulder region combined.
5. Torso items worked together.
6. Right leg items combined.
7. Left leg items combined.

A further summary cuts the process down to four items:

1. Both arms are worked together.
2. Face and head items worked together.
3. Torso and neck movements combined.
4. Both legs are tensed together. (People who find this difficult should work the legs separately.)

Relaxation through recall

PRT continues with relaxation through recall. This is described in Chapter 7 (p. 54).

EVALUATION OF PROGRESSIVE RELAXATION TRAINING

Shortened and standardized versions of progressive relaxation, such as Bernstein & Borkovec's, are favoured by researchers and clinicians alike, although Lehrer (1982), reevaluating Jacobson's work, argues for the superior benefit of the lengthy original. Lichstein (1988), reviewing studies comparing the two approaches, finds the evidence inconclusive.

The debate about the value of the initial contraction continues. As mentioned earlier, a recent study investigating whether relaxation using initial muscle tensing was more effective than using no muscle tensing, found that the initial tensing was detrimental to relaxation (Lucic et al 1991), thus endorsing Jacobson's view.

Because of its many advantages however, PRT is widely practised and its use is supported by a wealth of clinical findings.

PITFALLS OF PROGRESSIVE RELAXATION TRAINING

The pitfalls of muscular approaches are listed in Chapter 6 (p. 50).

FURTHER READING

Bernstein D A, Borkovec T D 1973 Progressive relaxation training: a manual for the helping professions. Research Press, Champaign, Illinois
Bernstein D A, Given B A 1984 Progressive relaxation: abbreviated methods. In: Woolfolk R L, Lehrer P M (eds) Principles and practice of stress management. Guilford Press, New York.

CHAPTER CONTENTS

Introduction to the method 43

The exercises 43
Breathing (1) 44
Arm 44
Leg 45
Toe flexion and extension 46
Breathing (2) 47
Abdominal muscle tensing 47
Shoulder bracing 47
Shoulder hunching 47
Head back 48
Upper face 48
Lower face 49
Termination 49

Pitfalls of muscular approaches 50

6

A tense–release script

The script set out below lies in the tradition of progressive relaxation. In procedure, however, it more closely resembles progressive relaxation training, except that reduced effort is put into the repeats in the manner of Jacobson's diminishing tensions. The exercises themselves are drawn from a variety of sources. Trainees may be lying or sitting to perform them, although, while the procedure is being introduced a sitting position is more suitable.

Introduction to the method

I am going to lead you through some of the major muscle groups of the body, asking you to contract and relax them, one by one. Tensing and releasing muscles can help to induce a feeling of physical relaxation. You may also feel mentally relaxed. As you carry out the items, you'll experience sensations in the muscles. These sensations indicate tension which you will learn to identify and to release. This is a skill which enables you to relax yourself any time you want to and the more you practise it the easier it will become.

The following exercises should first be demonstrated by the trainer in order to familiarize participants with the procedure. Participants are then invited to try them out. It is worth spending time on the demonstration so that group members feel they know the exercises before the instruction begins.

THE EXERCISES

- Breathing (1).

- Arm: spider hand, rod-like arm.
- Leg: dorsi and plantar flexion (foot bending up and down).
- Toe flexion (bending down) and extension (bending up).
- Breathing (2).
- Abdominal muscle tensing.
- Shoulder bracing.
- Shoulder hunching.
- Head pressing back.
- Upper face: brow raising, frowning, eye exercises.
- Lower face: jaw, lips, tongue.

Authors hold varying opinions as to the optimal duration of the tension and relaxation periods: based on their collective judgements, the present author suggests 5–10 seconds for tensing, and about 30–40 seconds for relaxing.

It is explained to participants that each tension phase is carried out on the command 'Now'. The signal for the release of tension is the word 'Relax'. When calling the items, the tone of voice can be varied from slightly crisp during the tension phase to soothing during the relaxation phase.

Participants may have their eyes open or closed. When they have taken up their lying positions, the instructor begins.

Breathing (1)   Breathing throughout

The section on hyperventilation in Chapter 15, (p. 119) is relevant to this exercise.

Please make yourself as comfortable as you can. Let your breathing settle down and observe its natural rhythm. After a minute or two, follow a natural breath out, making it a little bit longer than usual . . . then let the air in . . . let it gently fill your lungs . . . and . . . breathe out slowly, releasing your tensions with the air . . . and now let your breathing take care of itself . . . do not immediately repeat this deep breath.

You will recognize the exercises which follow. Please wait for the word 'Now' to perform the action.

Arm

Spider hand

This is adapted from Wallace (1980) (Fig. 6.1)

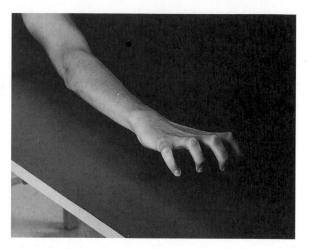

Figure 6.1 Spider hand.

I'd like you to focus attention on your right arm, whether it's lying alongside you, propped on the arm of your chair or on your lap. With the hand placed palm downwards on a surface (floor, chair arm or thigh), slowly press the fingertips into the surface, drawing them towards your palm so that your hand gradually takes on the shape of a spider . . . don't force the movement, just put a moderate amount of effort into it . . . Now . . . as you hold the position, notice the tensions in the hand and the underside of the forearm . . . feel them build up . . . then . . . Relax . . . let the tension go . . . relax the muscles . . . let the tension disappear and go on disappearing as you give the hand time to get more and more relaxed . . . notice how it feels when it's fully relaxed . . .

The 'spider' exercise is repeated once using less effort.

Rod-like arm (Fig. 6.2)

Still with the right arm, I want you slowly to tense up all the muscles so that the arm becomes rigid. Begin with a little tension in the fingertips . . . let it grow until the fingers are drawn into the palm making a fist shape. Then stretch out the arm, creating tension in the forearm and upper arm until the arm gets rigid like a rod . . . Now . . . feel the tension throughout the arm, but don't overdo it . . . and . . . Relax . . . let it flop down . . . feel the muscles going slack and the arm becoming limp . . . notice the relief, the pleasant tingling and the sense of warmth . . . let the arm go on relaxing . . . and relaxing a bit more . . . imagine the last remnant of tension flowing out through your fingertips . . . notice how the arm muscles feel when they are fully relaxed.

The exercise is performed again, using less effort the second time.

'Spider' and 'rod' are then carried out with the left arm.

Leg

Next is a group of leg exercises. The first two are for those lying down and the second pair are for those who are seated.

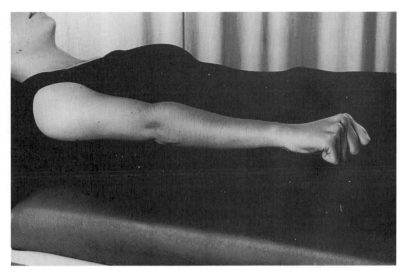

Figure 6.2   Rod-like arm.

Feet pointing towards face

From a supine position, the feet are pointed towards the face (Fig. 6.3).

Turning your attention to your legs which are lying flat on the ground, point your feet up towards your face, keeping the backs of your knees on the ground . . . Now . . . hold the position and notice the sensations you are getting in the working muscles around the shin bones . . . and then . . . Relax . . . as you let go your leg muscles, feel the tension draining out of them . . . and continuing to drain out as your legs and feet become more and more relaxed . . .

Feet pointing away from face

Still from a supine position, the feet are now pointed away from the face (Fig. 6.4).

This time I'd like you to point your feet down, as if you were using them to indicate something. Don't overdo it especially if you are prone to develop cramp . . . Now . . . as you hold the position, study the tensions in your calves . . . and then . . . Relax . . . let go . . . let all the tension dissolve . . . feel comfort returning to your lower legs . . . notice all the sensations you get from relaxing the muscles . . . continue letting go until you feel they won't relax any further . . .

These two exercises are repeated once with diminishing tension.

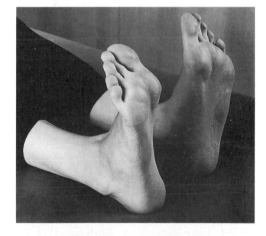

Figure 6.3   Feet pointing towards face.

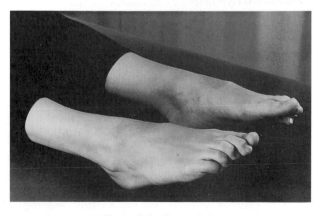

Figure 6.4   Feet pointing away from face.

The following two leg exercises are addressed to seated participants.

Heel raising

In the first, the heels are raised off the ground (Fig. 6.5).

Begin by making sure your feet are flat on the floor . . . then, keeping your toes firmly in contact with the floor, raise your heels up in the air . . . Now . . . feel the tension in your calf muscles . . . hold the action . . . then . . . .Relax . . . drop your heels to the ground . . . notice the relief . . . the comfort . . . the warm, tingling sensation in your calves . . . the enjoyable feeling of relaxing your feet . . . go on letting those feelings continue until your feet and calves are completely relaxed . . . then, a little bit further . . .

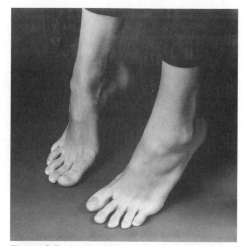

Figure 6.5 Heel raising.

Toe raising

In the second exercise, the front part of the foot is raised off the ground (Fig. 6.6).

This time, keep your heels on the ground, and raise the front part of your feet as if you were about to tap a rhythm . . . Now . . . keep your toes up in the air while you take notice of the tension sensation in the muscles around the shinbones . . . and . . . Relax . . . let the feet fall down . . . notice the relief in the shin area . . . feel the sense of tension leaving you . . . draining out through your feet and toes . . . and continuing to drain out a bit longer . . .

These two exercises are repeated with diminished tension.

The next exercise is addressed to both lying and seated participants.

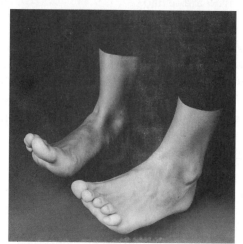

Figure 6.6 Toe raising.

Toe flexion and extension (Fig. 6.7)

Let your attention focus on your toes. Whether you are lying or sitting, curl your toes down, restricting the action to the toes themselves. Some people can do it more easily then others, but just do what you can . . . Now . . . feel the tension in the sole of the foot and the calf of the leg . . . then . . . Relax . . . let it go . . . feel the muscles going slack . . . feel them going slacker as the tension disappears . . . notice how the muscles feel when they are relaxed.

The exercise is repeated once using less tension.

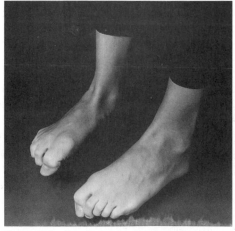

Figure 6.7 Toe flexion.

It is followed by a similar exercise in which the toes are bent upwards. Here, tension is felt along the top part of the foot and the shin.

Breathing (2)

At least a minute can be allotted to this item.

Turn your attention to your breathing again . . . notice its rhythm . . . place one hand over your upper abdomen and notice the gentle swell and recoil of the area underneath it . . . avoid any inclination to alter the rhythm . . . just let the breathing take care of itself . . .

Abdominal muscle tensing

Focus now on the abdominal muscles . . . make the area over your internal organs go flat and hard as you pull the muscles in . . . Now . . . feel the tension under your ribs, over your organs and around the back of your pelvis . . . then . . . Relax . . . let go . . . allow your muscles to spread themselves . . . feel a sense of deep relaxation . . . and let that relaxation become deeper as the moments pass . . .

One repeat is carried out using less tension.

Figure 6.8 Shoulder bracing.

Shoulder bracing (Fig. 6.8)

Moving to the region of the back, bring your attention to the blade-bones behind your shoulders. Draw them back so that they get nearer to each other (without putting too much effort into it) . . . Now . . . feel them being gently squeezed together . . . notice also, how your chest is lifted away from the supporting surface . . . and then . . . Relax . . . release the tension . . . let the muscles soften . . . feel your back lying once again in contact with the supporting surface . . . notice the feeling of relaxation and let that feeling continue on and on . . .

The exercise is repeated once with less tension.

Shoulder hunching (Fig. 6.9)

Moving to the neck region, I'd like you to lift your shoulders . . . hunch them up as if to touch your ears . . . Now . . . feel the tension in the lower neck . . . register the sensation . . . and . . . Relax . . . let the shoulders drop . . . and go on dropping . . . further and further as the tension ebbs away . . . feel your shoulders completely relaxed . . .

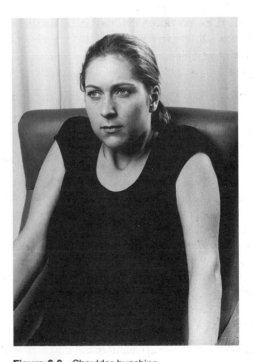

Figure 6.9 Shoulder hunching.

The exercise is performed once more using diminished tension.

Head back

And the head: keeping your chin in, press your head back against the support (against the floor or back of the chair) . . . press it back, making double chins in the front . . . stop short of discomfort . . . Now . . . notice the feelings you get from the working muscles . . . tension in the back of the neck . . . and . . . Relax . . . let go . . . feel the area relax . . . notice the sense of ease that floods into the area . . . allow the relaxation to deepen until all the tension has left your neck . . .

One repeat is carried out using less tension.

Upper face

Eyebrow raising (Fig. 6.10)

Moving to the face, to the many muscles responsible for subtle changes of expression: would you now raise your eyebrows . . . raise them high, creating horizontal furrows . . . Now . . . feel the tension in the muscle that stretches across the brow . . . and . . . Relax . . . let the tension flow out . . . feel the furrows being smoothed . . . continue until there is no tension left in your brow . . . then a little bit further . . .

The repeat is carried out using less tension.

Frowning (Fig. 6.11)

Focus on your frowning muscle . . . bring the eyebrows closer together, buckling the skin between them into a deep frown . . . Now . . . hold it a few moments, taking note of the sensation you get from the action . . . then . . . Relax . . . release the tension . . . feel the eyebrows spread sideways . . . imagine the space between them getting wider and continuing to get wider . . . notice the comfortable feeling that accompanies this idea . . . continue until all the tension dies away . . .

The exercise is repeated once using diminished tension.

Eyes

We come to the eyes. First, I'd like you to screw them up and notice the sensation you get from the action

Figure 6.10 Eyebrow raising.

Figure 6.11 Frowning.

. . . Now . . . spend a moment registering it . . . then . . . Relax . . . let go . . . let the muscles loosen . . . notice the feeling you get from loosening them . . . feel the skin smoothing out . . .

The exercise is performed once more using diminished tension. For the following exercise, the trainee's eyes should be closed. The format is slightly different in that, because there are so many eye movements, the relaxation is postponed until the end.

Next, without moving your head, turn your eyes upwards behind your closed lids . . . Now . . . hold your gaze up for a few moments . . . notice the tension in the muscles . . . and . . . bring your eyes back to a central position . . . and, look down, as if towards your feet . . . Now . . . hold it a few moments . . . then return to the centre . . . look to the right . . . Now . . . keep a steady hold . . . and return to the front . . . and, to the left . . . Now . . . hold it . . . then bring your eyes back to the front . . . and . . . Relax . . . let your eyes feel relaxed . . . as they rest in a middle position, notice how they feel . . . compare this with how they felt when they were working . . . let them go on relaxing . . . continue relaxing for a full minute . . .

Finally, roll your eyes in a clockwise circle . . . Now . . . notice the sensations of tension . . . pause . . . roll them now in an anticlockwise direction . . . again, notice the feelings . . . and . . . Relax . . . let them fully relax . . . let them go on relaxing until all the tension has left them . . .

One repeat may be carried out using less tension. A further exercise consists of focusing at different distances behind closed lids: first on a faraway object, then on an object placed close to the eyes (adapted from Madders 1981).

Imagine you are looking at an object on the distant horizon. You can't see it clearly but you are trying to make it out . . . Now . . . notice how it feels as you strain to identify it . . . then, releasing the tension, bring your eyes to focus on a piece of writing held very close . . . Now . . . notice the sensations as you make the effort to read the contents . . . and, Relax . . . let your eyes settle on the middle distance . . . feel the relief as you let go the tension in the muscles which control the focus . . . enjoy the feeling of releasing that tension . . .

After a short rest, repeat the action with reduced tension.

Lower face

Jaw

Bring your back teeth together . . . do it firmly but without actually clenching them . . . Now . . . feel a sensation in your jaw as if you'd been chewing tough meat . . . hold it . . . and . . . Relax . . . release the jaw muscles . . . feel the tension fading . . . continuing to fade . . . and then further still . . .

The exercise is repeated with diminished tension.

Lips

Press your lips tightly together as if you were rejecting some unpleasant medicine . . . Now . . . hold your lips pursed . . . then . . . Relax . . . let them go . . . and as they relax, notice feelings such as the warmth of the blood flowing back into your lips . . . tune in to the feelings of relaxation . . .

One repeat is carried out using less tension.

Tongue

Finally the tongue: press your tongue against the roof of your mouth and hold it there . . . Now . . . feel the tension in the tongue . . . and . . . Relax . . . notice how it feels when your relax it . . . and press it against the inside of your right cheek . . . Now . . . hold . . . and Relax . . . and against your left cheek . . . Now . . . hold . . . and Relax . . . and pull it back towards your throat (not too strongly) . . . Now . . . hold . . . and Relax . . . and then let your tongue settle in the middle of your mouth, just touching the backs of your front teeth . . . feel it releasing tension . . . let it go on relaxing . . . enjoy the feeling of relaxation . . . let that feeling spread throughout your mouth and over your face, making them feel warm, glowing and relaxed . . .then, let it spread to cover your neck and shoulders . . . your arms . . . back . . . abdomen . . . and legs, so that your entire body experiences a feeling of complete relaxation . . . continue relaxing for several minutes . . .

Termination

And now, I'm going to bring this session to an end . . . gradually I'd like you to return to normal activity, but first I'll count from one to three to help you make the adjustment . . . when I get to three, I'd like you to open your eyes, feeling fresh and alert and ready to carry on with your life . . . one . . . two . . . three . . . before getting up, give a few gentle stretches to your arms and legs.

PITFALLS OF MUSCULAR APPROACHES

It would seem that progressive relaxation is appropriate in any circumstances where rest is prescribed (McGuigan 1984). The method is unlikely to create negative effects and Jacobson did not refer to any.

Some points however, need to be considered:

1. Training in relaxation should never be viewed as a substitute for medical treatment; wherever a disorder is present or suspected, medical help should be sought.

2. Relaxation training is not recommended for people suffering from hallucinations, delusions or other psychotic symptoms, as the exercises can lead to out-of-body sensations. Imagery is never appropriate, but benefit has been derived from a tense–release and physical exercise approach during a non-active period of psychotic illness (Bloom & Gonzales 1981). Keable (1989) has emphasized the value of this finding for individuals who experience stress in addition to their psychosis. Discussion with the attending psychiatrist or psychologist would first be necessary.

3. Variations in the blood pressure may occur in the course of relaxation training: it can rise when limbs are being tensed and fall during deep relaxation. The first can be counteracted by allowing a rest between the tensings, and the second by asking trainees to bend and stretch their limbs a few times before resuming active life. The fall in blood pressure which accompanies deep relaxation is only that which occurs under any resting conditions. It is however, important to allow time for the individual to adjust to active life following a session of relaxation. Suddenly jumping up from a relaxed lying position can induce giddiness.

For people whose blood pressure is already high, a release-only method (Ch. 7) may be preferable to one which consists of muscle tensings.

4. Tense–release procedures performed with excessive tightening may lead to cramp. In order to avoid this, trainees can be advised to stop short of discomfort. Recurrent cramp would indicate the unsuitability of the technique for that individual. Overtensing the spine and the neck should also be avoided since it can lead to spinal damage.

5. Some researchers have reported a fear of relaxing in certain individuals (Lehrer 1979), and others report that relaxation occasionally induces anxiety (Borkovec & Heide 1980). It can be recognized by excessive perspiration, trembling, rapid breathing or general restlessness. The training (for that individual) should immediately be stopped. These symptoms may however, be the result of a fear that letting-go might lead to loss of control. To individuals who harbour such fears, the wording can be changed to 'as relaxed as you want to be'. It is worth mentioning that the researchers who studied the reaction (Borkovec & Heide 1980) were not using Jacobson's original method, but one of its modifications.

Disturbing feelings may rise to the surface during any kind of relaxation: in letting down the wall of tension, psychological defences can be weakened (Hough 1991).

6. Abromowitz & Wieselberg (1978) reported that a few individuals undergoing relaxation training became angry when asked to relax. It was unclear what had caused the anger but one reason suggested was that they had found difficulty in mastering the technique.

7. Progressive relaxation training has been found to be effective for many people suffering organic pain. It provides a physical approach to a physical disorder (Davidson & Schwartz 1976). Some individuals however, find that focusing on the body intensifies their perception of pain (Snyder 1985), and for them, muscular approaches may be less useful than mental ones such as imagery or meditation.

8. Trainees who, because of disability or disorder, are in doubt as to the suitability of any exercise, should begin by performing it very gently. This applies for example, to individuals

with back or neck problems.

9. As attention to breathing is a feature of most muscular approaches, the hazards of hyperventilation should be borne in mind (p. 119).

10. Some tense–release scripts make use of imagery. They will therefore, in addition, be subject to the pitfalls listed in Chapter 18 (p. 143).

CHAPTER CONTENTS

Introduction 53

Relaxation through recall 54
Relaxation through recall with counting 55

Passive neuromuscular relaxation 55
The relaxation ripple 56

A passive relaxation approach 57
Introductory remarks to trainees 57
Procedure for participants who are lying down 57
Termination 58
Adapted procedure for seated trainees 59

Kermani's scanning technique 59
Another passive method 59

Pitfalls of passive relaxation 59

7

Passive muscular relaxation

INTRODUCTION

Muscular relaxation is a process by which contractile tension in voluntary muscles is reduced. The methods described in the previous three chapters are principally examples of the tense–release technique. Because of the contraction component, this is essentially an active procedure. Relaxation performed without the contraction however, is a passive procedure. Jacobson's work covers both tense–release and passive relaxation.

Passive muscular relaxation consists of a systematic review of the skeletal muscle groups in the body. As attention is focused on each one in turn, the individual identifies any tension and then releases it. Passive relaxation has certain practical advantages over active methods in that:

1. The sequences can be carried out without drawing attention to the individual performing them. They are thus potentially useful in the workplace or other public location where stress arises.

2. Passive routines take less time to work through than tense–release ones.

3. The method is available to those with physical disabilities, the nature of which might preclude some of the tension routines.

Passive muscular relaxation, on the whole, requires previous knowledge of the tense–release approach. It is through tense–release that the individual learns to become aware of the sensations associated with muscle tension; sensations that help him to identify and release the tension.

Recent evidence of the value of passive relaxation comes from Lucic et al (1991), whose work supports the view that the tensing of muscle groups prior to relaxation hinders their capacity to relax. Their findings are thus in line with the view of Jacobson, whose work was essentially passive (though he did not use that word to describe it). Although his method has already been described in Chapter 4, reference must be made here to the position he holds as the preeminent exponent of the passive muscular approach. It is true that he used tensing procedures, but the central idea of his work is the release of tension.

The authors whose work is described here are:

- Bernstein & Borkovec (1973)
- Everly & Rosenfeld (1981)
- Madders (1981), and
- Kermani (1990).

These authors have been included primarily because of the precise form of their presentations. Bernstein & Borkovec (1973) present a release-only routine which they call 'relaxation through recall' in which muscle groups are relaxed by recalling the sensations associated with the release of tension.

Everly & Rosenfeld (1981), have also developed a release-only approach which they call 'passive neuromuscular relaxation', defining it as a focusing of sensory awareness on particular muscle groups followed by their relaxation. These researchers see passive neuromuscular relaxation as a form of mental imagery which, together with its overtones of suggestion, departs from the strictly physical nature of Jacobson's progressive relaxation. On this account, the pitfalls of visualization (Ch. 18, p. 151) as well as those for muscular relaxation (Ch. 6, p. 50) should be read in connection with this approach.

The authors mentioned above are psychologists. Madders, a physiotherapist, includes passive relaxation in her book. *Stress and Relaxation* (1981). As well as addressing the muscle groups of the body, her version has an element of imagery.

Finally a scanning procedure from the work of Kermani (1990), an autogenic training therapist is described.

RELAXATION THROUGH RECALL

This technique is adapted from Bernstein & Borkovec (1973) whose work is described in Chapter 5. While giving prominence to tense–release sequences in their approach, these authors also offer a release-only technique. 'Relaxation through recall' is the name given to this technique. It requires the trainee to have first learned the active form of progressive relaxation training, since the passive form is based on the memory of those routines.

The muscle groups involved are the final summarized groupings of arms, head and neck, trunk, and legs (p. 41). Two steps are involved.

1. The individual focuses on one of the groups, noticing any tension.
2. He recalls the sensation associated with releasing tension, and spends 30–45 seconds relaxing any tension that he finds.

Trainees are prepared by a short introduction (adapted from Lichstein 1988):

Tensing and relaxing has made you highly sensitive to the feelings which accompany changes in the muscles, and now that you know the technique, I want to lead you to a more advanced version of it. I would like you to cast your mind back to the four-group tense–release procedure, but this time, to drop the tensing part. As we travel through these four groups, I'm going to ask you simply to look for any tension, and then, by recalling the sensations associated with its release, to let it go.

The trainee sits in a reclining chair or something that resembles it and the following script is presented:

Would you close your eyes please. I'd like you first to concentrate on the muscles of your hands and arms. See if you can identify any feeling of tension in them. If so, notice where it is . . . notice how it feels . . . and relax it away, remembering previous feelings of releasing tension in these muscles . . . go on releasing tension as you recall those sensations . . . go on until the muscles become more and more deeply relaxed . . . until you feel relaxation flowing through all the muscles of your arms . . . until they are totally free of tension . . . signal with a lifted finger when the arms feel fully relaxed.

The trainer continues in this way for 30–45 seconds.

Next, bring your mind to focus on the muscles of your face and neck. Is there any tension there? If so, notice where it is and what it feels like . . . then relax it, recalling the feeling of letting the tension go . . . feel the tension leaving the muscles . . . note the pleasant feeling of relaxation . . . allow the relaxation to deepen and go on deepening as you concentrate on the peaceful state of those muscles . . .

Next, concentrate on the muscles of the trunk. Pick up any sensation of tension . . . notice where it is and what it feels like . . . remember what it felt like when you relaxed the tension in those muscles . . . and relax them now . . . relax any tension you find . . . continue letting the tension go until your muscles feel quite loose. Go on relaxing them . . . feel them getting looser and looser.

Finally, give your attention to your legs . . . do you notice any tension there? . . . notice exactly where it is . . . notice how it feels . . . and release it . . . recalling the sensation of releasing it . . . remembering that feeling . . . letting all the tension dissolve . . . further . . . then further still . . . until the muscles feel entirely relaxed . . . .

By practising relaxation through recall the trainee will be able to reduce the time it takes to relax each muscle group from 45 to perhaps 15 seconds.

Relaxation through recall with counting

When the trainee feels skilled at relaxing through recall, the procedure can be still further shortened by introducing counting. Here, recited numbers correspond to the relaxation of the groups in the recall procedure.

I'm going to count slowly from one to ten. As I count, I'd like you to focus on the same muscle groups as in the recall procedure, relaxing them as you did then.

One . . . two, focusing on the arms and hands as they become more relaxed . . . three . . . four, relaxing the face and neck muscles . . . five . . . six, focusing on the muscles of the chest, back, shoulders and abdomen, feeling them becoming more and more relaxed . . . seven . . . eight, allowing relaxation to flow through the muscles of the legs and feet . . . nine . . . ten, relaxed all over . . .

It is suggested that the counting be done at a pace which corresponds with the trainee's respirations. Once mastered, this technique can be used by the trainee when preparing for challenging situations.

PASSIVE NEUROMUSCULAR RELAXATION

The technique described here is the work of Everly & Rosenfeld (1981). This method owes much to autogenic training (Ch. 19) in its use of suggestion and its images of warmth and heaviness. It is however, considered by its authors to be a muscular method and so belongs in this chapter.

Trainees are introduced to the approach with a short explanation on the following lines:

Tension in the muscles is associated with tension in the mind. If tension is eliminated from the muscles, then the subjective feeling of stress is reduced. In this method you will be asked to focus attention on one muscle group at a time, releasing any tension that exists. No activity is involved; the method is a passive one. It has been found that by concentrating on the muscles in this way, deep levels of relaxation can be achieved. Of course, the more you practise, the more effective it becomes.

The necessary conditions include a warm, quiet room where interruptions are unlikely to occur, and a comfortable chair to sit in or flat surface to lie on. The following script is adapted from Everly & Rosenfeld (1981). The authors suggest allowing a pause of 10 seconds between each item:

Settle into the chair you're in or the surface you are lying on, letting your body weight sink into it. Close your eyes. To start with, I'd like you to turn your attention to your breathing . . . follow the next breath out . . . then, let the air in . . . feel it gently filling your lungs . . . pause for a moment . . . and breathe out slowly . . . then allow your breathing to follow its natural rhythm: gentle and slow . . . getting gentler and slower . . .

Now bring your attention to the muscles of your head. Begin to feel a slow warm wave of relaxation gathering at the top of your head and beginning to descend towards your forehead . . . focusing on the muscles above your eyes . . . feel those muscles becoming heavy and relaxed . . . concentrate on the heavy feeling you are getting from them . . . now shift your attention to the muscles of your eyes and cheeks and feel them also becoming heavy and relaxed . . . now, focus on the muscles of your mouth and jaw . . . allow them to grow heavy and relaxed . . .

Pause for 10 seconds.

As your head and face continue to relax, let the wave of relaxation slowly descend into your neck . . . focus your attention on the neck muscles and feel them becoming heavier and more relaxed with every moment that passes . . .

Pause for 10 seconds.

The wave of relaxation continues to roll down, this time spreading warmth over your shoulder muscles . . . focus on these muscles . . . allow them to become heavy and relaxed as you concentrate your attention on them.

Pause for 10 seconds.

The head, neck and shoulders remain relaxed while you focus on your arms . . . letting the wave of relaxation bring heaviness and warmth to those muscles . . . concentrate on the feelings in the arms . . ..

Pause for 10 seconds.

Now feel the wave of relaxation descending into your hands as you focus on them . . . feel the muscles of your palms and fingers relaxing . . . feel warmth flowing into them as they become more relaxed . . .

Pause for 10 seconds.

Now, as the upper part of your body remains in deep relaxation, switch your attention to your abdomen and legs . . . begin to feel the wave of relaxation descending into your thigh muscles . . . and as you concentrate on

them, feel them becoming heavy . . . heavy as lead . . .

Pause for 10 seconds.

The wave of relaxation continues to descend into your lower legs . . . focus on your calf muscles . . . feel the sense of heaviness and relaxation in your calves . . .

Pause for 10 seconds.

Now, as the rest of your body remains relaxed, turn your attention to your feet . . . feel the warm wave of relaxation descending into your foot muscles . . . feel them becoming warm, heavy and relaxed . . .

Pause for 10 seconds.

Then, as you feel all your muscles to be in a state of relaxation, start to repeat the phrase, 'I am relaxed'; repeat it every time you breathe out.

After a 5-minute pause:

I'd like you now to bring your attention back to the room in which you are lying. I am going to count from one to five, and as I count, begin to feel more and more awake, more and more refreshed, with a clear head. When I reach five, I'd like you to open your eyes. One, begin to feel alert . . . two . . . three, more alert still . . . four . . . five . . . open your eyes and gently stretch your arms and legs . . .

The relaxation 'ripple'

Closely related to the above method is the relaxation 'ripple'. Adapted from Priest & Schott (1991), the technique consists of one continuous wave of relaxation which begins at the crown of the head and progresses down through the body to the toes. As the wave descends, the individual briefly scans the muscle groups, releasing tension. If he is lying down, all tension can be released; if he is standing, excess tension can be released. The effectiveness of the exercise is increased if it is timed to coincide with the outbreath. However, the participant should be discouraged from extending the outbreath too long.

The exercise can be better understood if the first relaxation ripple is preceded by a tensing of the whole body (Priest & Schott 1991). Thereafter, it can be performed in a passive manner.

A PASSIVE RELAXATION APPROACH

The script presented here is adapted from Madders (1981). It is addressed to trainees who are lying down. A supplementary section enables the instructor to adapt it for the seated participant.

Introductory remarks to trainees

This is a method which helps to relax your muscles and your thoughts. It consists of focusing on different parts of the body in turn and releasing any tension you find. There are no physical actions involved; relaxation occurs by virtue of a thought process. In spite of its length, the method is one which you can easily use to induce relaxation on your own.

Procedure for participants who are lying down

A firm support with a soft surface is needed, e.g. a length of foam spread out on the floor. The script could begin with the passage called 'Sinking' in Chapter 2 (p. 14), and continue as follows:

With your eyes closed, let your attention focus on your breathing . . . notice how gentle, slow and regular it is becoming . . . imagine each breath out carrying your tensions away, leaving you more relaxed than you were before . . . if you want to, take one deep breath . . . then allow your breathing to settle into its own rhythm . . . easy, calm and even . . . and forget about it.

I'm going to ask you to take a trip round the body, checking that all the muscle groups are as relaxed as possible and letting go any tension that might still remain. If outside thoughts creep in, hold them in a bubble and let them float away. I'll begin with the feet.

Bring your attention to your toes . . . are they lying still? If they are curled or stretched out or in some way not entirely comfortable, waggle them gently. As they come to rest, feel all the tension leaving them . . . feel them sinking down, heavy and motionless.

Let your feet roll out at the ankles. This is the most relaxed position for them. Let all the tension flow out of them . . . enjoy the sensation of just letting them go.

Moving on to the lower legs: feel the tension leaving the calf muscles and the shins. As the tension goes, so they feel heavier . . . so they feel warm and pleasantly tingling.

The thighs next: to be fully relaxed they need to be slightly rolling outwards . . . feel the relaxing effect of this position . . . make sure you have released all tension, and feel your thighs resting heavily on the floor.

Focus for a moment on the sensation of sagging heaviness throughout your legs . . . let the muscles shed their last remaining hint of tension and settle into a deep relaxation.

And now, think of your hips. Let them settle into the surface you are lying on . . .recognize any tension that lingers in the muscles . . .then relax it away . . . let it go on relaxing a bit further than you thought possible.

Settle your spine into the rug or mattress . . . become aware of how it is resting on the floor. Let it sink down, making contact wherever it wants to . . . all tension draining out of it.

Let your abdominal muscles lose their tension. Let them go soft and loose. Feel them spreading as they give up their last vestige of tension . . . notice how your relaxed abdomen rises and falls with your breathing . . . rises as the air is drawn in and falls as the air is expelled . . . abdominal breathing is relaxed breathing.

Moving up to your shoulders, to muscles which are prone to carry tension . . . feel them letting go . . . feel them spreading . . . feel them easing into the floor, limp and heavy . . . feel them dropping down towards your feet . . . imagine them shedding their burdens . . . and as the space between your shoulders and your neck opens out, imagine your neck a bit longer than it was before.

Now, direct your thoughts to the muscles of your left arm. Check that it lies limply on the ground. Notice the feeling of relaxation and allow this feeling to sweep down to your wrist and hand. Think of the fingers, are they curved and still? . . . neither drawn up nor stretched out . . . neither open nor closed, but gently resting . . . totally relaxed. As you breathe out, let the arm relax a little bit more . . . let it lie heavy and loose . . . so heavy and loose that if someone were to pick it up, then let go, it would flop down again like the arm of a rag doll.

Repeat the last paragraph with the muscles of the right arm.

Your neck muscles have no need to work with your head supported, so let them go . . . enjoy the feeling of 'letting go' in muscles which work so hard the rest of the time to keep your head upright. If you find any tension in the neck, release it and let this process of releasing continue, even below the surface . . . feel how pleasant it is when you let go the tension in these muscles.

Bring your attention now to your face, to the many small muscles whose job it is to manage your expressions. At the moment there's no need to have any expression at all on your face, so allow your muscles to feel relaxed . . . imagine how your face is when you are asleep . . . calm and motionless . . .

Now, think about the jaw . . . and as you do, allow it to drop slightly so that your teeth are separated . . . feel it relaxing with your lips gently touching. Check that your tongue is still, and lying in the middle of your mouth, soft and shapeless. Relax your throat so that all tension leaves it and the muscles feel smooth and resting.

With no expression on your face, your cheeks are relaxed and soft. If you think of your nose, it is just to register the passage of cool air travelling up your nostrils while the warmer air passes down . . . breathe tension out with the warm air . . . breathe stillness in with the cool air.

Check that your forehead is smooth . . . not furrowed in any direction . . . and as you release its remaining tension, imagine it being a little higher and a little wider that it was before . . . continue this feeling into your scalp and behind your ears . . . feel a sense of calm as you do this.

Let your thoughts focus on your eyes as they lie behind gently closed lids. Think of them resting in their sockets, floating rather than fixed . . . and as they come to rest, so do your thoughts also.

Spend a few minutes continuing to relax, deepening the effect of the above sequences . . .

You have now relaxed all the major muscle groups in your body. Think about them now as a whole . . . a totally relaxed whole . . . soothed by your gentle breathing rhythm, feel the peacefulness of this idea . . .

Images may drift in and out of your mind . . . see them as thoughts passing through. Feel yourself letting go of them. Say to yourself: 'I am feeling calm, I am feeling peaceful'. Let your mind conjure up a scene of contentment.

Imagery

The instructor picks one of the following: a sunny beach, a river bank or a scented garden. If trainees suffer from hay fever the first item is the best choice.

A sunny beach

See yourself lying on the hot sand of a sunny beach within an enclosed bay. It is sheltered from storms and protected from ocean currents. It is safe. You watch the light dancing on the water; you smell the sea air as it fills your nostrils; you hear the gulls calling above the sound of waves; you feel the warm sun on your skin. The grains of dry sand run through your fingers, forming little humps and hollows beneath your hand.

A river bank

Imagine you are lying in the soft, juicy long grass of early summer. You are in a green meadow that rolls down to the river. Scents rise up from the wild flowers, sweeping over you in waves. The sun is warm but a gentle breeze softens its intensity. Closing your eyes you become aware of the sound of water flowing, of birds calling and of leaves rustling.

A scented garden

Picture yourself lying on a newly mown lawn with the sun beating down on the moist cuttings, drawing out their fragrance. Reach out and feel the coolness of the damp grass. Through your half-closed eyelids you can see the tops of the trees swaying against the sky. Light breezes carry the scent of honeysuckle.

Following one of these short passages of visualization, trainees can relax quietly for a few minutes, before the session is brought to an end.

Termination

I am going to ask you to bring yourself slowly back to the room you are lying in. Gradually become aware of it. Gently move your arms and legs . . . wriggle your spine, and in your own time, allow your eyes to open. Slowly sit up and take in your surroundings. Give your body plenty of time to adjust from the relaxed to the alert state.

Before the meeting breaks up, the value of

practice should be emphasized. If carried out on a daily basis, the technique will help the trainee to relax himself more effectively.

Adapted procedure for seated trainees

The trainee picks the chair he finds most comfortable, although in a public building the choice may be limited. For deep relaxation the body needs to be well supported. The procedure begins in the following way:

Settle into your chair, sitting well back into the seat, your feet flat on the floor and your hands in your lap. Close your eyes. Become aware of the parts of your body that touch the chair and the floor. Feel the weight of your body passing through those points: hips, thighs, feet, back and arms, some of them carrying more weight than others. If the back of the chair is high enough, use it to support your head. If not, your head may be dropping forwards which is all right if you find it comfortable, but it tends to put a strain on the neck muscles if held for a long time. Try raising your head and seeing it as a weight supported by a pole. If you can balance it in this way, on your spine, you will be giving your neck muscles a rest.

The same script as for the lying position may be used, substituting the word 'sitting' for 'lying', and 'chair' for 'floor'. The paragraph about the neck muscles can be deleted, and also that referring to the feet.

KERMANI'S SCANNING TECHNIQUE

To 'scan' in this sense, is to run the attention over all the voluntary muscles.

Scanning may be used for at least two purposes: on the one hand, as a means of checking to see if tension exists, and on the other, as a device to enable the individual to feel in touch with his body as a whole. Both purposes are relevant in the context of relaxation, and the method forms a quick and simple version of the passive relaxation approach.

Here is an example adapted from Kermani (1990).

I'll ask you to spend a moment getting in touch with the different parts of your body, acknowledging them as part of you and checking that they feel relaxed and comfortable. Begin by bringing your attention to your feet. First the toes . . . working up through the ankles . . . to the calves and shins . . . over the knees . . . along the thighs . . . the abdomen . . . then the chest. Think now of your shoulders . . . of travelling down to the elbows . . . through the forearms . . . and into the wrists . . . hands and fingers. Become aware even of your fingertips.

Next, move across to the lower spine and the pelvis. Give your attention to the lumbar region . . . rising to the back of the chest and the blade bones . . . continuing up into the neck and scalp . . . to the crown of the head . . . then slowly begin to descend to the forehead . . . ending with the jaw . . . feel that every part of your body is relaxed . . .

You might like to think of a giant paint brush sweeping over your body, following the same route.

Another passive method

A release-only method is described in Chapter 8 (p. 64) as one component of Ost's applied relaxation.

PITFALLS OF PASSIVE RELAXATION

Passive relaxation is subject to the pitfalls of other muscular approaches (Ch. 6, p. 50). Because passive methods often include imagery and suggestion, the pitfalls relating to visualizations should also be taken into account (Ch.18, p. 151).

FURTHER READING

Bernstein D A, Borkovec T D 1973 Progressive relaxation training: a manual for the helping professions. Research Press, Champaign, Illinois
Everly G S, Rosenfeld R 1981 The nature and treatment of the stress response. Plenum Press, New York
Jacobson E 1976 You must relax. Souvenir Press, London

Kermani K S 1990 Autogenic training. Souvenir Press, London
Madders J 1981 Stress and relaxation: self-help ways to cope with stress and relieve nervous tension, ulcers, insomnia, migraine and high blood pressure, 3rd edn. Martin Dunitz, London

CHAPTER CONTENTS

Öst's applied relaxation method 61
    Introductory remarks to participants 63
    Conditions for training sessions 63
    Tense–release 64
    Release-only 64
    Cue-controlled or conditioned relaxation 65
    Differential relaxation 66
    Rapid relaxation 67
    Application training 67
    Maintenance programme 67

Evaluation of Öst's method 67

Pitfalls of applied relaxation 68

8

Applied relaxation

The methods described in previous chapters have, on the whole, been concerned with the induction of deep relaxation. Their purpose is to equip the individual with routines to be performed in the privacy of his own home. As such, these methods are useful for unwinding after a stressful day, but may not, however, provide strategies for coping with stress as it occurs. For this, some kind of shortened version that can be linked into life activities is required. Jacobson's (1938) differential relaxation (p. 95) and Wolpe's (1958) systematic desensitization (p. 149) represent early attempts at applied formats. However, it was Goldfried (1971) who, recognizing the extent of the gulf between relaxation in the therapeutic environment and relaxation in the stressful situation, focused expressly on the issue of the application of the skills. He emphasized the need for a portable and shortened form of progressive relaxation; a form which could be used to defuse anxiety as it occurs, and one which the individual could use as a general coping skill in everyday life. In so doing, he gave the individual a new role, defining him as an active agent in his treatment rather than a passive client. The approach was called 'training in self-control' because it implied active mastery of anxiety by the individual himself.

ÖST'S APPLIED RELAXATION METHOD

Öst's (1987) applied relaxation method is a recent version of Goldfried's approach. Using progressive relaxation as a core technique, the method teaches the individual to relax in successively shorter periods and to transfer these relaxation effects to everyday situations. Thus the individual is equipped with a strategy to control his reactions to stressful events as they occur.

The method consists of six components, in each of which a particular aspect of relaxation is taught:

- tense–release technique
- release-only technique
- cue-controlled (conditioned) relaxation
- differential relaxation
- rapid relaxation
- application training.

It is estimated that by using the tense–release method taught here (Wolpe & Lazarus 1966), the trained individual can achieve a relaxed state in 15–20 minutes; by using the release-only technique he can achieve it in 5–7 minutes; using the cue-controlled, in 2–3 minutes; the differential, in 60–90 seconds and using rapid relaxation, in 20–30 seconds. The final goal is to be able to apply relaxation skills to the experience of everyday stressful events.

The components must be taught in a precise order since progression to each depends on mastery of the preceding one. A total of 8–12 sessions of tuition is required, backed up by home practice which should be carried out twice a day, and is itself an important part of the programme.

Anxiety and Öst's method

Although applied relaxation can be used to cope with day-to-day stress, Öst's method is designed for use with people who suffer from panic and other kinds of anxiety. In this context, an understanding of anxiety as a state is crucial to the success of the training and an explanation should be given to the participant at the outset.

Anxiety may be seen as having three aspects: the physiological, the cognitive and the behavioural. The physiological aspect is represented by such phenomena as raised heart rate and blood pressure, palpitations, sweating and increased muscle tension; the cognitive aspect by negative thoughts such as 'This is too much for me to cope with' or 'I'm going to have a heart attack', and the behavioural aspect, by tense posture and different kinds of unrelaxed activity. These effects can escalate with one inflaming the other. In particular, the physiological and cognitive aspects can create a vicious circle with negative thoughts leading to sympathetic changes which are themselves interpreted in a negative way. The result can be a spiralling of anxiety (Fig. 8.1).

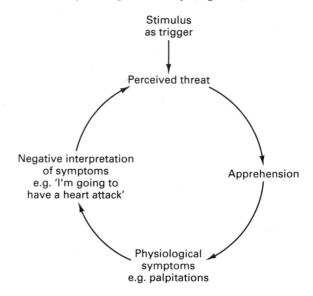

Figure 8.1 A cognitive view of anxiety. (Adapted from Clark D M 1986, A cognitive approach to panic. Behaviour, Research and Therapy 24:463 with kind permission from Elsevier Science, Kidlington.)

One way of breaking the circle would be to reinterpret the bodily changes in a more positive light, i.e. instead of thinking he is about to collapse with a heart attack, the individual could reassure himself that everyone gets palpitations sometimes. Another way of breaking the circle would be to neutralize the anxiety with the use of a relaxation technique such as progressive relaxation. Both ways are incorporated into this method.

Because anxiety is easier to relieve when it is mild, it should be addressed before it reaches a peak. Early signals or signs of rising anxiety levels such as a pounding heart, sweating, fast breathing or tense muscles can be used as cues to employ the technique. Experiences of anxiety-provoking events can be recorded by means of

Date	Situation	Reaction, i.e. anxiety signals	Intensity (0 – 10)	Action taken

Figure 8.2 A form for recording self-observed early anxiety signals. (Adapted from Öst L-G 1987, Applied relaxation: description of a coping technique and review of controlled studies. Behaviour Research and Therapy 25: 399, with kind permission from Elsevier Science, Kidlington.)

'self-monitoring', where the individual notes on a printed form the situations, the intensity of his anxiety and the remedial action taken by him (Fig. 8.2). This form, over time, reflects his progress in coping with such events.

Introductory remarks to participants

Before beginning the programme of relaxation, the rationale of the treatment is presented to participants:

As its name suggests, this method shows you how to apply relaxation skills in everyday life. This means the skills have to be quick-acting and unobtrusive. The aim is to be able to relax in 20–30 seconds and to transfer this skill to situations of stress.

The approach starts by introducing you to progressive relaxation which consists of tensing and releasing the muscles throughout the body. When that is learned and practised daily, the tensing part of the exercise is dropped.

Next, you'll be asked to repeat the word 'relax' to yourself when you are in a state of relaxation. Attaching the word to the state has the effect of turning the word into a cue; a cue to invoke a state of relaxation. This only happens of course, after it has been repeatedly associated with the experience of relaxation.

Learning how to use reduced amounts of muscle tension when carrying out specific tasks, is the next procedure, followed by a rapid-acting technique for maintaining low levels of stress throughout the day. Finally, these skills are applied to particular situations of stress.

These exercises enable you to achieve relaxation in progressively shorter periods of time. Success depends on practice.

If you are troubled by anxiety and suffer from symptoms such as pounding heart, breathlessness, nausea and muscle tension which you've been told have no medical foundation, try seeing these symptoms purely as bodily sensations, which they are. If you regard them as threatening they will tend to escalate, increasing the feeling of distress. If you dismiss them and relax your body they'll tend to subside. Bodily sensations of stress can be controlled in this way and since, as with anything else, they are easiest to deal with when they first appear, it is useful to train yourself to recognize early signals.

Conditions for training sessions

It is suggested that participants sit for the exercises since daily stress frequently occurs in this posture rather than in a lying one. The chair should be comfortable and have arm rests. The procedures are first demonstrated by the trainer and carried out by the trainee to ensure that they have been understood. The trainee then closes his eyes while the instructor runs through the programme. At the end, the trainee rates the degree of relaxation gained on a 0–100 scale.

Each component requires one or two weeks of practice for the trainee to become proficient in it.

Tense–release

Two sessions of tuition are devoted to learning this version of progressive relaxation.

First session

The first is spent working on the hands, arms, face, neck and shoulders. Each muscle group is taken through one tense–release cycle in which 5 seconds are allotted for the tension and 10–15 seconds for the release, as follows:

Begin by clenching the right hand . . . make a fist . . . make it tight . . . notice the sensation of tension in the hand and forearm while you hold it for five seconds . . . then let it go . . . feel the hand and forearm becoming relaxed and comfortable . . . warm and relaxed . . . relaxed and heavy . . .

The release is continued for 10 seconds.

The other actions featuring in session one are:

- clenching the left hand
- bending the right elbow
- straightening the right elbow by pressing the wrist down on the arm of the chair
- bending the left elbow
- straightening the left elbow
- raising the eyebrows and wrinkling the forehead
- bringing the eyebrows together and frowning
- screwing the eyes up tight
- biting the teeth together
- pressing the tongue against the roof of the mouth
- pressing the lips together
- pressing the head against the back of the chair
- pressing the chin down on to the collar bone
- hunching the shoulders up to the ears
- bracing the shoulders back to bring the blades together.

Termination. When the above exercises have been worked, the session is brought to an end.

The relaxation session is over now, and to help you

return to activity, I'm going to count from one to five, and when I get to five, I want you to open your eyes feeling calm and relaxed . . . one, feeling calm . . . two, feeling relaxed . . . three, very calm . . . four, very relaxed . . . five . . . open your eyes.

Second session

Session two starts with a review of the work done in the first session followed by tense–release exercises for the chest, stomach, back, legs and feet. These are:

- tensing the muscles which pull the stomach in
- arching the back so that the spine leaves the back of the chair
- tensing the buttock muscles by pressing the feet down into the floor
- raising the heels with the toes remaining on the ground
- raising the front part of the foot keeping the heels on the ground.

The second session is terminated in the same way as the first.

Participants are instructed to practise for 15 minutes twice daily. They are asked to record the level of relaxation achieved, using a 0–100 scale where 0 = total relaxation, 100 = maximum tension, and 50 represents normal. They are also asked to keep a note of the length of practice time taken to reach the level achieved. The form shown in Figure 8.3, serves to motivate the individual to practise as well as to record the details of the homework session.

Release-only

In this phase of instruction, the 'tension' part of the sequence is eliminated, leaving just the 'release' part. As a result, the relaxed state can be achieved in less time than when working with the full sequence; 5–7 minutes are suggested instead of the 15 of the tense–release session.

The training session begins with breathing instructions, followed by a scanning of all the voluntary muscles starting with the head and working down to the toes. The following instruc-

0 = totally relaxed
100 = maximum tension

Date	Time	Component	Degree of relaxation (0 – 100)		Time taken to achieve it
			Before	After	

Figure 8.3 Form for recording relaxation training homework. (Adapted from Öst L-G 1987, Applied relaxation: description of a coping technique and review of controlled studies. Behaviour Research and Therapy, 25: 400, with kind permission from Elsevier Science, Kidlington.)

tions are adapted from Öst (1987):

In a moment I'm going to ask you to focus your attention on your breathing, and in particular, on the movement of your upper abdomen . . . notice how it swells slightly as you breathe in, and sinks back as you breathe out . . . do not change it in any way . . . just tune in to its rhythmic pattern . . . feel yourself relaxing more with each breath . . . feel your muscles letting go from the top of your head . . . your forehead . . . eyebrows . . . eyelids . . . cheeks . . . temples . . . jaws . . . throat . . . tongue . . . lips . . . feel your entire face relaxed . . . now . . . your neck . . . shoulders . . . arm . . . and down to the tips of your fingers . . . and while you are doing this, let your breathing continue at its own pace, expanding the stomach region in particular . . . Now, relax your back . . . now, the lower part of your body . . . hips . . . thighs . . . knees . . . calves . . . shins . . . feet . . . toes . . . still breathing gently and noticing the relaxing effect of each breath . . . feel yourself relaxing more and more . . .

The sequence is terminated in the same way as for the first component.

Again, the homework assignment is a twice-daily practice, the trainee being asked to record

afterwards, the level of relaxation achieved and how long it took to reach it.

Cue-controlled or conditioned relaxation

In this training component, the individual picks a word such as 'relax'. 'Peace', 'calm', or 'control' would serve as well, but 'relax' is adopted here. Next he relaxes himself by employing the release-only method of progressive relaxation. Once relaxed, he begins silently to recite his chosen word; he recites it once each time he breathes out. Following many repetitions, an association is built up between the word and the relaxed state whereby the word alone becomes capable of inducing a measure of relaxation. The word has thus become a cue. The stronger the association, the greater the power of the cue word. Expressed in other terms, a conditioning process has been set up, as a result of which the trainee feels himself relaxed whenever he thinks the word 'relax'.

A training session would begin with the 'release-only' method of relaxation. The trainer then proceeds as follows:

Spend a few moments quietly relaxing with your eyes closed . . . signal to me by raising your right index finger when you feel fully relaxed . . . if you are ready, turn your attention now to your breathing . . . tune in to its rhythm . . . let it adopt its own pace . . . do not be tempted to alter it . . . and just before you breathe in, think the word 'inhale' . . . just before you breathe out, think the word 'relax' . . .

The trainer leads with the instructions of 'inhale' and 'relax' for five breaths, and then asks the trainee to continue on his own for a further five breaths. After a few minutes' rest, the full sequence is repeated.

If there is more than one participant, the trainer will not attempt to synchronize their respirations but will let them conduct their own exercise. As proficiency increases, the command 'inhale' can be dropped, and the word 'relax' used on its own.

Homework consists of 20 pairings a day of the cue word 'relax' with exhalation, performed when the individual is fully relaxed. Participants should be warned against overbreathing, i.e. allowing the breathing to become deeper or more rapid (p. 119). The trainee keeps a record of the level of relaxation achieved and the time taken to reach it.

Once learned, it takes only 2 or 3 minutes to get fully relaxed by this method.

Differential relaxation

So far, the sessions have been concerned with teaching basic techniques. The application of those skills now begins. Differential relaxation focuses on controlling the levels of muscle tension while the individual is engaged in some activity. Although some tension is needed in order to carry out the task, the level is often greater than is necessary. This applies both to the muscles actively involved in the task, and to the muscles not directly engaged in it. Different levels of tension (or relaxation) are required for each.

Since an ability to recognize muscle tension at its varying levels is essential for developing this skill, differential relaxation is presented after the individual has been trained in progressive relaxation.

Two sessions of tuition are indicated, one

dealing with sitting and the other with standing activities. Both sessions begin with a revision of cue-controlled relaxation.

The first session: sitting

In the first, the trainee, seated in an armchair, is instructed to make certain movements while maintaining a relaxed state in the rest of the body.

Please make yourself as comfortable as possible. Settle into the chair with your feet flat on the floor. With your eyes closed relax yourself using your cue word with breathing . . . when you are ready, would you raise your right index finger . . . I'd like you now to open your eyes and look around the room without moving your head . . . notice the tension in the eye muscles but keep the body relaxed . . .

Next, look around the room allowing your head to move in order to increase your range of vision. Keep a minimum of tension in the neck muscles while you do this, and check that the rest of your body is free from tension . . .

Would you now lift one arm, and as you do, remember to keep the other parts of your body relaxed . . . and, lower the arm. Continue to scan your body for signs of unnecessary tension.

Now, lift one leg off the ground, keeping the rest of your body as relaxed as possible . . . and, let it down.

If you had any difficulty with this exercise, perhaps we could discuss it before moving on.

The routine is then carried out on the other arm and leg, after which the trainee is moved from his armchair to an upright chair. He relaxes himself in this new sitting position before being led through the same procedure of eye, head and limb movements. Next, he is seated at a table and asked to write something short such as his name and address, using the minimum of muscle tension needed to accomplish the task. As an alternative, in practice sessions, he could make a short telephone call, adopting the same relaxed state.

The second session: standing

In the second session of differential relaxation, the trainee stands. His position should be near a wall in case he feels unsteady, but he should not be leaning on it. The session begins with cue-controlled relaxation, after which the same schedule of head, arm and leg movements is worked through.

Lastly, the trainee is asked to practise relaxation while walking. Emphasis is placed on finding an easy way of moving, and on relaxing the muscles not used, such as those of the face and hands. Any initial awkwardness will disappear as the individual discovers more relaxed ways of holding his body.

With the skills he has learned and practised, the individual will now be able to achieve a state of relaxation consistent with effective task performance within about 60–90 seconds. Differential relaxation is expanded in Chapter 12.

Rapid relaxation

As its name implies, this component is designed to reduce still further the time it takes to get relaxed. First, the trainee's environment is arranged so that a regularly used appliance acts as a cue to relax; for example, the wristwatch or the telephone are marked with a coloured dot which reminds the individual to relax whenever he sees it. Every time he looks at his watch or makes a telephone call he is reminded to release tension. This means that stress is in general held at low levels in the everyday setting. Rapid relaxation consists of the following routine performed each time the individual sees the coloured dot:

Take a slow breath . . .think 'relax' . . . then exhale.
Repeat this twice . . . scan the body for unnecessary tensions . . . and release them.

Regular practice of this short sequence (15–20 times a day) makes the technique more effective and results in the trainee being able to reduce further the time taken to relax. It has been found that after one or two weeks' practice, he can relax himself by this method in as little as 20–30 seconds.

Application training

Applying relaxation skills in situations of anxiety is the subject of this phase. The goal is not to extinguish anxiety but to control it at a level at which the task can be efficiently performed. The recognition of early signals of anxiety is emphasized, since they are easier to control than full-blown ones.

Take yourself to a situation that you know is likely to provoke stress for you. Relax yourself before entering the scene. Observe your reactions. If you feel anxiety levels beginning to rise, bring out your cue word 'relax'. Continue to apply it until you feel your anxiety levels falling.

It may not work the first time because, like any skill, practice is necessary to achieve success, but gradually, you will find you are gaining more control over your anxiety levels.

The technique can be applied across a wide range of stress — and anxiety — provoking situations. As a preliminary, the individual could visualize himself successfully coping in the stress-provoking situation before exposing himself to the same event in real life (see Chapter 18).

Maintenance programme

However successful the treatment, Öst suggests keeping up the habit of scanning the body for unnecessary tension and using rapid relaxation to release it.

EVALUATION OF ÖST'S METHOD

Öst addresses three modes of anxiety with the applied relaxation approach: the physiological, the cognitive and the behavioural. The physiological aspect is addressed through muscle relaxation; the cognitive through the cue word; and the behavioural through differential relaxation and exposure to the stressor. A multivariate approach such as this, has advantages in a condition such as anxiety where changes occur in different modes.

Applied relaxation has been tested in the treatment of a large number of conditions including panic disorders, headache, pain, epilepsy, tinnitus, migraine and gastric catarrh. In a review of 18 controlled studies, it was found to be significantly more effective than no treatment or placebo conditions. When compared with other behavioural methods, it was found to be as effective. Follow-up, at varying times from 5–19 months, showed that the effects were maintained and in some cases augmented (Öst 1987).

A study which compared it with progressive relaxation (the version of Bernstein & Borkovec 1973), showed applied relaxation to be more effective on most measures immediately following treatment. On follow-up at 19 months, applied relaxation was shown to be more effective on all measures (Öst 1988). Thus the method seems to provide long-term benefit.

PITFALLS OF APPLIED RELAXATION

Since applied relaxation is based on progressive relaxation, the same pitfalls are relevant to both methods. They may be found in Chapter 6 (p. 50).

FURTHER READING

Öst L G 1987 Applied relaxation: description of a coping technique and review of controlled studies. Behaviour, Research and Therapy 25: 397–407

Hawton K, Salkovskis P M, Kirk J, Clark D M 1989 Cognitive behaviour therapy for psychiatric problems. Oxford Medical, Oxford

CHAPTER CONTENTS

Protocol for behavioural relaxation training 70
Setting 70
Introduction of method to participants 70
Training procedure 70
Arousal 71
Variations of the protocol 72
Script for trainee sitting in an upright chair 72
'Mini-relaxation' 72

Pitfalls of behavioural relaxation training 72

The Behavioural Relaxation Scale 72
Using the Behavioural Relaxation Scale 73
Reliability and validity of the Behavioural Relaxation
Scale 73

**Other methods of assessment of behavioural
relaxation training 74**
Self-report 74

**Evaluation of the effectiveness of behavioural
relaxation 75**

9

Behavioural relaxation training

A person who is tense adopts a characteristic pattern of muscular activity in the form of frowning, clenching and general body tenseness. The muscles of a relaxed person by contrast, are free from excessive muscle tension. As a result, people who are relaxed look different from people who are tense. Their feelings are associated with a different posture in each case. Schilling, working in the early 1980s, found the converse also occurred, that is, people adopting a relaxed posture reported feeling more relaxed.

Schilling, who was teaching progressive relaxation to adolescent boys, noticed they were better at tensing than releasing; in fact they found it difficult to respond to the request to relax. He suggested to his pupils that instead of trying to *become* relaxed, they should adopt the more concrete objective of trying to *look* relaxed; to take up postures they would expect to see in people who were relaxed. The result was that the pupils not only succeeded in looking relaxed, but reported actually feeling more relaxed. Thus, by adopting postures characteristic of relaxation, they had induced a subjective feeling of relaxation.

The idea is reminiscent of the facial and postural feedback hypotheses which state that feedback from facial expression and posture induces feelings that match those expressions and postures. In other words, people feel the emotions that correspond with their poses. This theory is referred to again in Chapter 25 (p. 198).

Based on these ideas, Schilling & Poppen

(1983) set up a method of relaxation which they called behavioural relaxation training (BRT).

PROTOCOL FOR BEHAVIOURAL RELAXATION TRAINING

Setting

The ideal setting is a warm, quiet room with dimmed lighting. A padded recliner is the chair of choice but since this may not be available, any flat surface will serve. Pillows may be used under the knees, forearms and head, as required. Women will find it convenient to wear trousers.

Introduction of method to participants

Participants are introduced to the method in the following way:

We can all recognize signs of tension: tightly drawn face muscles, clenching of teeth and fingers. These are typical postures that people adopt when under stress. When people are relaxed, muscle tensions are released and a new posture results. The central idea of behavioural relaxation training is that by adopting the posture of a relaxed person, we can make ourselves feel more relaxed.

In this method you will be asked to make different parts of your body look as relaxed as possible and then to notice the effect the new position has on you; to notice how the new position feels. I'll describe and demonstrate each item before we begin. Please try out the items on yourself.

The postures, as described in Table 9.1, are then demonstrated and the trainee asked to copy them. The unrelaxed postures are also demonstrated to emphasize the point. Feedback is provided by the trainer in the form of praise or corrective instructions. The trainee is asked particularly to take note of the proprioceptive events, i.e. the joint and muscle feelings which convey the sense of body position as each new posture is adopted.

Following the demonstration, the trainee rests quietly with his eyes closed. After a few minutes, the instructor may make an initial assessment (see the section on the Behavioural Relaxation Scale, p. 72).

Training procedure

The training procedure is then presented in its entirety. Below is a slightly paraphrased version of the protocol laid out in Poppen (1988), where it is suggested that each relaxed posture be held for 30–60 seconds. Trainees are again asked to close their eyes.

Feet

Starting with the feet: these are relaxed when you feel they are flopping, with the toes slightly pointing away from each other. No effort is involved; it is the posture of rest. If you are putting any effort into it, then your muscles will be working and your feet will be tensed. Notice how your feet feel in the relaxed position.

Body

The next area is called 'body'. Your body is relaxed when your hips and shoulders are in line with each other and resting on the supporting surface. If you are lying in a crooked fashion, your body is not relaxed. If there is any movement you are not relaxed. Make a note of the sensation of having a relaxed body.

Hands

This posture is called 'hands'. Your hands are relaxed when they are resting on a surface with the fingers gently curled, that is to say, neither clenched nor stretched out. Notice the sensations in your hands as you relax them.

Shoulders

And now the shoulders; these are relaxed when they are level and dropped. If you feel one is twisted or higher than the other, then they are not relaxed. Register the feeling of having relaxed shoulders.

Head

The next posture is called 'head'. Make sure your head is resting on its cushion and facing forwards. Feel it

Table 9.1 Relaxed and unrelaxed behaviours. (Adapted from Lichstein 1988 Clinical Relaxation Strategies, p137, with permission from John Wiley, New York)

Item	Relaxed	Unrelaxed
Breathing	Breaths regular and fewer in number than recorded on the baseline	Breaths irregular and greater in number than recorded on the baseline
Quiet	No audible sounds such as sighs, words or movements	Talking, whispering, sighing, coughing, snoring or other audible sounds
Body	Symmetrical and fully resting on supporting surface	Holding any part tense or twisted
Head	Motionless and supported with nose in midline	Head-turning or other movements; head unsupported or tilted; nose outside midline
Eyes	Lids lightly closed with eyes still	Eyes open; or if closed, darting about under tense and fluttering lids
Mouth	Lips parted at centre of mouth with teeth separated	Lips firmly closed with teeth held together; or mouth uncomfortably open
Throat	No activity	Swallowing, twitching or preparing to speak
Shoulders	Dropped, and level with each other; resting against support	Both hunched or one higher than the other; not resting on support
Hands	Both resting at sides, on armrests or on lap; palms down, fingers gently curled	Clasped, clenched tight or gripping the armrest
Feet	Comfortably rolled out so that the toes point away from each other	Pointing vertically, crossed or excessively rolled out

being supported. Any attempt to turn or twist it will cause your neck muscles to work. Notice the feelings you get as you relax your neck muscles.

Mouth

The next posture is called 'mouth'. Your mouth will be relaxed if your teeth are parted and your lips gently touching at the sides. If you are smiling, grimacing, licking your lips or pressing them together, your mouth is not relaxed. Take note of the feelings you get as you relax your mouth.

Throat

The next relaxed area is called 'throat', and this is relaxed when you can feel no movement there. If you are swallowing or if your tongue is twitching, then your throat is not relaxed. However, if you need to swallow, do so, then return to your relaxed state. Notice the sensations in your throat as you relax it.

Breathing

The next item is called 'breathing'. Relaxed breathing is slow and gentle. Unrelaxed breathing is rapid, jerky and may be interrupted by coughing, sighing and yawning. Register the effect of your relaxed breathing.

Quiet

The next item is called 'quiet'. This means that you

are not making any sounds such as sniffing, umm-ing, or talking. If you feel you have to clear your throat, that's all right, but return to your state of quiet afterwards, noticing the sensation of stillness.

Eyes

The last relaxed area is called 'eyes'. These are relaxed when the lids rest over them in a lightly closed position and when the eye movements are brought to rest. Eyes are unrelaxed when they dart about and when the lids are twitching. Notice the feelings you are getting from your eyes as you relax them.

The order is not important but it is suggested that the eyes are left until the end, since the trainee needs to use them to mentally observe the other behaviours (Poppen 1988).

A training session will last about 15–20 minutes after which, the trainee is instructed to continue relaxing as he silently reviews the items for a further 10–15 minutes. At the end of this period, the trainer may carry out a posttreatment assessment (see p. 72).

Arousal

Arousal takes place in the following manner:

Very slowly, I would like you to prepare to end the session. To help you transfer from your deeply relaxed state, I am going to count slowly from one to five: one . . . two . . . three, slowly open your eyes . . . four . . . five . . . begin to move your limbs . . . and in your own time, sit up.

Practice. Since behavioural relaxation training is a skill, practice is necessary. Trainees are urged to spend 20 minutes a day practising.

Variations of the protocol

Variations of the above protocol exist for different situations: first, where the only available chair is an upright chair and second, where the need for relaxation occurs in the middle of a task (termed 'mini-relaxation' by Poppen).

Script for trainee sitting in an upright chair

Where the trainee is seated in an upright chair, the following four areas of back, head, arms and legs should be substituted for body, head, hands and feet in the protocol given above.

Back

The next area is called 'back'. It is relaxed when your shoulder blades and hips touch the chair symmetrically. It is unrelaxed when you are bending forwards, arching backwards or leaning to one side. Register the feelings you get from the relaxed posture.

Head

Now we come to the area called 'head', and this is relaxed when it is held upright and is looking forwards. The head is unrelaxed when it is tilted or turned in any direction. Notice the feelings you get from holding your head in the relaxed position.

Arms

The next area to relax is called 'arms'. These are relaxed when the wrists are resting on the thighs; they are unrelaxed when hanging down, when crossed or when being leant on. Notice the sensations as you relax your arms.

Legs

The next area is called 'legs', and these are relaxed when you have both feet flat on the floor with a right angle at the knees. Allow the knees to fall outwards into a comfortable position. The legs are unrelaxed when crossed, extended or tucked under the chair. Notice the sensations in your legs when they are in the relaxed position.

'Mini-relaxation'

Any activity uses particular muscle groups. The muscles which are not involved, however, can be relaxed. This is what Poppen means by 'mini-relaxation'. For example: the hands can be relaxed while talking; the shoulders while typing; the mouth, throat and breathing while working alone. Thus, mini-relaxation is a form of differential relaxation (see Ch. 12).

Mini-relaxation can be practised throughout the day and reminders to do so provided by placing coloured dots on the telephone, watch, steering wheel, typewriter, kettle-handle or any other frequently used appliance.

Poppen suggests that benefit can be derived from combining behavioural relaxation training with other relaxation methods such as autogenics and meditation. In this way the one can augment the effects of the other.

PITFALLS OF BEHAVIOURAL RELAXATION TRAINING

As with any relaxation approach, possible pitfalls should be considered before taking it up. Chapter 6 (p. 50) contains a discussion of hazards relating to muscular approaches.

THE BEHAVIOURAL RELAXATION SCALE

There are no universally accepted procedures of assessment in relaxation; a reliable and valid measuring device has yet to be found. Schilling & Poppen's (1983) Behavioural Relaxation Scale (BRS) is an attempt to fill one aspect of this gap. It was designed as an easy method for measuring the motor element of relaxation, i.e. that relating to the voluntary muscles. Although it specifically measures the behaviours taught in behavioural relaxation training, it may be used to assess the motor aspect of any relaxation procedure.

The scale is based on the assumption that a person who feels relaxed, also looks relaxed. As a result, some kind of judgement of the degree to which a person is relaxed can be made by an onlooker. Using the same items that feature in behavioural relaxation training, the scale allows an objective assessment to be made, without the need for expensive equipment such as electromyographic instruments. Each posture is checked for the degree of relaxation with reference to the table of relaxed and unrelaxed postures (Table 9.1). The order of the items in Table 9.1 is seen by Poppen (1988), as being the most convenient for assessment purposes.

Using the Behavioural Relaxation Scale

Establishing the baseline breathing rate

The first measure concerns the breathing rate. This is counted over a 30-second interval (each count representing a complete cycle of inhalation and exhalation). The process is repeated 15 times and the total sum of the respirations divided by 15 to give the mean or average number of respirations in 30 seconds. The mean is then entered in the box marked 'breathing baseline' on the score sheet (Fig. 9.1).

General assessment

A general assessment covers five 1-minute periods in which the individual is observed for outward signs of relaxation. Each minute begins with a further count of the breathing rate lasting 30 seconds; it is entered in the empty box in the column marked '1' in Figure 9.1. If the answer is less than the baseline rate, then the adjacent plus sign is ringed; if it is more, the minus sign is ringed. The following 15 seconds are spent scanning the trainee's key postures, picking out any unrelaxed ones and repeating the appropriate word label for example, 'shoulders' for a hunched arm. The succeeding 15 seconds are spent ringing the items; plus for relaxed postures, minus for any that continue to be unrelaxed.

After the first minute, the procedure is re-peated and the answers recorded under the figure '2', and so on until five columns have been completed. The ringed plus signs are added up and entered under 'total'.

Working out the score

Scoring is expressed as a percentage arrived at in the following way: the total number of ringed 'plus' signs is counted and the sum divided by the total number of observations (i.e., the 10 behaviours multiplied by the five minutes). The resulting figure is then multiplied by 100. For example: if there were a total of 40 ringed plus signs, they would be divided by the 50 observations. After multiplying the resulting fraction by 100, a figure of 80% would be obtained.

The pretreatment baseline

One pretreatment assessment (p. 70) acts as a baseline against which to measure progress, but should itself be carried out after a short period of rest to avoid confounding the effects of training with those which occur naturally whenever a person enters a restful environment (Lichstein et al 1981). Thereafter, assessment follows each training session to monitor progress.

Reliability and validity of the Behavioural Relaxation Scale

The reliability of the scale, i.e. its ability to produce the same scores when used on different occasions, has been tested. It was found that higher levels of reliability were obtained with trained observers than with untrained ones. Thus the training of observers is important.

The validity of the scale, that is, the extent to which the device measures what it purports to measure, has been demonstrated by Schilling & Poppen (1983); subjects receiving accepted forms of relaxation training showed statistically significant changes in relaxation scores on the Behavioural Relaxation Scale while controls did not. Also, significant correlations were found between electromyographic measures of frontalis muscle and BRS scores, i.e. low EMG readings were

Name..Date.......Time.......Session no.......

Breathing baseline [ ] + relaxed
− unrelaxed

INTERVALS

	1		2		3		4		5		Total
Breathing	−	+	−	+	−	+	−	+	−	+	
Quiet	−	+	−	+	−	+	−	+	−	+	
Body	−	+	−	+	−	+	−	+	−	+	
Head	−	+	−	+	−	+	−	+	−	+	
Eyes	−	+	−	+	−	+	−	+	−	+	
Mouth	−	+	−	+	−	+	−	+	−	+	
Throat	−	+	−	+	−	+	−	+	−	+	
Shoulders	−	+	−	+	−	+	−	+	−	+	
Hands	−	+	−	+	−	+	−	+	−	+	
Feet	−	+	−	+	−	+	−	+	−	+	
										Score	

Self-ratings 1 2 3 4 5 6 7

Figure 9.1 Behavioural Relaxation Scale score sheet. (Adapted from Poppen R 1988 Behavioural relaxation training and assessment, Pergamon Press with permission from Allyn and Bacon, Needham Heights, MA.)

associated with BRS scores which reflect relaxed postures as described in the BRS, while high readings were associated with scores which reflect unrelaxed postures (Schilling & Poppen 1983).

OTHER METHODS OF ASSESSMENT OF BEHAVIOURAL RELAXATION TRAINING

Because relaxation involves responses in subjective, physiological and behavioural spheres, a full assessment would take account of all three modalities. Poppen indicates the need to view behavioural assessment as part of a broader system of measurement. One of its components is self-report.

Self-report

As relaxation and anxiety are subjective states, it is appropriate and customary to include a self-rating measure when assessing their levels. Self-report can take the form of free description, but since this is difficult to quantify, pre-set descriptive phrases with associated numbered ratings are often used. The individual rings the number corresponding with the phrase that most accurately reflects his state.

A behavioural relaxation self-rating scale, adapted from Poppen (1988) is shown below.

Behavioural Relaxation Self-rating Scale

1. Feeling extremely tense and upset throughout my body.
2. Feeling generally tense throughout my body.
3. Feeling some tension in some parts of my body.
4. Feeling relaxed as in my normal resting state.
5. Feeling more relaxed than usual.
6. Feeling completely relaxed throughout my entire body.
7. Feeling more deeply and completely relaxed than I ever have.

Discrepancy between self-report and objective testing

There are often wide discrepancies between self-reports and objective measurements. One of the reasons is that self-report may be coloured by factors of social desirability, for instance where the trainee gives the answer he thinks is expected of him. These matters are discussed further in Chapter 24 (p. 189).

EVALUATION OF THE EFFECTIVENESS OF BEHAVIOURAL RELAXATION

Behavioural relaxation offers both therapy and a scale of assessment. As a therapy it provides a form of body scanning in which relaxed postures are adopted and feelings of relaxation experienced. As an assessment tool it provides a numerical measure of the level of relaxation present in the muscles.

A comparison of behavioural relaxation training with progressive relaxation and biofeedback and control, using the Behavioural Relaxation Scale, showed decreasing tension scores in all relaxation groups. The behavioural relaxation training group alone maintained their low tension scores at follow-up (Schilling & Poppen 1983). This suggests that the benefits of behavioural relaxation training are not short-lived.

Behavioural relaxation training does not demand expensive equipment or long training sessions. It is easily learned and readily applied. Minimum levels of unrelaxed behaviour have been apparently achieved within as few as two training sessions (Schilling & Poppen 1983).

FURTHER READING

Poppen R 1988 Behavioural relaxation training and assessment. Pergamon Press, Oxford
Schilling D J, Poppen R 1983 Behavioural relaxation training and assessment. Journal of Behaviour Therapy and Experimental Psychiatry 14: 99–107.

CHAPTER CONTENTS

Rationale of Mitchell's method 77

Procedure for Mitchell's Method 78
   Starting position 78
   Instructions 79
   Introductory remarks to participants 79
   Items of the Mitchell method of relaxation 79
   Working through the schedule 79
   Practice 82

Further aspects of the Mitchell method 82
   'Keys' and 'triggers' 82
   The 'three-point pull' 83
   Application of the method to specific conditions 83
   Comparison with other approaches 83

Evaluation of Mitchell's method 83

Pitfalls of Mitchell's method 83

10

The Mitchell method

RATIONALE OF MITCHELL'S METHOD

Mitchell (1987) argues that it is useless to ask a person to notice tension in his muscles since there are no nerve endings in muscle tissue capable of conveying such information to the conscious brain. The sensory apparatus in the muscle connects only with the lower brain and spinal cord. Consequently, exhortations to become aware of the presence or absence of muscle tension are inappropriate. However, proprioceptive structures in the joints, and skin pressure receptors do have links with the conscious brain. The first tell us where our limbs are in space, and the second tell us where the skin is being stretched or compressed. It is only, she claims, by moving the joints and stretching the skin that information about muscle tension is relayed to the higher centres. Thus, the joints and the skin are the organs on which we need to focus attention.

Mitchell's approach is based on the physiological principle of reciprocal inhibition, i.e. when one group of muscles acting on a joint is working, the opposing group is obliged to relax. As the fibres of one group contract, the fibres of the opposing group become slack. It is a built-in mechanism to allow the smooth performance of muscular activity.

Mitchell exploits this principle and makes it the nub of her approach. Stress-related posture, or what she calls 'the punching position' is studied, the working muscle groups are identified, and then relaxed by activating the opposing groups.

The resulting changes of position of the joints, and the accompanying skin sensations, are then mentally registered as the part settles into the posture of ease. Thus, her approach consists of moving the body out of the position of defence or stress and training it to recognize and adapt the position of ease or relaxation.

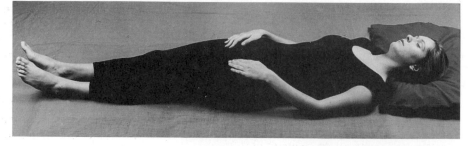

Figure 10.1 Starting position: supine.

Her method is composed of 13 items, referred to as joint changes (although they do not all involve joint activity). These changes reverse different aspects of the punching position which is described below:

- shoulders hunched
- arms held close to sides
- fingers curled into the palms
- legs crossed
- feet dorsiflexed (drawn up towards face)
- torso bent forwards
- head held forwards
- breathing rapid with noticeable movement in the upper chest
- jaw clenched
- lips pursed
- tongue pressed into upper palate
- brow furrowed into a frown.

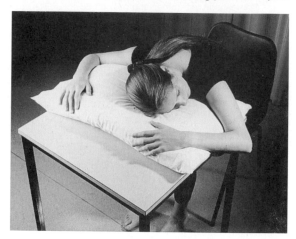

Figure 10.2 Starting position: forward-lean-sitting.

Mitchell does not assert that the punching position is actually adopted under stress; rather, that the muscles responsible for it are contracting to a slight extent.

PROCEDURE FOR MITCHELL'S METHOD

Starting position

Three starting positions are described:

1. supine lying, on a firm surface (Fig. 10.1)
2. sitting, leaning forwards with head and arms resting on a table, i.e. forward-lean-sitting (Fig. 10.2)
3. sitting in a straight, high-backed chair with

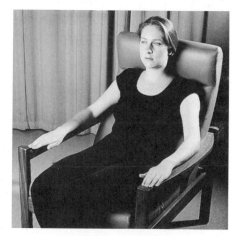

Figure 10.3 Starting position: sitting.

arm rests on which the hands are supported, palms downwards (Fig. 10.3).

Varying the starting position is useful in order to extend the range of application of the method. The eyes may be open or closed.

Instructions

The instructor begins by giving an order to direct a part of the body into a posture of ease. Each order is followed by the word 'Stop'. This means that the part is no longer being actively moved; it also means that the muscles responsible for the movement are no longer contracting. The part however, remains in the position of ease. This position is then mentally registered.

Introductory remarks to participants

Trainees are introduced to the method by a short description of the rationale and procedure.

I just want to say something about physiological relaxation before we begin. When people are under stress, there is a position which they tend to adopt. We could call this 'the punching position'. Although people don't actually present themselves in a punching posture, the muscles which create it are tensing to a minute degree.

If we move the body into the opposite of the punching position, we will be taking it into a position of ease or relaxation.

You might ask: 'How do we get the punching muscles to relax?' This is where the physiological principle comes in: when one group of muscles acting on a joint is tensed, the opposing group is obliged to relax.

The trainer demonstrates.

When I bend my wrist forwards, the bending-back muscles relax, and vice versa. It's a reciprocal mechanism without which smooth action could not take place.

The method itself consists of a succession of changes of position. Each change moves a body part out of its position of defence and into its position of ease. As the part settles into the position of ease, you'll be asked to notice how it feels. The aim is to learn to recognize the relaxed position so that you can reproduce it more easily. I'll first demonstrate the items.

Items of the Mitchell method of relaxation

1. Pull your shoulders towards your feet.
2. Elbows out and open.
3. Fingers and thumbs long.
4. Turn your hips outwards.
5. Move your knees until they are comfortable.
6. Push your feet away from your face.
7. Breathing.
8. Push your body into the support.
9. Push your head into the support.
10. Drag your jaw downwards.
11. Press your tongue downwards in your mouth.
12. Close your eyes.
13. Think of a smoothing action which begins above your eyebrows, rises into your hairline, continues over the top of your head and down into the back of your neck.

Each item is modelled by the instructor who asks the trainee to copy it.

Working through the schedule

The schedule is then worked through in its entirety. It is presented here with the orders expressed in inverted commas:

1. Shoulders

'Pull your shoulders towards your feet'. Do this gently, but go on until you can't pull them down any more. Feel the space between your shoulders and your ears getting greater. 'Stop pulling.' Notice the feel of the new position. Take plenty of time to register the sensations you are getting from it.

2. Elbows (Figs 10.4, 10.5 and 10.6)

'Elbows out and open'. For participants lying supine or sitting in a high-backed chair: slide your elbows sideways, carrying your arms away from your body until you reach a comfortable point (Figs 10.4, 10.6). For participants in forward-lean-sitting: slide your arms away from your body, opening your arms at the elbow joint (Fig. 10.5). 'Stop moving'. Check that your arms are resting on the supporting surface and notice how it feels to have a space between your arms and your body. Feel this position.

3. Hands (Figs 10.7 and 10.8)

'Fingers and thumbs long'. Stretch and separate your

Figure 10.4 'Elbows out and open' in supine position.

Figure 10.5 'Elbows out and open' in forward-lean-sitting position.

Figure 10.6 'Elbows out and open' in sitting position.

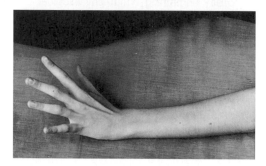

Figure 10.7 'Fingers and thumbs long.'

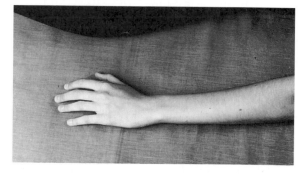

Figure 10.8 Fingers recoiling.

fingers and thumbs while the heels of both hands remain in contact with the floor, the table or the arm of the chair. While the fingers and thumbs spread (Fig. 10.7), feel the palms getting taut. 'Stop'. As you stop, the fingers recoil and fall on to the supporting surface where they lie with the hand gently open, fingertips touching the surface underneath (Fig.10.8). Notice how the hand feels; notice also, without disturbing your fingers, the texture of the surface under your fingertips. Spend a moment or two taking in these sensations.

Extra time should be spent on the hand because of its disproportionately large sensory area in the brain.

4. Hips (Fig. 10.9)

'Turn your hips outwards'. If you are lying, this means rolling your thighs outwards (Fig. 10.9). If you are sitting, it means swinging your knees apart. 'Stop'.

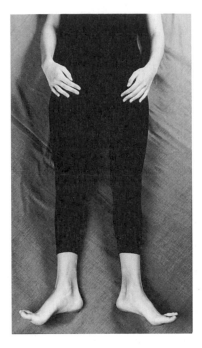

Figure 10.9 'Turn your hips outwards.'

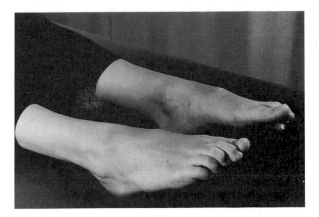

Figure 10.10 'Push your feet away from your face' in supine position.

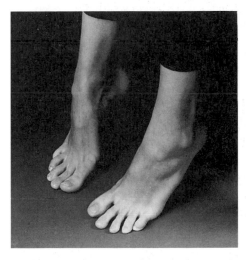

Figure 10.11 'Push your feet away from your face' in sitting position.

Let your legs settle comfortably, noting how they feel in this position.

5. Knees

'Move your knees until they are comfortable'. This simply means adjusting their position in whatever way enhances their comfort. 'Stop' and register that sense of ease.

6. Feet and ankles (Figs. 10.10 and 10.11)

'Push your feet away from your face'. If you are lying, point your feet and toes down, being careful not to induce cramp. If you are sitting with your feet on the floor, keep your toes in contact with it and raise your heels. You are working the calf muscles and reciprocally relaxing the muscles around the shin. 'Stop'. As you stop, your calf muscles stop working too. (If you are sitting, your heels drop down.) Take in the feelings you are now getting from your feet and ankles. Spend a few minutes enjoying the sensation of ease in your legs.

7. Breathing

There are no orders for this item because people have their own breathing rates. I'll describe the action first, then you can perform it in your own time.

I'd like you to think of the soft triangle between the front edge of your ribs and your waist. As you breathe you can feel it swelling slightly; at the same time you can feel your ribs spreading outwards. As you breathe out, that soft area sinks back and your ribs recoil.

Allow your breathing to take place slowly and comfortably, without putting any effort into it and without attempting to alter its rhythm.

8. Torso

'Push your body into the support'. Press against the support whether it is underneath you or behind you.

'Stop'. Feel your body slumped into the floor, table or chair. Feel its weight being supported. Notice the points where your body touches the support.

9. Head

'Push your head into the support'. This will be the floor for those lying down, the table for those leaning forwards and the back of the chair for those seated. 'Stop'. As you stop pushing, notice that the support carries the weight of your head. Feel your head being supported.

10. Jaw

'Drag your jaw downwards'. Let your teeth come apart and your jaw hang down inside your mouth. 'Stop'. Feel the new position. Notice also the contact between your gently touching lips.

Spend a bit longer on this item because the lips, in common with the fingertips, are richly supplied with sensory nerve endings.

11. Tongue

'Press your tongue downwards in your mouth'. Draw it away from the upper palate. 'Stop'. Feel your tongue lying loosely behind your teeth. Notice also your throat slackening.

It is worth spending extra time on this item, for the same reason as for the jaw.

12. Eyes

'Close your eyes' (if they are not already closed). Simply lower your eyelids and gently keep them down. Let your eyes be as still as they can be. Feel the peace of the darkness.

13. Forehead and scalp

'Think of a smoothing action which begins above your eyebrows, rises up into your hairline, continues over the crown of your head, and down to the back of your neck.' Savour the effect.

The above 13 items may be repeated.

Mind

Mitchell ends with a sequence for the thoughts.

Let your mind focus on a topic you find pleasant. Pick one that flows and develops like a poem or a walk in the country and let it hold your attention as it unfolds. Continue for a few minutes.

Termination

When you are ready, I'd like you to begin to make a gradual return to normal activity. Give your arms and legs a good stretch. Perhaps yawn. Give your body plenty of time to adjust to an active state.

Practice

The Mitchell method of physiological relaxation is a skill which can be learned; the more it is practised, the greater will be the benefit gained from it.

FURTHER ASPECTS OF THE MITCHELL METHOD

'Keys' and 'triggers'

The items in Mitchell's schedule cover the whole body. Many individuals however, have characteristic ways of displaying tension. This means that they will be likely to benefit more from some joint changes than from others. The joint change that an individual finds most effective in reducing tension is referred to by Mitchell as the 'key change', because it is instrumental in releasing tension in other parts of the body. The key change can be identified by asking the individual how he tends to react when experiencing anger, pain, anxiety or conflict. If he tends to make fists, his key change will be finger-lengthening; if he tends to clench his teeth, it will be jaw-dropping. Key changes, by their generalizing effects, can promote a sense of ease throughout the whole body.

Mitchell applies her technique to everyday activities, using the concept of 'triggers of tension', i.e. events which tend to provoke feelings of stress such as waiting at traffic lights or being interrupted by bells and alarms. She suggests sticking coloured tabs on potentially stressful appliances such as the steering wheel and the telephone as reminders to adopt the key change.

Thus, to become more relaxed in daily life, there is first a need to recognize the triggers, and second, a need to diminish their effect by using the key change to move the body into the ease position.

Benefit can also be gained from a partial use of the schedule. Mitchell suggests that selected joint changes be used during specific activities, for example, the face items can be carried out while driving, or the leg items while reading. The idea is not far removed from differential relaxation (Ch. 12).

The 'three-point pull'

This is a variation of the shoulder item where, in addition to pulling the shoulders down, the head gently reaches upwards. (It should be done without tilting the head backwards.) The action is useful for stretching the joints in the neck, and may be practised in public situations without attracting attention.

Application of the method to specific conditions

The Mitchell method lends itself to a range of conditions as well as to everyday stress. It is widely used in the field of obstetrics where its advantage lies in its avoidance of tensing procedures (p. 185). The required relaxation is achieved by simply moving the body part.

Mitchell's insistence that breathing should be slow and easy and never include breath-holding, is another reason for the method being favoured by those working in the obstetric field (Williams & Booth 1985, Polden & Mantle 1990). For the same reasons the method is often adopted by those who work in the field of respiratory medicine (Hough 1991).

Comparison with other approaches

Like Jacobson, Mitchell avoids using the order 'Relax'. Her reason is that she finds it 'vague, generalized and ambiguous'. Jacobson avoided using it because he felt it provoked the trainee into making an effort which was superfluous, when 'going negative' was the effect he wanted. On other points, they are of course, fundamentally opposed: Mitchell placing the highest value on joint and skin sensations and rejecting the idea of information coming from the muscles, while Jacobson is only interested in muscle feelings, dismissing any value that joint sensations might have.

A greater resemblance may be found between Mitchell and Alexander where the 3-point pull of Mitchell recalls the 'neck lengthen' injunction of Alexander (p. 88).

EVALUATION OF MITCHELL'S METHOD

The method is simple and quick and many of the 'changes' can be carried out unobtrusively. It is widely practised as a stress-relieving strategy, and clinical findings testify to its effectiveness. Scientific evaluation of the method however, has only just begun. Jackson (1991) studied four rheumatoid arthritis sufferers trained in the Mitchell method, comparing them with untrained controls. Using electromyography to measure activity in the frontalis muscle (a sensitive indicator of general muscle state), she found a marked reduction of tension in the study group and very little change in the control group. No statistical analysis was reported.

In systematically avoiding contraction of the muscles which make up the tension posture, Mitchell's method departs from the principles of progressive relaxation. Studies comparing the two approaches do not exist to date, to the author's knowledge. It would however, be interesting to know what research might reveal about the relative merits of these two methods.

PITFALLS OF MITCHELL'S METHOD

These are similar to the pitfalls of other muscular approaches (Ch. 6, p. 50).

FURTHER READING

Mitchell L 1987 Simple relaxation: the Mitchell method for easing tension, 2nd edn. John Murray, London

ACKNOWLEDGEMENT

The author acknowledges the permission granted by the publisher John Murray to reproduce the phrases from Simple Relaxation 1987 by L. Mitchell.

CHAPTER CONTENTS

Principles of the Alexander technique 86
Primary control 86
Use and misuse 86
Faulty sensory perceptions 86
Inhibition 87
'End-gaining' and the 'means whereby' 87
Integration of mind and body 87

The technique 87
The three elements of primary control 88
Other directions 89
Recognizing and correcting misuse 91
Relaxation effects 92
Teaching the Alexander technique 93

Evaluation of the Alexander technique 93

11

The Alexander technique

A person's posture is the way that individual habitually holds himself against the forces of gravity and is one of his recognizable features. A look round our acquaintances tells us that they all have characteristic ways of holding themselves; each one stands differently, walks differently and sits differently. Although a person's posture may be largely of genetic origin and thus beyond his control, we are inclined to think that it is also governed by the way he looks at and reacts to life.

Teachers of the Alexander technique point to the way young children use their bodies, describing the effect as 'poise'. They also indicate how this natural poise can become distorted by emotional and physical influences as the child grows towards maturity, resulting in the development of tension habits which interfere with healthy functioning.

This notion had earlier captured the attention of Matthias Alexander, at a time when he was suffering from a problem with his voice. An actor by profession, he noticed that he was developing hoarseness and a painful throat whenever he began to perform. Intuitively, he felt that posture lay at the root of it. Mirrors revealed that he was pulling his head back and tightening his neck muscles to the extent that he could not breathe properly. By freeing his neck and lengthening his spine he discovered he could regain control of his voice, and the manner in which he accomplished this forms the basis of the Alexander technique.

PRINCIPLES OF THE ALEXANDER TECHNIQUE

The following principles underpin the technique:

- primary control
- use and misuse
- faulty sensory perception
- inhibition
- 'end-gaining' and the 'means whereby'
- integration of mind and body.

Primary control

Alexander believed that the primary control of human posture lay in the relationships of the head to the neck and of the neck to the rest of the spine. So convinced was he of their crucial nature, that an almost magical significance was attached to these relationships in his day. This status has, however, been modified over the years, and the Alexander teacher of today sees primary control less as an inviolable principle than as a useful starting point.

Primary control has three components:

- a neck that is free and whose muscles contain only enough tension to keep the head upright.
- a head moving forward and up (Fig. 11.1), not back and down to crumple the spine (Fig. 11.2).
- a spine that feels lengthened, thus counteracting any tendency towards sagging.

Use and misuse

'Use' refers to the characteristic way we have of holding our bodies. It is a neutral term. When there is harmony between the tension necessary to support the body and the relaxation necessary to allow it to move, the use is said to be 'balanced'. When, however, this is upset by too much or too little tension, a state of misuse is said to prevail (Barlow 1975). Examples of misuse are hunching of the shoulders, head sinking into the spine, chin thrusting out.

The regaining of 'balanced use' means the recovery of natural movement patterns, which can only occur if we review the messages we are getting about the position of the body in space.

Figure 11.1 Head held forward and up.

Figure 11.2 Head held back and down.

Faulty sensory perceptions

All movement in the healthy organism is accompanied by sensory feedback in the form of proprioceptive impulses from the moving part. This gives us information about the position of body parts in space. In the young child these messages lead to responses which are natural, economic (in terms of energy consumption) and uncontaminated by emotional factors while those in the adult may be distorted by trauma (mental or physical).

Responses carried out repeatedly, turn into habits which are then interpreted by the higher centres as normal, i.e. the way we habitually use our bodies will feel normal to us simply because we are used to it. Alexander's experience with the mirror showed him he was still pulling his head back even after he felt he had corrected it. This could only be because his body had got used to the 'bad' posture and had internalized it as normal, so that even the smallest degree of correction was interpreted by his conscious mind as overcorrection.

The phrase 'faulty sensory perception' refers to the way messages are interpreted in a misused body.

Inhibition

Many of our movements are automatic. If they show patterns of misuse which we want to change, it will be necessary to intercept them, that is, to examine them before they are automatically executed. A pause is required. This act of pausing constitutes what Alexander called 'inhibition'. It allows the individual to question the validity of his response. It gives him the chance to reconsider his action and to redirect his movement.

Inhibition, not to be confused with the Freudian meaning, is what happens when the individual ceases to react automatically to stimuli, thereby leaving him free to respond appropriately; to do nothing for a moment while the maladaptive, automatic response pattern is broken. 'When you stop doing the wrong thing, the right thing does itself' (Alexander 1932).

'End-gaining' and the 'means whereby'

Inhibition provides the opportunity to focus on the means whereby we achieve a certain end. It draws attention away from 'end-gaining', where action is performed too quickly and too energetically for one to give any thought as to the manner in which the end is gained. Alexander would say that the goal is not the only consideration: it is the journey, as well as the arrival, that counts.

Integration of mind and body

Central to the teachings of Alexander is a belief that the mind and the body are interdependent. Not only does the body posture reflect the individual's thoughts, but his mind responds to the way he uses his body. Such notions introduce a new dimension to the concept of body movement, and can be said to lie at the heart of the statement that 'we *are* our posture' (Barlow 1975).

THE TECHNIQUE

The technique itself reeducates the body to perform in a balanced and energy-economical way (Gray 1990). Habits of misuse are identified and replaced by more appropriate ways of using the body. Assessment and correction are carried out in positions of lying, sitting, standing and walking. Gently using her hands, the teacher guides the pupil's body both in motion and at rest while the pupil mentally focuses on the message he is getting from the teacher's hands. For example, a supine pupil might be told to think of the words: 'Shoulder release and widen', as the teacher is repositioning one of his shoulders. Thus, without actively performing the movement, the pupil directs his body to cooperate.

Some of the principal orders or directions are listed below, beginning with the three elements of primary control:

1. 'neck free'
2. 'head forward and up'
3. 'back lengthen.'

Other directions include:

4. 'keeping length'

5. 'back widen'
6. 'shoulder release and widen'.

The three elements of primary control

1. 'Neck free'

This means that the head is carried in such a way that no undue strain is put on the neck muscles. The image of the nodding-dog-in-the-back-of-the-car may help to convey the feeling of a free neck.

2. 'Head forward and up'

The phrase applies to pupils who are sitting or standing. 'Head forward and out' is the phrase for those who are lying. It means that the head is held with the chin pointing to the toes, not poking out. It also means that the head is lifted up or out of the vertebral column. The result is that the individual feels taller or longer, having 'grown' from a point at the back of the crown of the head. It is the opposite of a head that sinks into the shoulders with the chin thrust out. At the same time no excessive effort should be made to extend the body. The described effect can often be achieved simply by 'thinking up'. Figures 11.1 and 11.2 illustrate the correct and incorrect ways of carrying the head.

3. 'Back lengthen'

An erect spine anteroposteriorly displays a succession of natural curves: concavities in the cervical and lumbar regions, convexity in the dorsal region. In urging 'back lengthen', it is not implied that efforts should be made to obliterate these natural curves, but rather, that the curves should not be allowed to become overemphasized, since that would result in shortening or crumpling of the spine. Actions which particularly shorten the spine are:

1. Overextension of the cervical vertebrae (thrusting out the chin)
2. Overextension of the lumbar vertebrae (exaggerated lumbar concavity) (Fig. 11.3).

Figure 11.3 Standing with exaggerated cervical and lumbar curves.

Similarly, slumping is to be avoided. Slumping occurs when the whole spine is rounded into a long C-shaped curve, with the neck hyperextended in order to allow the eyes to look forwards. Slumping also creates shortening of the spine (Fig. 11.4).

'Back lengthen' indicates that the spine should be allowed to reach its full length as opposed to being either crumpled (where spinal curves are exaggerated) or slumped (where the back is too rounded). An image that evokes the idea of lengthening the back is that of a jet of water springing up in the spine and lifting it gently. The head should feel lightly balanced on top.

Alexander's view of a balanced standing posture is one in which the body weight passes through the front of the heel, the knees are unbraced, and the pelvis is in midposition, with

Figure 11.4 Standing with spine slumped into a long C-shaped curve.

Figure 11.5 Balanced standing posture.

the 'tail' neither thrown out, nor forcibly tucked under. The direction to 'think up' evokes the idea of standing straight but without making any forced effort to do so. Some teachers use the analogy of a helium-filled balloon lifting the head (Gray 1990). Figure 11.5 illustrates the correct standing position.

'Neck free', 'head forward and up' and 'back lengthen' are fundamental to the technique.

Other directions

4. 'Keeping length'

The order 'keeping length' is related to 'back lengthen'. Alexander applies it to the action of sitting down where he sees particular benefit to be gained from the avoidance of crumpling. His

method of sitting is illustrated in the following passage (Leibowitz & Connington 1990):

Place your feet slightly apart and positioned so that the backs of your legs are lightly in contact with the chair seat. Let your arms hang loosely by your sides. Before lowering yourself, let your mind focus on the idea of 'keeping length', i.e. not crumpling the spine. Keep the head and neck in the same relation as they were in the standing position and as you lower yourself, flatten the lumbar curve. Although you are looking at the floor as you go down, make a point of thinking 'UP' to prevent any tendency of the spine to crumple.

Figure 11.6 demonstrates the correct way of lowering the body into a chair.

The wrong way of sitting down, Alexander, is to overextend both

Figure 11.6 Sitting down with the spine 'keeping length'.

Figure 11.7 Sitting down with a 'crumpled' spine.

lumbar regions, i.e. to thrust the chin out and exaggerate the lumbar concavity. Their combined effect crumples and shortens the spine (Gray 1990). Figure 11.7 shows an incorrect way of lowering the body into a chair.

On rising from the chair, the head should start the movement and lead the body forwards. From that point the motions of sitting down are put into reverse.

What Alexander is saying is that the lumbar spine should be slightly flexed and the cervical spine prevented from extending itself in the actions of sitting down and rising. He urges applying the same ideas to other activities which carry the centre of gravity forwards, such as leaning over a basin to clean the teeth.

Alexander compared the action of toothbrushing in humans, to the peeling of fruit by erect primates in the wild. Both actions take place anterior to the body itself. On noticing that primates adopted a particular stance to carry out their task, he concluded that mechanical advantage was being gained from it. The stance itself is characterized by bent knees, and slightly flexed

(flattened) lumbar and cervical spines; a posture which is referred to as the 'monkey position'. (Fig. 11.8).

The effect of the monkey position is to keep the centre of gravity as close to the spine as possible, thereby relieving the strain on the lumbosacral junction. Where the monkey posture is not adopted for comparable tasks, a position of mechanical disadvantage is created. Figure 11.9 illustrates this idea: the arms and head reach forwards, pulling the centre of gravity with them while the cervical and lumbar spines retain their concavities.

Common to both the monkey position and the act of sitting (as recommended by Alexander) is a slight flexion of the lumbar spine. Alexander's insistence on the value of this posture has been supported by research (Adams & Hutton 1985, Adams et al 1994) which is discussed later in this chapter.

5. 'Back widen'

This phrase applies to the posterior part of the thorax which should be allowed to feel wide in

Figure 11.8 Task performance in a position of mechanical advantage (the monkey position).

Figure 11.9 Task performance in a position of mechanical disadvantage.

order to permit full expansion of the ribs. To convey the sensation of 'back widen' Gray (1990) refers to the rib cage filling out into the back as the air enters the lungs.

6. 'Shoulder release and widen'

This is aimed at relaxing the muscles of the shoulder girdle since they are often held more tensely than they need to be.

Recognizing and correcting misuse

Test for body alignment

As mentioned in the section on faulty sensory perception, an habitual posture, whether balanced or not, will feel 'right' to its owner. This makes it difficult for him to recognize misuse in himself. A procedure to solve this matter has been worked out by Barlow (1975):

Stand with your heels 5 centimetres (2 inches) from a wall, with your feet 46 centimetres (18 inches) apart. Let your body sway back until it touches the wall.

Figure 11.10 shows this position.

If your shoulders and hips touch simultaneously with each side level, your alignment is correct. However, you may find that one side touches the wall before the other or that your shoulders touch before your hips. Do what you can to realign yourself. Next, bend your knees slightly and notice that this action will tend to bring the lumbar vertebrae into contact with the wall (lumbar curve flattened).

Figure 11.11 demonstrates this effect.

If you can hold this position with relative comfort, then your body is not in a misused state. If you find it unduly tiring, then practice will make it easier and help to restore alignment.

Changing posture

Alexander sees misuse as resulting from mental

Figure 11.10 Testing for body alignment 1: leaning against wall.

Figure 11.11 Testing for body alignment 2: flattening the lumbar concavity as the body is lowered.

stress and the demands of contemporary life; in its turn, misuse can be the cause of physical stress leading to muscle and joint problems. A person wishing to change his posture needs to consider three points. He should:

- Be aware of the particular habit-governed movement that he wants to alter.
- Refuse to react automatically. This implies stopping to reassess the 'means whereby', i.e. being ready to say 'no' to the old method.
- Redirect his muscles by a thought process. This signifies *thinking* about the corrected movement rather than driving the muscles to perform it. 'The mind gives the instruction, and little by little, the body absorbs the message' (Fontana 1992).

Regularly practising new responses will result in a gradual weakening of the old ones and turn a pattern of misuse into one of more balanced use. There are no defined stages of progress nor specified goals of perfection. Individual problems call for individual remedies. The purpose of the Alexander technique is to cultivate a sensitive approach to the movement of one's own body (Barlow 1975).

Relaxation effects

Although proponents speak of 'balanced use' rather than relaxation, the technique can nonetheless be seen as a method for promoting relaxation. Balanced use results in the elimination of excess muscular activity and in the establishing of minimum levels of muscle tension. These are concepts that are found in Jacobson's differential relaxation. For Alexander however, they form the basis of his technique, whereas for Jacobson, the

Figure 11.12 Promoting body symmetry in a relaxed position.

main concern is with the release of residual tension.

Alexander suggests a daily 15-minute session of rest, to be carried out in a crook lying position (knees bent up, feet flat on the ground) with a book under the head (where the height of book is determined by the shape of the spine). The object is to allow the body to regain its natural symmetry. The procedure is also a relaxing one (Fig. 11.12).

Teaching the Alexander technique

The purpose here is to give a general idea of the principles underlying the Alexander technique, rather than to show how to teach it; such training involves a 3-year course. The principles however, may be woven into other approaches, particularly where posture is a key item.

Trained teachers of the Alexander method often work in the field of the performing arts. The technique however, has universal relevance.

EVALUATION OF THE ALEXANDER TECHNIQUE

Alexander's method is among the few approaches to focus systematically on relaxation of the body while it is in motion (Woolfolk & Lehrer 1984). As such it is a form of kinesthetic reeducation. The technique is based on the assumption that the way we use our bodies affects our general functioning. However, there is no ideal; it is for each to explore his or her possibilities and find better ways of using the body. For this, and other reasons, the technique does not readily lend itself to systematic investigation and has not until recently begun to receive scientifically rigorous assessment.

Among the few controlled studies is that of Valentine (1993). Valentine investigated the effects of the Alexander technique on performance anxiety. She looked at experiential, behavioural and physiological aspects of anxiety associated with performance of music, and found that anxiety was lowered by training in the Alexander technique on all measures in low stress situations. These effects on the whole, however, did not transfer to the highly stressful recital situation.

The work of the anatomist Adams (Adams & Hutton 1985, Adams et al 1994) has implications for some of the postural claims made by Alexander. Adams has studied the effect of actions which impose physical stress on the lumbar spine. He has found that a moderate degree of flexion (i.e. flattening of the lumbar curve) is mechanically advantageous, which supports Alexander's views about sitting down and the monkey position.

There is however, a need for more research, both psychological and physiological. Until that has been carried out, and conclusions drawn the technique must, in Barlow's words, continue to be regarded as a hypothesis (Barlow 1975).

FURTHER READING

Alexander F M 1932 The use of the self. Dutton, New York

Barlow W 1975 The Alexander principle. Arrow, London

Gray J 1990 Your guide to the Alexander technique. Gollancz, London

Leibowitz J, Connington B 1990 The Alexander technique. Souvenir Press, London

CHAPTER CONTENTS

Definition and methods 95
Jacobson's method 95
Bernstein & Borkovec's method 96

Examples of the use of differential relaxation 96
Seated at a desk typing 96
Driving to the supermarket 96
Digging the garden 96
Stressful situations 96
Standing and walking 96

Prerequisites 97

Comparison with other methods 97

12

Differential relaxation

DEFINITION AND METHODS

Differential relaxation, a phrase introduced by Jacobson (1938), means, in his own words: 'the minimum of tensions in the muscles requisite for an act, along with the relaxation of other muscles' (Jacobson 1976). This is to say that, ideally, the muscles engaged in performing any activity, for instance typing, exhibit a minimum level of tension consistent with task efficiency, while those not directly engaged in the task are relaxed. The body is as relaxed as it can be while achieving the objective, i.e. typing the page. Thus, differential relaxation is progressive relaxation applied to everyday tasks.

We need muscle tension in order to live our lives. It is essential for carrying out purposeful activity, of the type that Jacobson calls 'primary'. Purposeful activity however, may be accompanied by tension in muscles whose action does nothing to promote the outcome, such as grimacing while writing. This is referred to by Jacobson as 'secondary activity'. Differential relaxation calls for the recognition and elimination of all secondary activity and of any excessive tension in the muscles performing the primary activity.

Jacobson's method

Jacobson's method is to isolate the task, reduce muscle tension to below the level at which the task can be performed then, gradually, to reintroduce tension to the minimum level where the task can be carried out efficiently. He gives an example (Jacobson 1976):

Sit holding an open book on your lap. Reduce the tension in your posture so that the book nearly falls off your lap. Relax your eye and speech muscles so that you are unable to follow the words. Then little by little, increase the tension until the book is secure on your lap and you can see the words . . . then, gradually increase the tension enough to take in their meaning.

A similar routine can be applied to writing:

Take up a pen with the intention of writing your name, but using too little energy to make a mark on the paper. Repeat the action, this time putting a little more force into it. Continue putting slightly more force into it until you reach a point where you are able to write in a way which you recognize as your style. Keep it relaxed. You are now combining effective outcome with economy of effort.

A good time to test for the presence of secondary tensions is when opening the morning mail. The anticipation and apprehension of what it might reveal can raise tension levels far beyond what is necessary for the simple task of opening envelopes.

Bernstein & Borkovec's method

In their manual on progressive relaxation training, Bernstein & Borkovec (1973) develop the idea of differential relaxation. They single out three aspects of complexity; position of the body, level of activity and the situation in which the activity takes place. Variations of each are worked into an 8-step schedule starting with 'sitting, doing nothing in a quiet room', and ending with 'standing, performing some activity in a busy environment'. Four of the items occur in the sitting position while the level of activity and the situation are varied; the other four occur in the standing position. During the performance of these exercises the pupil is asked to monitor his tension levels, using 'recall' (p. 54) to relax himself.

EXAMPLES OF THE USE OF DIFFERENTIAL RELAXATION

Seated at a desk typing

. . . just enough power in the hands to control the

keys, type a few sentences. Then break off to check your body for tension. If you find any, relax it away using 'recall' (p. 54) or cue-controlled breathing (p. 65). Resume typing, checking again for tension. Make a telephone call, maintaining a relaxed posture, using only enough tension to hold the receiver.

Driving to the supermarket

As you settle yourself into the driving seat, spend a minute checking all your muscle groups for tension. Identify the muscles you need for driving. If you notice excess tension in any of these muscles, relax it. Check that the muscles you don't need, such as the face muscles, are relaxed. Maintain relaxation while steering and changing gear until you arrive at the store. Park the car and walk towards the entrance, relaxing any tension in your face and shoulders. Pick a trolley and as you push it around, continue to check your body, relaxing those muscles you do not need and putting the minimum of tension into the ones you need for the task. Pause regularly to scan your body for unnecessary tension.

Digging the garden

As you pick up the spade, feel the weight of it in your hand, fleetingly judging the degree of muscle work required to use it. Remind yourself that you can put too much effort into tasks of this nature. Relax your face muscles while you carry out the digging.

Stressful situations

Differential relaxation is relatively easy to achieve in activities which do not pose any threat but is more difficult in situations of stress, e.g. delivering a speech. In such cases additional strategies may need to be employed, such as mental rehearsal of the event and positive self-talk, to help reduce excessive tension (see Ch. 18).

Standing and walking

The principles of differential relaxation can also be applied to the postures of standing and walking, where certain muscle groups such as those of the back and the legs, hold the body vertical and propel it along while uninvolved groups such as those of the face can be relaxed.

The following two examples illustrate these ideas.

Standing

Have your eyes open. Stand with shoes off, feet parallel and two or three inches apart. Release excess tension with cue-controlled breathing. Unlock your knees, slightly bending and stretching them a few times to feel the weight falling evenly down through them to your feet. Rock forwards and backwards over them until you find a comfortable position for your hips. Feel your spine rising above your hips . . . feel it supporting your head, and let your head reach up as high as it wants to go. Nod it gently to find its best position. Relax your face muscles. Let your arms hang down by your sides with your shoulders dropped. Feel your body relaxed and resilient. Enjoy being inside it. There should be no effort involved. When the posture feels as comfortable as possible, notice what makes it feel like that.

Walking

One way of finding your own energy-economical way of walking is to experiment with different kinds of walking. Marching, sailor's roll and tiptoeing are of course, artificial ways of walking; however, by exploring different styles, you may find it easier to distinguish between unnatural and natural forms, and be helped to find your own natural way of walking. This will be the one that gives you most comfort and pleasure. Practise it, enjoy it. Feel your whole body relaxing into the rhythm of your walking. Feel that the muscles responsible for propelling you along are no more tense than they need to be . . . and that your face and shoulder muscles are relaxed.

PREREQUISITES

Differential relaxation is thus concerned with minimum tension levels during activity and task performance. There are two prerequisites: knowing which muscle groups are needed for each activity, and possessing the skill of muscle relaxation.

COMPARISON WITH OTHER METHODS

The Alexander technique, with its concept of 'balanced use' (p. 86), is grounded in the principle of differential relaxation. Here, the crucial elements are the relationships of head, neck and spine which, when correct, allow the body to adopt balanced and relaxed postures while engaged in activity. Alexander's procedures for the actions of sitting down and rising are essentially techniques of differential relaxation.

Mitchell (1987) is advocating differential relaxation when she urges the partial use of her schedule during task performance; for example, practising 'joint changes' for the shoulders and the jaw while driving or typing. Her 'key changes' can also be seen as a differential technique, in that they are directed at switching off unnecessary global tension while allowing specific movements to take place (p. 82).

Poppen's (1988) mini-relaxation is another differential form. Here, relaxed-looking postures are adopted in the muscle groups not engaged in the task; for example, the legs can be relaxed while writing a letter (p. 72).

Differential relaxation also forms one component of Öst's applied relaxation and is discussed further in Chapter 8 (p. 66).

FURTHER READING

Bernstein D A, Borkovec T D 1973 Progressive relaxation training: a manual for the helping professions. Research Press, Champaign, Illinois
Jacobson E 1976 You must relax. Souvenir Press, London

Öst L G 1987 Applied relaxation: description of a coping technique and review of controlled studies. Behaviour Research and Therapy 25: 397–407

CHAPTER CONTENTS

The benefits of stretching 99

On the floor 100

Sitting 101

Standing 103

Pitfalls of stretching exercises 107

13

Stretchings

THE BENEFITS OF STRETCHING

Elasticity is one of the properties of muscle tissue. Stretching helps to maintain that elasticity. Elasticity not only enables muscles to function better, but also gives them some protection from injury. Thus the stretching exercise is useful for warming up prior to strenuous sports activities.

Gentle stretchings help to maintain the mobility of the joints by stimulating the flow of synovial fluid. This fluid lubricates the joint and creates smooth action.

In the case of the spinal joints, stretchings help the discs to recover after activity which changes their shape. The intervertebral discs are soft structures whose shape is altered when the spine is moved. Bending in any direction transforms the discs into wedge-shaped bodies with their fluid content squeezed towards the thick end of the wedge. When a body position is held for long periods and under load, i.e. the load of the body's own weight, this effect becomes more pronounced (Twomey 1993). It is known as 'creep' and is defined as the progressive deformation of a structure under constant load by forces which are not large enough to cause permanent damage (Kazarian 1975). The condition rights itself as the body resumes its normal position, but it takes time. Stretchings in the opposite direction can aid the recovery and may help to reduce the risk of injury, since the spine is vulnerable during the interval.

For this reason, motorists who have driven long distances, creating conditions in which creep occurs, should avoid lifting heavy loads immedi-

Figure 13.1 Body rotations.

ately afterwards and should perform stretchings, not only at the end of the journey, but at regular intervals throughout its course (Twomey & Taylor 1987). Stretchings will not guarantee protection from injury, but they may make it less likely to occur. (See the sections on Back-arching and Crouching/squatting.)

Stretching is something we do unconsciously after being in one position for a long time. The body seems to ask for it. We stretch after sleeping, after working at a desk, after bending down to weed a flower bed. All three trigger the need, or the desire to stretch the body. Subjectively, stretchings result in a feeling of comfort, pleasure and relief.

The stretchings presented here are primarily designed to induce a sense of well-being and relaxation. They are grouped according to their starting positions.

ON THE FLOOR

The floor or ground provides the best surface, softened by a mat or a carpet. Grass or firm sand also give the degree of hardness required. A bed is too soft.

Body rotations (Fig. 13.1)

Lie flat on your back. Bend both knees and place the feet flat on the ground. Now roll your bent knees to one side; roll them as far as they will easily go. At the same time, carry both your arms and your head to the other side. You are now twisting your body and stretching one set of oblique trunk muscles. Keep it a comfortable stretch. Hold the position for a few seconds. Then bring your knees back to midline, resting your feet on the ground and your arms by your sides. Repeat the exercise in the other direction.

Curling into a ball (Fig. 13.2)

Lie flat on your back. Draw your knees up. Gather them in your hands and gently pull them towards your face. Still holding your knees, release the pull. Repeat the pull a few times.

Some lower back conditions respond favourably to this exercise and the previous one, Body rotations.

Figure 13.2 Curling into a ball.

Hip joint stretches (Fig. 13.3)

Sit on the ground (cushion optional) and draw your legs into a bent position with your knees pointing sideways. Have the soles of your feet facing each other and in contact. Place your hands around your ankles and rest your elbows on your thighs. Apply pressure to your thighs, gently and slowly. Then take a rest. Reapply the pressure.

You should feel a comfortable stretching in the hip area. However, the range of movement in hip joints varies greatly, so do not compare yourself with other people. Perform the exercise just to the point where you feel it is giving you a comfortable stretching sensation and no further.

SITTING

An upright chair or a stool is used. For the first exercise a long stick, for example a broomhandle is needed.

Body turning (Fig. 13.4)

Sit with your feet flat on the ground. Grasp the broomhandle with your hands 90 cm (3 ft) apart and raise your arms so that the stick just clears your head (your elbows are bent). Turn the upper part of your body to the left. This moves the stick through about 90°. Just go as far as you need to in order to get a comfortable stretch. Do not overstretch or bounce. Then return to the starting position. Repeat in the other direction.

Figure 13.3 Hip joint stretches.

Figure 13.4 Body turning.

Shoulder circling (Fig. 13.5)

Bend your elbows and place your fingertips on your shoulders. With your elbows, draw slow circles in the air. After two or three circles, break off and repeat in the opposite direction.

Arms stretching above head (Fig. 13.6)

Bend your elbows and lift your arms above your head. Feel yourself pushing the air above you with your open hands. When your elbows are straight, spread your arms sideways and lower them to your sides. Let them rest limply. Repeat once or twice.

Head pressing backwards (Fig. 13.7)

Clasp both hands behind your head and, pressing your head against them, arch backwards. Take care not to lean back too far if you are in a lightweight chair. Return your body to a vertical position.

Figure 13.5 Shoulder circling.

Figure 13.6 Arms stretching above head.

Figure 13.7 Head pressing backwards.

STANDING

Trunk bending sideways (Fig. 13.8)

Stand with your feet apart and your hands by your sides. Bend your body sideways, giving it a good stretch. Return to the upright position and repeat on the other side.

Arm and trunk bending sideways (Fig. 13.9)

This exercise resembles the previous one except that the sideways bend is performed with one hand over your head. Maintain an easy stretch in each direction.

Arms stretching back (Fig. 13.10)

Clasp both hands behind your back and straighten your elbows, drawing your shoulders back at the same time. Feel a stretch in the shoulder area, but do not overdo it. Then relax your arms and repeat the exercise.

Figure 13.8 Trunk bending sideways.

Figure 13.9 Arm and trunk bending sideways.

Figure 13.10 Arms stretching back.

Arms reaching upwards (Fig. 13.11)

Stand with your feet together or apart. Clasp your hands, then raise your arms above your head, turning the palms towards the ceiling as you straighten your elbows. Hold them there a few seconds, then lower them.

Arms stretching sideways (Figs. 13.12 and 13.13)

Stand with your feet apart, and your arms bent at the elbow and raised to shoulder level. Gently swing one arm sideways and as you do so, allow your elbow to straighten. Return your arm to the bent position. Repeat with the other arm.

The previous five exercises are particularly useful for people who are leaning over a desk or a workbench. The last two can also be performed in a sitting position.

Figure 13.12 Arms stretching sideways: 1.

Figure 13.11 Arms reaching upwards.

Figure 13.13 Arms stretching sideways: 2.

Trunk twisting (Fig. 13.14)

Stand with your hands on your hips. Slightly bend your knees and twist the upper part of your body to the left. Feel a comfortable stretch, then return to the starting position. Repeat on the other side.

Back arching (Fig. 13.15)

Place the palms of your hands over the bones that run sideways from your lumbar spine. Using that point as a fulcrum, bend over backwards. Go as far as is comfortable. No further! Then return to an upright position. Repeat. If the exercise makes you feel dizzy, keep your head and eyes looking forwards as you perform it.

Benefit can be gained from this exercise when driving long distances, brushing paths, vacuuming carpets or leaning over a table to sort papers.

Figure 13.14 Trunk twisting.

Figure 13.15 Back arching.

Crouching/squatting (Fig. 13.16)

Get into a crouching or squatting position with your head down. Hold the position for 10–20 seconds. If you can, lay your feet flat on the ground; otherwise, perch on your toes. That is all that most people can do.

This is another exercise which may be found to ease the lumbar spine when carried out at breaks during long-distance drives. Its somewhat bizarre appearance will escape attention if the driver pretends to be examining the tyres of his vehicle. The squat position seems to be beneficial for back health in general since it has been found that in populations where it is habitually adopted, lumbar disc degeneration is rare (Fahrni & Trueman 1965). For people with painful knees however, it is not advisable.

Figure 13.16 Crouching.

Calf stretching (Fig. 13.17, Read 1984)

Take your shoes off and stand facing a wall with your toes about 30 cm (12 in) away from it. Have your feet parallel and 10 cm (4 in) apart. Raise your arms and lean your forearms vertically on the wall. Rest your body weight on your forearms. With your heels on the ground and your knees straight, let your hips sink forwards.

You will feel a stretching in the calf muscles. Let it be a comfortable stretch, not a punishment. If you do not feel any stretching, take your feet further back until you do. As you stretch the calf muscles, hold the position for 5 seconds, then release it. Repeat a few times.

When carried out prior to athletics, sporting activities or workouts, calf stretching helps to protect the calf muscles from strain.

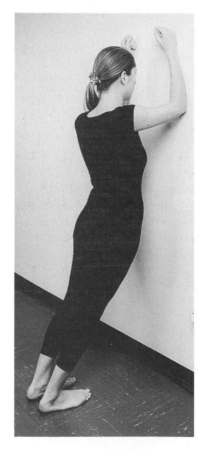

Figure 13.17 Calf stretching.

Inner thigh stretching (adductor stretching) (Fig. 13.18)

Stand with your feet about 50 cm (20 in) apart, hands on your hips. Swing your weight over the left knee, bending it as you do so. This puts a stretch on the inside of the right thigh. Hold the position for about 5 seconds, then release the stretch. Repeat. Then swing over the other leg.

This exercise is protective for the leg adductor muscles of athletes and sportsmen and women.

PITFALLS OF STRETCHING EXERCISES

1. A participant may be undergoing medical treatment which contraindicates a particular stretching exercise. Priority should always be given to any medical instructions he has received.

2. Stretchings should be done gently without straining. At no time should any exercise feel uncomfortable. If it does, it should be stopped. Reasons for possible discomfort are that:

　a. the trainee is overdoing it

　b. he has an innate restriction of joint movement

　c. he has an incipient disorder.

3. The number of repetitions carried out is a matter for the individual to decide. Only he knows if he is still benefiting from the exercise.

4. When working in a group of people there is often a temptation to do better than, or at least as well as, the others. Many minor injuries occur from participants feeling challenged by neighbours (perhaps older than they) who outshine them. People often feel they have a duty to prove themselves. This of course is mistaken thinking. The only 'duty' imposed on the individual in this context is to make his body feel as comfortable as possible.

Figure 13.18 Inner thigh stretching.

CHAPTER CONTENTS

Exercise recommendations 109

The cardiovascular system and exercise 110
  Moderately raised blood pressure 111

The bones 111
  Bone mineral content and exercise 111
  Type of exercise 112

The muscles, ligaments and joints 112

Psychological aspects of exercise 112

Pitfalls of exercise 113

14

Physical exercise

There is now solid evidence that exercise contributes to the well-being and consequent peace of mind of the individual. So convincing is this evidence, that a book like this would be seriously deficient without some reference to it. However, as small group work does not usually provide opportunities for exercise of the type recommended below, the myriad ways of taking exercise will not be described. Nevertheless, the topic may be discussed within a group, along with plans for the introduction of exercise into the lives of hitherto inactive participants. Individuals can be encouraged to take up a form of exercise of their choice, since enjoyment adds to any resulting sense of well-being.

In this chapter, recommendations concerning exercise will first be discussed. The effects of exercise are then examined, in the cardiovascular system, in the bones, in the muscles, ligaments and joints, and from the psychological aspect. Finally, the pitfalls associated with exercise are considered.

EXERCISE RECOMMENDATIONS

Studies investigating the fitness-promoting effects of exercise in healthy individuals have, for the past four decades focused on three factors: intensity, duration and frequency. Intensity is linked to the idea that minimum levels of activity are needed to improve fitness. These levels bear a direct relationship to the individual's maximum capacity, or maximum heart rate as estimated from his age. The recommended duration of exercise varies from 20 to 60 uninterrupted minutes, while the optimum frequency is held to be 3–5 days a week; less fails to provide adequate benefit, and more provides negligible additional benefit (American College of Sports Medicine 1991).

This approach forms the basis of the recommendations of the National Fitness Survey (Allied Dunbar National Fitness Survey 1992). For building up fitness in healthy individuals, exercise should:

- Be of a kind, such as walking, running or swimming, which is rhythmic and uses most of the large muscles of the body, i.e. aerobic (Table 14.1).
- Be introduced gradually in both intensity and duration, and progress by small stages, each one covering a period of 8–10 weeks.
- Be moderately vigorous in intensity and make the participant sweat and feel out of breath for some part of the time (Table 14.2).
- Be kept at a level of intensity where the heart, as measured by the pulse rate, works at between 60–80% of the estimated maximum heart rate of the individual concerned.
- Last at least 20 minutes.
- Be carried out regularly, i.e. three times a week.

The maximum rate can be estimated as 220 minus the person's age. Thus, for a 40-year-old

Table 14.1 Aerobic and anaerobic exercise

Aerobic exercise
Aerobic exercise is sustained rhythmic activity such as distance running, swimming, walking, jogging, dancing and cycling. As defined by the Royal College of Physicians (1991), it is exercise which 'involves repetitive contractions of large muscle groups at levels of energy expenditure less than about 60% of maximum capacity ... performed for prolonged periods on the available oxygen supply'. It results in the improved endurance of muscles.

Anaerobic exercise
This consists of high intensity work of short duration. The demands are so great they exceed the availability of oxygen and create the need for anaerobic metabolism. Examples are jumping, sprinting and press-ups. Anaerobic activity also includes isometric muscle work (contractions unaccompanied by shortening of the muscle) such as weight-lifting. The intensity of the work compresses the arteries in the muscle, thus reducing its blood and oxygen supply (Royal College of Physicians 1991). Exercise of this nature is used to strengthen muscles.

Table 14.2 Grades of exercise activity. Adapted from Allied Dunbar National Fitness Survey (1992)

Vigorous
Activity in which the individual exerts himself to the point of getting out of breath and sweating. It includes squash, football, tennis, strong sustained swimming, long-distance running, cycling over difficult terrain and energetic aerobics.

Moderate
The same activities (except squash) are carried out but the individual stops short of getting out of breath and sweating. Less demanding activities such as golf, social dancing, table tennis, garden digging, long brisk walks are included, and because they are less demanding they *can* be carried to the point of getting out of breath and sweating.

Light
A few of the above activities such as golf, social dancing and table tennis are performed in a light manner; also included are fishing, darts, snooker, bowls, weeding, planting, light DIY and long walks at an average pace.

individual, the estimated maximum heart rate would be 180. After calculating 60–80% of this figure, a range of 108–144 is obtained. This means that the pulse rate of this 40-year-old healthy individual should be kept within the range of 108–144 during exercise for building up fitness.

People who are less fit, can take the figure 200 instead of 220 as their starting point; and those under medical supervision should seek the advice of their doctor.

The above intensity levels, originally adopted by the American College of Sports Medicine, are now considered unnecessarily high by the College, and lower levels of 40–60% are now recommended (American College of Sports Medicine 1991). In addition, it should be remembered that these figures are appropriate for healthy individuals.

However, reaching minimum levels of intensity is not universally regarded as important. Some research suggests that the total energy expended throughout the day is as critical for improving fitness as the intensity of the exercise, and that the benefit derived from three 10-minute sessions is equal to that gained from one 30-minute session (Blair et al 1992).

THE CARDIOVASCULAR SYSTEM AND EXERCISE

Inactivity can lead to coronary disease. It appears

to be so powerful a factor that some researchers suggest that it doubles the risk of the disease developing (Powell et al 1987). Dynamic exercise on the other hand, when carried out regularly, results in a decreased heart rate for any given level of activity. The demand for myocardial oxygen is thus reduced and exercise tolerance is increased (Royal College of Physicians 1991).

In a well-exercised body, changes occur in the peripheral vascular system which enable the voluntary muscles to function with a lower blood flow than they had hitherto needed. As a result, blood is not diverted from the viscera until a higher level of activity is reached. Thus, the circulatory system undergoes less disturbance during exertion than previously occurred (Royal College of Physicians 1991).

The value of exercise is underlined in the findings of the National Fitness Survey (Allied Dunbar National Fitness Survey 1992). In women over 54 years who had never carried out recreational activity, 15% of the sample suffered from heart disease, angina or breathlessness, compared with only 3% who had exercised for three-quarters of their adult lives. In men, these percentages were 21 and 14% respectively.

However, it is not clear how much exercise should be carried out by the healthy individual to achieve protection from coronary heart disease. Writers do not all hold the same view. Some research findings indicate that exercise should be vigorous to have any value (Morris et al 1990). Others point to the advantages of moderate exercise: Paffenbarger et al (1986) found that 5 hours of brisk walking or 3 1/2 hours of running a week was adequate. The recommendations to take a daily brisk of 30–60 minutes reflects this view and is considered by Blair et al (1989) to produce the required standard of fitness for most people. Light activities have also been shown to confer health benefit (US Preventive Services Task Force 1989).

Researchers agree however, that previous regular exercise, if it is not maintained into middle age, provides no protection from coronary disease (Paffenbarger et al 1986, Morris et al 1990).

Moderately raised blood pressure

Exercise has also been shown to have advantages where blood pressure is raised to a mild to moderate degree. A study conducted on people whose baseline blood pressures were in the region of 148/99 mmHg, showed that 45-minute periods of exercise carried out three times a week, with the heart working at 60–70% of its maximum rate, resulted in a fall in blood pressure of 11/9 mmHg. When this activity was carried out on a daily basis, the fall increased to 16/11 mmHg (Nelson et al 1986).

These results are associated with relatively high exercise intensity levels. Blair et al (1992) point to evidence which suggests that lower intensity levels are also effective, i.e. working at 60 or even 50% of maximum capacity. These researchers raise the possibility that the lower levels are more effective.

THE BONES

Bone mineral content and exercise

Bone mineral density in both men and women undergoes a progressive decline from its peak in the early thirties. In women, there is a sharp decline in the first 5 years following the menopause, as a result of diminishing oestrogens and the decline continues, although less sharply, into old age.

The mineral density of bone is determined by the concentration of calcium salts per unit volume. It is subject to two influences: the peak mineral content achieved during early life, and the rate of loss sustained during middle and old age. Recent data suggest that environmental influences are responsible for as much as half the variation in peak bone mass (or mineral density) among women (Krall et al 1993). This implies that factors such as exercise and nutrition play a role in establishing bone mass in the female child and young adult (Snow-Harter et al 1992). It has been suggested that these factors are also important in controlling the loss in later years.

Studies on women after the menopause have shown that bone mineral loss may be modified by exercise carried out three times a week. One study looked at the effect of different kinds of exercise and compared this with the effect of no exercise. Significant differences in bone mineral density were found between the groups who exercised and the group which did not, indicating an association between exercise and bone density. No differences however, were found between the two groups who exercised, one regularly carrying out 30 minutes of aerobic activity (walking, dancing or jogging), and the other, aerobic activity plus strengthening exercises (10 contractions to each muscle group) (Chow et al 1987).

Other studies suggest that, in middle-aged and older women, bone density may even be increased by exercise. A study conducted in 1983 by Krolner et al showed that systematic physical exercise was associated with increased vertebral bone density in postmenopausal women: 1 hour of walking, plus exercises twice a week for 8 months, resulted in an increase in bone mineral content of 3.5% in the exercise group, while the inactive control group suffered a decrease of 2.7% in the same length of time. It is interesting to compare these effects of exercise with those of oestrogen and progesterone therapy, where increases of 6.4% in vertebral bone density have been demonstrated, using continuous supplementation for a year (Munk-Jensen et al 1988).

Exercise offers some degree of protection against bone loss throughout life: the bone density of women who exercise at least three times a week is higher than the bone density of sedentary women in their age group, whether they are 20 or 80 years of age (Talmage et al 1986).

Further benefits of exercise are reported by Law et al (1991), who estimate that exercise can reduce the risk of hip fracture by at least half. This suggests that inactivity has contributed substantially to the high rate of hip fracture during the past few decades.

Type of exercise

A further question arises: what kind of exercise is most effective in maintaining bone mass? Although isometric arm work, in the form of squeezing a tennis ball 6 times a day for 3–6 weeks, has been shown to increase bone mineral density in the radius (Beverley et al 1989), particular value is gained from exercise which applies longitudinal pressure to the long bones, i.e. weight-bearing exercise (Astrand & Rodahl 1986). This means that swimming and cycling are less effective than walking, jogging and dancing.

This superiority of weight-bearing exercise applies only in the context of maintaining bone mineral content, since swimming and cycling offer substantial benefit to other body organs.

THE MUSCLES, LIGAMENTS AND JOINTS

Exercise benefits the muscles, ligaments and joints as well as the bones. The muscles become more resistant to fatigue as a result of aerobic activity; their strength increases as a result of isometric activity, and their elasticity is improved by stretchings.

Regular exercise strengthens the attachment of tendons and ligaments to bone. It also brings nourishment to the articular cartilages and helps to maintain their thickness which in turn, cushions the stress on the articular bone surfaces. The joint movement which accompanies exercise stimulates the flow of synovial fluid and helps to keep the joint healthy. When joints are not moved through their full range, their lubrication becomes reduced. Thus, it has been suggested that inactivity may sometimes be a contributing factor in the development of osteoarthritis (Alexander 1989).

The kind of movement which helps to preserve the health of the joint is active, nonstressful movement carried out through the full range of the joint.

PSYCHOLOGICAL ASPECTS OF EXERCISE

Exercise seems to be closely linked to mental health. Psychological assessment suggests that a sense of well-being is derived from regular exercise, with participants reporting less tension, fatigue, aggression, depression and insomnia (Royal College of Physicians 1991). The psychological benefits of exercise include distraction from worries, a sense of achievement, a feeling of improved physical appearance and enjoyment of the pleasant surroundings of the exercise activity (Royal College of Physicians 1991).

The National Fitness Survey (Allied Dunbar National Fitness Survey 1992) found that people who were active, at higher intensity levels on a regular basis, felt better than people who were not, while Hughes (1984) found that higher levels of self-esteem were reported among the physically active compared to the physically inactive.

There is evidence that moderate exercise reduces symptoms of depression and anxiety. Martinsen (1990), reviewing the literature, has shown that regular aerobic exercise contributes to the relief of mild to moderate depression and is not significantly less effective than other kinds of treatment. The level of activity adopted in Martinsen et al's (1985) controlled study was 1 hour three times a week for 6–9 weeks. The therapeutic effects of moderate exercise extend also to anxiety, although there are fewer controlled studies on this topic. Generalized anxiety however, seems to respond more favourably to exercise than does agoraphobia and panic disorder. It has also been shown that activity and exercise improve the individual's capacity to cope with daily emotional stressors (Brooke & Long 1987).

Both aerobic and anaerobic exercise have favourable psychological effects (De Coverley Veale 1987). After a period of moderate activity, the mood of a person who regularly takes exercise becomes altered: a depressed person will become less depressed, an anxious person less anxious, an angry person less angry. These mood-elevating effects, which may last for 2–6 hours, are thought to be associated with the raised levels of endorphins (endogenous morphines) which accompany exercise of moderate intensity (Ransford 1982, Sime 1990, Royal College of Physicians 1991).

PITFALLS OF EXERCISE

In recommending exercise to participants, the health care professional needs to be aware of its hazards. The activity can be excessive and be-

yond the capacity of the individual. There have been instances of muscles and tendons being injured and even death occurring in the course of exercise. It is important therefore to keep the activity within safe limits. The following points should be borne in mind:

1. Exercise should not be seen as a substitute for medical help in the presence of disease or suspected disease. People with cardiovascular problems should first consult their doctor before taking up exercise.

2. A medical examination is an essential preliminary for middle-aged or older people who wish to embark on activity at an unaccustomed level. Individuals who suddenly take up vigorous exercise would be seriously at risk if they had unrecognized cardiac problems.

3. Any programme of exercise should be introduced gradually in order to allow the organs to adapt to the new demands. Walking or swimming are useful ways to start. Unaccustomed strenuous activity is potentially hazardous.

4. All exercise should be preceded by some kind of 'warming up' activity to prepare the muscles for action (Safran et al 1989). Warming up usually takes the form of stretchings and mild activity such as running on the spot. This opens up the blood vessels in the working part and helps to protect against ischaemia (inadequacy of local blood supply) which can occur in unprepared muscles.

5. Warming down is also important. During vigorous or moderate exercise a higher than normal proportion of the total blood volume circulates through the voluntary muscles. This state continues for some time after the exercise has come to an end, and causes a lowering of the blood pressure. It carries real dangers for the elderly, but should be guarded against even in the young. As a remedy, the exercise can be slowly reduced in intensity or alternatively, some lighter activity can be performed to bring about a gradual return of normal blood distribution.

6. Exercise should not be too strenuous. To be safe, exercise should be well within the capacity of the individual and performed regularly. The individual should never feel he is exercising to

the limit of his strength. He should also know how to recognize signs of fatigue. Warnings of overwork in the form of chest pain or faintness for example, should never be ignored (Allied Dunbar National Fitness Survey 1992).

7. In the case of older people, the exercise should be light and regular. Demands should be kept low since ageing organs do not have the reserves of strength or the resilience of younger ones. Aerobic work should not be too arduous, while resisted work for muscle strengthening should be seen as potentially hazardous because of the rise in blood pressure which accompanies it.

In most other respects, older people derive the same benefit from exercise as younger people. They simply need to know when to stop.

8. The cardiovascular benefit of jogging has to be weighed against the stress it might impose on the weight-bearing joints (US Preventive Services Task Force 1989). Thus, if there is a family history of joint problems, it may be advisable to consider an alternative form of aerobic exercise such as cycling or swimming.

In their review of studies, Blair et al (1992) however, find little evidence of an association between running and increased risk of osteoarthritis in the hip or knee.

9. Bone mineral density in athletes has been found to be higher than it is among people who take no exercise. However, in the case of young women in endurance sports such as long-distance running and ballet dancing, there can be a temporary reduction in the level of oestrogen, creating amenorrhoea (cessation of menstruation). If prolonged, this can lead to loss of bone. As soon as the strenuous exercise stops however, the oestrogen level rises, menstruation returns and bone loss is halted.

10. 'Fatigue fracture' is a condition which sometimes afflicts rowers and long-distance runners. It is most likely to occur if the level of exertion exceeds what is customary for that individual.

11. Exercise is contraindicated during any kind of fever and should be avoided during viral infections such as influenza.

The gradient of risk

Blair et al (1992) refer to a gradient of risk across activity levels: the more intense and longer-lasting the exercise, the greater the risk it imposes. They emphasize the benefits of lower levels of activity since these are associated with reduced risk while yet conferring significant fitness benefit. Blair et al recommend as a public health message: 'A little exercise is better than none at all' rather than one which insists on minimum levels of exercise intensity.

While the advantages of exercise should be set against its potential hazards, it must be said that most people derive benefit from it. It should however, be carried out in a sensible manner (Royal College of Physicians 1991).

FURTHER READING

Allied Dunbar National Fitness Survey 1992 Activity and health research: a report on activity patterns and fitness levels. Sports Council and Health Education Authority, London

Bouchard C, Shephard R J, Stephens T, Sutton J R, McPherson B D (eds) 1990 Exercise, fitness and health: a consensus of current knowledge. Human Kinetics Books, Champaign, Illinois

Royal College of Physicians of London 1991 Medical aspects of exercise: benefits and risks. Royal College of Physicians, London

Steptoe A 1992 Physical activity and psychological well-being. In: Norgan N G (ed) Physical activity and health. Cambridge University Press, Cambridge

CHAPTER CONTENTS

The process of breathing 115

Breathing and relaxation 117
Level of breathing 117
General advantages of breathing as a method of
relaxation 117
Exploring respiratory movements 117

**General points regarding breathing awareness
exercises 117**

Breathing awareness exercises 118
Abdominal breathing 118
Breathing pouch 119
'Out tension, in peace' 119
Breathing meditation (1) 119
Breathing meditation (2) 119
Breathing with cue words 119

Hyperventilation 119
Treatment 121
Discussion 121

Pitfalls of breathing exercises 122

15

Breathing

Most relaxation methods, like imagery and the release of muscle tension, influence the autonomic system by indirect routes. Breathing is different. It leads directly into the autonomic nervous system, a fact which adds to its potential as a method of influencing physiological arousal (Lichstein 1988). In this Chapter the respiratory mechanism is described; exercises which induce relaxed breathing patterns are presented; there is a section on hyperventilation, and also one on the pitfalls of breathing exercises.

THE PROCESS OF BREATHING

Breathing is an automatic process governed by centres in the brain stem (pons and medulla). These activate the diaphragm and costal muscles to open the rib cage which expands in three directions: vertically, laterally and anteroposteriorly. Negative pressure in the pleural cavity pulls the lungs out, causing air to be sucked in. Relaxation of the same muscles results in the recoil of the thoracic structures and the expulsion of air. The respiratory organs are illustrated in Figure 15.1.

Oxygenated blood leaves the lungs bound for the heart which pumps it round the body where its oxygen is exchanged for waste products, amongst them carbon dioxide. These are carried back to the heart. The spent blood is then returned to the lungs where it gives up its carbon dioxide and collects a fresh supply of oxygen. The interchange of blood gases takes place in the alveoli (air sacs) which contain surfaces richly

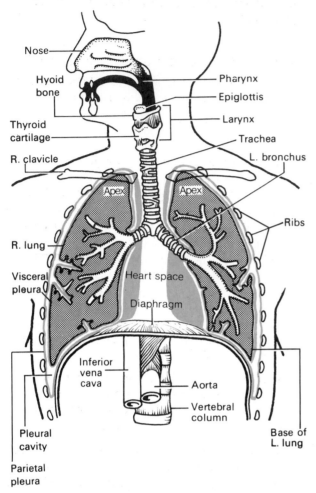

Figure 15.1 The organs of respiration. (From Wilson 1990 with permission.)

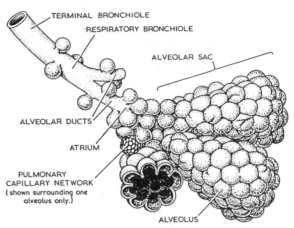

Figure 15.2 A terminal bronchiole with its air sacs. Reproduced from Waddington (1983). In: Downie P A (ed) Cash's textbook of chest, heart and vascular disorders for physiotherapists. Faber & Faber, London (with permission from Mosby-Wolfe, London).

supplied with hairlike blood vessels through which the gases diffuse (pass through membranes). The direction in which the gases pass is determined by their concentration, i.e. they move from a situation of high concentration to one of low concentration. Thus oxygen passes from the air in the bronchial tubes to the blood, and carbon dioxide passes from the blood to the air in the bronchial tubes. Each breath makes a contribution to the process. Figure 15.2 shows the structure of a terminal bronchiole with its air sacs.

Chemoreceptors in the walls of the aorta and the carotid arteries help to control breathing and are sensitive to changes in the amount of carbon dioxide circulating in the blood (Wilson 1990). The levels of carbon dioxide influence physiological activity, and are conventionally represented in terms of the partial pressure of carbon dioxide (P_{CO_2}). The arterial P_{CO_2} may range from 35 to 45 mmHg in the healthy individual (Hough 1991) although some writers regard 30 mmHg as the extreme lower limit of the normal range (Gardner & Bass 1989). Carbon dioxide levels are measured using arterial blood gas samples or end-tidal airflow (air delivered at the end of exhalation and measured at the mouth or nostril); the results from either the blood or the airflow are very similar in normal lungs (Gardner & Bass 1989).

Overbreathing and underbreathing

Overbreathing leads to excessive loss of carbon dioxide and a lowered arterial P_{CO_2} (hypocapnia); underbreathing to a build-up of carbon dioxide and a raised arterial P_{CO_2} (hypercapnia). A small rise of 2–5 mmHg (mild hypercapnia) is associated with lethargy, and symptoms resembling those of parasympathetic dominance i.e. relaxation (Slonim & Hamilton 1976). Further rises of 10–20 mmHg create an effect that mimics sympathetic dominance (fight–flight response). Even further rises can lead to unconsciousness.

BREATHING AND RELAXATION

Level of breathing

Given that a mild degree of hypercapnia has a relaxing effect, the question arises as to what level of breathing is associated with it. Lanphier & Rahn (1963) indicate that 5–10 seconds of breath retention will be likely to raise the Pco_2 by 2–5 mmHg. However, it must be said that breathholding is generally disliked by authors and is not advocated here.

Slow, shallow breathing will tend to have a similar effect, and although taking longer to achieve mild hypercapnia, has the advantage of promoting a smooth breathing rhythm. A further point in favour of slow breathing is its association with parasympathetic activity (p. 4).

General advantages of breathing as a method of relaxation

1. Respiration is directly linked with the autonomic nervous system which controls physiological arousal.
2. The techniques are easy to learn.
3. Breathing is particularly useful for individuals who find imagery difficult.
4. Most breathing exercises can be carried out anywhere.

Exploring respiratory movements

The exercises in this section are concerned with breathing awareness and introduce the individual to the mechanics of respiration.

During the inspiratory phase the chest expands through all dimensions. Participants can confirm this for themselves by carrying out the following exercises (plenty of time should be allowed).

1. Lying or sitting

Place your hands on the lower edge of your ribs, fingertips a few centimetres apart. Feel your hands rise and separate as the air flows in, and recoil as it flows out.

2. Sitting with head and arms resting on a table

With movement in the front of the chest now restricted, you can feel the chest expanding backwards.

3. Lying or sitting

Place your right hand over the solar plexus (the soft part between the ribs and the navel) and your left hand over the front of your chest below the clavicle (collar bone). Notice what happens under your hands when you breathe. As the air enters, feel the expansion growing, first under your right hand, then rising through the chest to reach the area under your left hand. Explore that idea for a minute or two.

The emotional state

Breathing is also subject to a person's emotional state:

Imagine for a few moments a situation that makes you feel uneasy . . . Next, imagine one in which you feel at ease . . . Did you notice any change in your breathing pattern from one to the other?

Breathing in a calm individual is associated with relaxed abdominal muscles and is characterized by visible movement of the upper abdomen; stressful breathing is associated with predominantly upper costal movement and often involves contraction of the shoulder girdle muscles. Calm breathing tends to have a slow rate, stressful breathing, a more rapid one.

GENERAL POINTS REGARDING BREATHING AWARENESS EXERCISES

1. Breathing should occur at the natural pace of the individual.
2. It should be seen in terms of 'letting the air in' rather than 'taking a breath'.
3. A smooth transfer should take place between inhalation and exhalation, and between exhalation and inhalation unless the exercise indicates otherwise.

4. Breathing through the nose is preferable to breathing through the mouth since the nasal passages both filter and warm the incoming air.
5. Although some exercises may emphasize particular aspects of the breathing cycle, the respirations should always be gentle.
6. Artificially deep breaths should not be repeated. (See the section on hyperventilation at the end of this chapter.)

As mentioned earlier, a slow rate of breathing is associated with relaxation: routines designed to lengthen the respiratory cycle will tend to have a calming effect. Abdominal breathing also is associated with relaxation. The exercises which follow are built around these ideas.

BREATHING AWARENESS EXERCISES

Slowing the breathing rate does not mean that the breath has to be deep. Slowed breathing does not mean that extra air is taken in or released; it means simply that the air travels more slowly. The result is a breath whose depth has not been changed by the exercise. Moreover, it is a relatively shallow breath, since shallow breathing is appropriate for a resting individual. Slow breathing is usually combined with abdominal breathing, and this forms the basic exercise presented here. Relaxing imagery also features in some of the exercises.

Counting strategies are another approach which is sometimes used. These are procedures which lengthen the breathing cycle either by extending the breath out or by introducing breath-holds. Such manipulations would appear to be a logical way of slowing the rate. However, unless skilfully managed, they can create tension if participants have to struggle to conform to their patterns. They may be found helpful by some people; others however, find the artificial rhythm unconducive to relaxation. As a result, controlled breathing of this kind is not included in the present work. Emphasis here is placed on methods which focus on the moving abdomen, or methods which incorporate relaxation-inducing imagery.

Exercises 1–5 below are described in this chapter.

1. Abdominal breathing.
2. Breathing pouch.
3. Out tension, in peace.
4. Breathing meditation: 1.
5. Breathing meditation: 2.
6. Breathing with cue words (cue-controlled relaxation). This has been described in Chapter 8 (p. 65).

One breathing exercise is probably enough in one session. It can be repeated a few times, then dropped and taken up again later in the session. Allowing breaks between the exercises is a safeguard against overbreathing which may occur if the exercises are too enthusiastically carried out. Overbreathing or hyperventilation is discussed in a later section of this chapter.

Abdominal breathing

This refers to the kind of breathing which emphasizes the downward expansion of the chest cavity. It was often referred to as diaphragmatic in the past, before it was realized that the diaphragm was involved in all normal breathing (Hough 1991).

The diaphragm is a sheet of muscle whose edges are attached to the lower ribs creating a floor to the chest. In the resting state it is dome-shaped. Contraction of the diaphragm flattens the dome, thereby lengthening the chest and sucking in air. Relaxation of the muscle causes it to reassume its dome shape which helps to push the air out. But the diaphragm also forms the roof of the abdomen and as such, its movements affect the position of the internal organs: as the contracting diaphragm presses down on the organs, it causes the abdomen to swell slightly. Similarly, as the relaxing diaphragm releases its pressure on the organs, the abdomen sinks back again.

To carry out an abdominal breathing exercise, the individual should first make himself as comfortable as possible, and spend a few minutes quietly resting. The following instructions may then be given:

Spend a few moments running through a sequence of pleasant imagery . . . then, as your body relaxes turn your attention to your breathing . . . lay one hand lightly over the solar plexus. Focus your attention on this area. Start the exercise with a breath out . . . a naturally occurring breath out. Notice a sinking of the area under your hand. Next, allow air to flow into the lungs, noticing the swelling which takes place under your hand. Then as the air is expelled, notice the area under the hand sinking back again. Allow the breathing to take place naturally.

Some writers teach abdominal breathing by urging pupils to 'think in and down' (Innocenti 1983). This helps to create a natural abdominal movement. Although most schools of relaxation adopt abdominal breathing in preference to thoracic breathing, research does not indicate that it changes the distribution of air in the lungs (Martin et al 1976). Abdominal breathing is however, associated with a relaxed state.

Breathing pouch

A variation of abdominal breathing, this exercise incorporates imagery. It is adapted from Everly & Rosenfeld (1981).

Concentrate on your breathing rhythm without trying to change it. Become aware of your upper abdomen swelling as you inhale and sinking as you exhale. Picture an imaginary, hollow pouch lying inside your abdomen . . . as you breathe in, air travels down to fill the pouch, making the abdomen swell . . . breathing out empties the pouch, causing the abdomen to sink back . . . if you place your hand over your abdomen, you can feel the gentle swelling and sinking taking place.

'Out tension, in peace'

Listen to your breathing without altering its pattern . . . imagine your tensions being breathed out . . . imagine them being carried away, a little at a time with each breath out . . . and now, imagine that every time you inhale, you are breathing in peace, a little at a time with each breath . . . breathe out tension . . . breathe in peace . . . gently breathing . . . feeling peace flowing through your body . . . always keeping your breathing natural . . .

Breathing meditation (1)

Let your mind follow the path of the breath, taking care not to change its pace or its rhythm. Think of the air flowing in through your nostrils, along your nasal passages, down your windpipe and into your lungs . . . then, gently and smoothly turning, it is carried out along the same route . . . turning again as the air is drawn back in . . . notice the feel of the air . . . warm as it leaves, and cool as it enters . . . continue on your own with this idea for a few minutes.

Breathing meditation (2)

This script illustrating 'breath mindfulness', is adapted from Lichstein (1988). It is particularly addressed to people with high blood pressure.

With your eyes closed, settle into your chair, couch or wherever you have chosen to be . . . let your body lose its tension and let your mind gradually become calm by using some pleasant imagery . . . allow your mind's eye to rest on the upper part of your abdomen . . . be aware of it swelling and sinking as you breathe . . . notice these breathing movements without trying to change them . . . just observe them in the knowledge that your body takes full care of your breathing . . . allow your breathing to continue on its own . . . flowing gently and smoothly . . . perhaps you can feel the rate getting slower . . . this is because your resting body doesn't need so much oxygen as when you are active . . . your heart rate also is lowered and your blood pressure falls, as a state of quiet settles on you . . . allow yourself to enjoy this feeling of tranquillity . . . let your mind continue to focus on your breathing for a few minutes longer.

Breathing with cue words

This exercise is described under the name of cue-controlled relaxation in Chapter 8 (p. 65).

HYPERVENTILATION

Exercises which succeed in slowing the breathing rate tend to reduce ventilation. This is a useful strategy to employ whenever a person is under stress, since stress tends to increase ventilation. Ventilation in a person under stress can be increased to such an extent that it disturbs body systems. At this level it is called 'hyperventilation'.

In the state of hyperventilation a person processes a greater volume of air than is required by his body at that moment (Innocenti 1983). Thus, a hyperventilating person is one who is breathing in excess of body needs: taking in too much oxygen and releasing too much carbon dioxide. This results in reduced levels of carbon dioxide in the arteries and body tissues. The arterial P_{CO_2}, normally around 42 mmHg, can fall to as low as 26 mmHg (Innocenti 1983). Since carbon dioxide is acid the pH value of the blood rises, creating alkalosis. This results in neuronal excitability, vasoconstriction and a widespread disturbance of the body chemistry.

Itself a symptom of stress, overbreathing thus creates symptoms on its own account. Cerebral vasoconstriction (Gardner & Bass 1989) causes:

- dizziness
- faintness
- headache
- visual disturbance

Other symptoms are (Gardner & Bass 1989):

- paraesthesia (tingling), caused by alkalosis
- chest pain, caused by coronary vasoconstriction
- palpitations, caused by paroxysmal dysrhythmia.

These symptoms are collectively referred to as 'the hyperventilation syndrome'. Many of them resemble the symptoms of sympathetic nervous system activity. The apprehension they create can itself release catecholamines which reinforce the initial symptoms, setting up a vicious circle as shown in Figure 15.3.

The breathing pattern of a hyperventilating person may display irregularities which include any of the following (Hough 1991):

- Rapid breathing, rising in some cases to 30 or more breaths a minute.
- Sighing, yawning, excessive sniffing.
- Halts in the breathing cycle.
- Marked movement in the upper regions of the chest.
- Difficulty getting the breath.

Contrary to what might be supposed, the overbreathing does not lead to a greater availability of oxygen because the hypocapnia causes

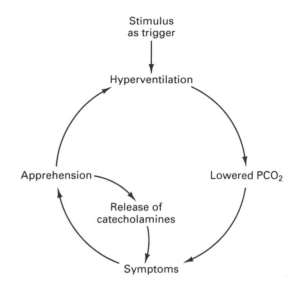

Figure 15.3 The cyclic pattern of hyperventilation.

vascular changes which result in a decreased amount of oxygen being transferred to the tissues (Lum 1981).

The condition may be acute or chronic. Acute hyperventilation, which occurs in some people during moments of extreme stress, can give rise to marked symptoms. In chronic hyperventilation however, there are often few visible symptoms: a process of adaptation appears to take place where the respiratory control mechanism undergoes 'resetting' to a lower level of P_{CO_2} (Gardner & Bass 1989, Gardner 1992). However, in order to maintain this level, the respiratory drive must be increased, i.e. the individual must take deeper than normal breaths or suffer chest discomfort.

Although there is no infallible way of testing for chronic hyperventilation, an indication of the state can be gained from simple tests (Hough 1991). Two are described below:

- The individual is asked to overbreathe rapidly for two minutes (provocation test). This not only reproduces symptoms which he is able to recognize if he is a hyperventilator, but also demonstrates to him that he has control over them. This test should not however, be carried out where the individual is suffering from heart disease. Therapists need also to be aware of the possibility of strong feelings being released in the course of the test.

• The individual is asked to hold his breath. Difficulty in holding it for as long as 10 seconds suggests that he is a hyperventilator.

Treatment

Whether the hyperventilation is acute or chronic, the aim of treatment is to raise the P_{CO_2}. Three ways of achieving this are:

1. Holding the breath for a few seconds.
2. Altering the rate and depth of the respirations, making the breaths slower and shallower.
3. Changing the composition of the inhaled air; rebreathing exhaled air.

Breathholding.   This may correct the condition momentarily but if breath holds are practised repeatedly, they tend to promote tension and irregular breathing patterns. Breathholding is therefore not advocated by practitioners in medicine or physiotherapy except to compensate for the effects of an unnaturally deep breath (Innocenti 1983).

Altering rate and depth.   The respirations can be made slower and shallower. This approach is the method of choice for chronic hyperventilation (Lum 1977, Innocenti 1983, Hough 1991, Rowbottom 1992). The individual is first made aware of his existing breathing pattern which is then gradually replaced by a new one through a process of reeducation. Abdominal breathing is a central feature and is carried out by asking the individual to lay one hand over the solar plexus and to focus on the swelling and sinking of the upper abdomen. 'Slow, gentle, shallow, smooth and abdominal' is the prescription of Hough (1991) who adds that the individual should be in control, although under the guidance of the physiotherapist. She suggests aiming at a breathing rate of 10 breaths a minute, although symptoms should be allowed to take priority over numbers. In the beginning, this controlled breathing may create air hunger. If this happens, the individual can be reassured and congratulated, with an explanation that the brain is recognizing change before it can adapt to new conditions (Rowbottom 1992).

Changing the composition of inhaled air: rebreathing.

Air is made up of a variety of gases, of which oxygen contributes 21% and carbon dioxide 0.04% (Wilson 1990). However, this applies only to the air which enters the lungs. The air which leaves the lungs contains a lower proportion of oxygen and a higher proportion of carbon dioxide (exhaled air contains about 4% carbon dioxide). If a person in acute hyperventilation rebreathes his own exhaled air, the condition will be temporarily corrected; a convenient way of doing this is by breathing into a paper bag with the neck of the bag firmly held over the nose and mouth. Powell & Enright (1990) suggest rebreathing four or five times, taking a rest, then repeating the process if necessary. Hough (1991) emphasizes that the rebreathing should be gentle.

The hyperventilating person may feel that the bag procedure draws attention to him when used in a public place. A more convenient although less effective alternative is to cup the hands over the nose and mouth and, without releasing the hands, continue to breathe into them.

Rebreathing exhaled air is useful in acute hyperventilation and particularly if symptoms rise to panic level. Where symptoms are chronic, rebreathing techniques will do little more than temporarily relieve them (Gardner & Bass 1989). Treatment should therefore focus on the reeducation of normal breathing patterns (as above).

Relaxation

Because of the association between anxiety and hyperventilation, relaxation and stress management are useful components of treatment.

Home practice

Reeducating the respiratory centres of chronically hyperventilating individuals to accept higher levels of P_{CO_2} takes time. Only practice can restore a normal breathing pattern. This practice consists of slow, smooth, shallow abdominal breathing performed little and often (Hough 1991).

Discussion

It is difficult to distinguish hyperventilation in the

acute form from panic attack. Similar symptoms occur in both conditions, being a result either of overbreathing or of stimulation of the sympathetic nervous system (Clark 1986). Some researchers discuss the likelihood of an interaction between the two conditions; a possibility which is supported by the tendency for panic attacks to decline following treatment that focuses on respiratory control (Clark et al 1985). However, Clark (1986) does not see hyperventilation alone as being the cause of panic attacks. Cognitive factors predominate in his model; but inasmuch as hyperventilation occurs, Clark suggests that resulting bodily sensations must be both perceived as unpleasant and interpreted in a catastrophic way for panic to develop. Figure 15.4 illustrates this idea.

In its chronic form, the hyperventilation syndrome is gaining ever-increasing recognition.

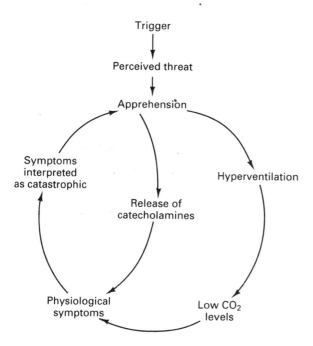

Figure 15.4 How hyperventilation might interact with cognitive factors to create a panic attack. Adapted from Clark (1986). A cognitive approach to panic. Behaviour, Research and Therapy 24: 463 (with kind permission from Elsevier Science, Kidlington).

PITFALLS OF BREATHING EXERCISES

1. Breathing exercises for inducing relaxation should not be seen as a substitute for medical treatment where a disorder exists. They may however, be used as a complement if the physician or physiotherapist agrees.

2. The individual should never feel he is straining or forcing the breaths; they must always feel comfortable.

3. Dizziness during the exercises is probably a symptom of hyperventilation, i.e. the exercises are being performed too deeply or too quickly. Remedies may be found in the section on hyperventilation. Alternatively, the individual could take a rest from the exercise. It is useful if the instructor describes the condition of hyperventilation at the outset.

4. Since individuals vary in their breathing rates, routines imposed by the instructor are not recommended in a group situation. The instructions can be phrased in such a way that participants individually decide on a pace that suits them.

5. Although slow, abdominal breathing can be an effective way of inducing relaxation, it may not suit everyone. In particular, people who suffer from different kinds of air hunger may not find it helpful to manipulate their breathing rate.

6. Although people who suffer from panic disorder have been shown to derive benefit from relaxation, a few individuals occasionally report the occurrence of panic attacks during periods of relaxation. Two possible explanations are offered here. The first comes from Hough (1991), who points out that relaxation weakens psychological defences and may allow disturbing feelings to rise to the surface.

Ley (1988) puts forward an alternative explanation: if a person who is already hyperventilating begins to relax, he lowers his metabolic rate. This reduces his production of carbon dioxide. If he does not make a corresponding reduction in ventilation, his hypocapnia will increase and his symptoms become more marked.

FURTHER READING

Hough A 1991 Physiotherapy in respiratory care: a problem-solving approach. Chapman and Hall, London

Innocenti D 1983 Chronic hyperventilation syndrome. In: Downie P (ed) Cash's textbook of chest, heart and vascular disorders for physiotherapists, 3rd edn. Faber and Faber, London

Webber B A, Pryor J A 1993 Physiotherapy for respiratory and cardiac problems. Churchill Livingstone, Edinburgh

Mental approaches to relaxation

SECTION CONTENTS

16. Self-awareness 127

17. Imagery 133

18. Goal-directed visualization 143

19. Autogenic training 155

20. Meditation 161

21. The relaxation response 171

CHAPTER CONTENTS

Introduction 127

Exercises in self-awareness 128
Awareness of thinking style 128
Awareness of the capacity for intuition 129
Awareness of feelings (emotions) 129
Awareness of the body 130
Awareness of the environment 130
Awareness of the way we relate to others 130

Benefits and pitfalls of self-awareness exercises
132

16

Self-awareness

INTRODUCTION

'Being aware' or 'being conscious' convey similar ideas. Their use when applied to the self however, is very different. Being aware of the self is defined as 'the tendency to focus attention on the private aspects of the self' (West 1987). This signifies a process of self-exploration; a getting-to-know oneself. Being conscious of the self as we use the phrase in everyday language, on the other hand, implies the sense of being 'painfully aware of being observed by others' (Burnard 1991). A person who is self-conscious sees herself as being critically scrutinized by the observer, and in this role, allows herself to be turned into an object. The result of self-consciousness is embarrassment; the result of self-awareness is self-knowledge.

Increased self-knowledge comes from listening to ourselves: to who we are, what we are and how we are (Tschudin 1991). It relates to questions such as 'Am I the person I want to be?' and if not, 'What is stopping me become that person?' or 'Why don't I allow myself to develop to my fullest?' The answers help us to understand ourselves. The better we know ourselves, the easier it is to make decisions which further our life plans. Without this knowledge, we may find decisions being made for us.

Self-awareness also puts us in touch with our outward behaviour, and the way others may be responding to it. In this way, self-awareness can enhance our personal relationships.

The notion of self-awareness is fundamentally

linked to the notion of living in the present, responding in the here-and-now, and being aware of the present moment, since that is where we express ourselves and make our impact on life. Of course, we need to take into account lessons learned from the past and goals set for the future, but it is all too easy to dwell on these and let the present take care of itself. This can lead to our losing whatever control we had of it. Being aware of the self helps us perform in the present.

Greater control of our lives, enhanced relationships and the capacity to live in the present all contribute to our peace of mind. Self-awareness exercises can thus be seen as relaxation techniques.

Authors have structured self-awareness in different ways. Stevens (1971) divided it into three parts: an outer world of sensory information, an inner world of feelings (visceral and emotional), and an inner world of mental activity (thoughts and images). Burnard (1992) sees the internal part as corresponding with Jung's four functions of the mind (thinking, feeling, sensing and intuiting), to which he adds a visceral component which includes muscle tension and bodily relaxation. The external part refers to what other people see: our verbal and nonverbal behaviour together with other aspects of the way we present ourselves.

To Tschudin (1991), the inner world consists of thoughts and emotions and the outer world of people and environments with a 'go-between' world relating to the senses. A composite view is presented here (Fig. 16.1). The inner aspect includes thinking, intuition, emotions and bodily sensations which include those of muscle tension; the outer aspect refers to the way we relate to other people, and the intermediary area is concerned with the five senses.

The exercises presented here are adapted from Stevens (1971), Burnard (1992) and Bond (1986).

EXERCISES IN SELF-AWARENESS
Awareness of thinking style

We have different ways of thinking: sometimes we think in a vertical or focused way as when doing arithmetic. At other times our thinking may be more inclined to a lateral style, as, for instance, when we are engaged in creative work. We also have our own personal styles of thinking: some people tend towards a cause–effect style, others to a broader canvas style. The individual can review her own style in the following manner:

Take a few moments off to make a list of the thoughts that go through your mind and the dialogue that accompanies them. Write them down. Repeat this twice later in the day. Compare the items on your three lists and notice if a pattern emerges. Is some particular thought claiming your attention? If so, how do you approach it? Do you see it as a problem to be solved or do you let it dominate you? If you are trying to solve it, are you using a focused method or are you keeping your mind open and receptive to fresh ideas? Both approaches are useful. Do you have a tendency to favour one more than the other?

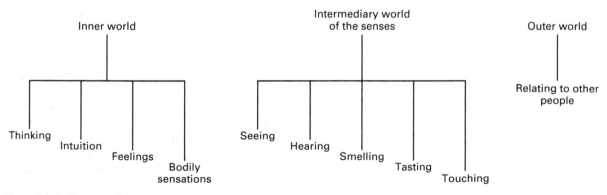

Figure 16.1 Aspects of the self.

Awareness of the capacity for intuition

Our glorification of the rational has all but eclipsed the imagination in everyday affairs. We distrust intuition, or at best, give it short shrift. Our belief in the undeniable value of logical thinking does not however, mean we must stifle the imagination, and those who underestimate its power may do so at their peril for it communicates with the inner self.

Sit quietly and allow yourself to become relaxed. Follow your breathing, and next time you breathe out, release all your tension in a long sigh. Scan your body, checking that all your muscles are relaxed. Imagine yourself in a place of beauty and peace. Allow your thoughts to drift in and out. Focus on a matter that has been claiming your attention recently . . . keep it light . . . there's no compulsion to resolve it at this moment . . . just listen to yourself . . . tune into yourself . . . be receptive to any ideas that float into your head . . . listen to your gut feeling; you can judge its merits later . . . just be open for yourself . . . When you are ready, bring your visualization to an end.

Awareness of feelings (emotions)

To focus on emotions need not be seen as self-indulgence. Rather, it is a form of self-examination which can provide us with insights and perhaps indicate useful paths of change. While our emotions may be said to enrich our lives on the one hand, they give us trouble on the other; some feelings can be so strong they cloud our judgement and others may be so uncomfortable we repress them.

Heron (1977) reminds us that society urges us to control rather than express emotion, and this he claims, blocks our development as full human beings. Anger and grief are two examples where this occurs. He sees the handling of emotions as a skill and has developed a model which identifies four aspects of this skill. They consist of the degree to which we:

1. are aware of our emotional patterns
2. express ourselves in controlled or spontaneous ways
3. share our feelings
4. use catharsis to move forward.

1. Awareness of emotional patterns

We need to recognize our feeling patterns and tendencies to react in certain ways. Only when we are aware of them can we see how they may be influencing our behaviour.

2. Control or spontaneity

Many situations require us to hide our feelings, but there are other occasions when a more spontaneous response is called for. Whether we express our emotion or hold it back is governed not only by the circumstances but also by whatever decision we make at the time. Some individuals may have a tendency to respond in one or the other way? If so, are they aware of it?

3. Sharing our feelings

Self-disclosure is part of the process of deepening a relationship, and this applies whether the individual is making the disclosure or listening to another making hers. Although the sharing of feelings involves taking a risk, the relationship is unlikely to develop without it. Most relationships are enriched by some degree of self-disclosure; the extent to which it occurs depends on the nature of the relationship and the inclination of the individual. Is she *inclined* to share her feelings?

4. Releasing emotions in a process of catharsis

This aspect of emotional skills provides a safeguard against the bottling-up of emotions. If emotions are not expressed or dealt with at the time they are aroused, they get suppressed. In this latter case, a subsequent environmental trigger may stir them up and lead to inappropriate behaviour of two kinds: first we may overreact if we see the issue as a safe channel in which to let off the pressure of our suppressed emotions, or second, we may underreact, having trained ourselves to keep a tight rein on our feelings at all times. Either way our response is a maladaptive one. The process of catharsis helps to free the individual from the tyranny of unresolved emotions. Heron lists three elements of cathartic release:

1. Letting-go of feelings. This can take place in a controlled way such as going for a jog or a workout; it can also be achieved in less restrained ways such as shouting into a pillow or kicking a cushion.

2. Gaining insights. The release of emotions may be accompanied by intuitive insights which deepen the individual's understanding of the situation and of herself.

3. Decision making. If emotional release has cleared her mind of its burden, and newly found insights have enriched her perceptions, the individual is better able to plan and carry out constructive changes to her life.

A self-awareness script based on Heron's model is presented below.

Spend a few minutes considering your feeling patterns . . . do you tend to react in characteristic ways? . . . what are these ways of reacting? . . . for example, do you tend to control your feelings or do you make spontaneous responses? . . . can you think of occasions when you have used one or other of those responses? . . . and to what effects? . . . (pause) . . .

Do you tend to share your feelings or are you reluctant to trust people? . . . have you been let down in the past by sharing your feelings? . . . if so, has it affected your readiness to trust others? . . . (pause) . . .

How do you deal with situations which make you angry? . . . do you answer back (as the occasion permits), or do you tend to bottle up your feelings? . . . having bottled them up, are you able to find ways of releasing that pent-up anger? . . . if so, do you feel more content afterwards? . . . think of occasions when you have used catharsis . . .

Awareness of the body

From time to time, the body needs attention. In between, we spend periods of varying length without giving it a thought. Breathing, digestion, skin sensations can all be ignored; muscle tension also passes unnoticed. If we are interested in reducing muscle tension, it can be useful to make a point of listening to the body occasionally.

Allow your thoughts to focus on your body. Notice any sensations, such as stomach rumblings, joint discomfort, itches or the tendency to sigh . . . things you normally disregard as you concentrate on your work. Perhaps you are also ignoring feelings of tension in your muscles, in your back, your shoulders, your face or your writing arm . . . try focusing on those areas and releasing the tension . . . realize that you could just as easily increase it . . . try for a moment deliberately exaggerating the feeling of muscle tension . . . notice that you have the power to switch it on or off . . . simply by making a conscious effort you can increase or decrease those feelings of tension. Explore that idea for a few moments.

Awareness of the environment

This aspect of the self is concerned with information from the five senses: sight, sound, smell, taste and touch. Much of this activity never gets through to our consciousness which may be to our advantage if we are concentrating on a piece of work. However, it is through our senses that we experience our environment and are able to relate to the world.

Sit on your own. Allow the breath out to carry all your tensions with it. Bring your mind to focus on what is happening around you: the sounds inside the building and outside . . . the smells of the kitchen/office/shop/classroom/factory . . . the taste of the coffee you just drank . . . the arrangement of the furniture in the room . . . the colour of the decoration . . . the temperature of the room . . . the feel of the chair underneath you, the pen or the peeler in your hand . . . focus on each one separately for a few moments. If you are driving notice the countryside. If you are waiting in a bus queue pick out the different sounds in the street . . . if you are walking to the letterbox, notice the front gardens along the way . . .

Notice how the exercise has the effect of taking you away from your preoccupations and giving you an acute experience of the present moment.

Awareness of the way we relate to others

People can only know about us from what we show of ourselves: our appearance, general demeanour and what we say. These are outer aspects of the individual, and disclose much or little of the inner self depending on the level of intimacy. All that can be known about a person is what he or she consciously or unconsciously reveals, so that what we reveal is important since it establishes our identity in the world. Our behaviour whether verbal or nonverbal, creates us as individuals in other people's eyes.

Verbal behaviour refers to the actual words spoken. Nonverbal behaviour includes aspects of speech such as tone of voice, timing, emphasis, accent (paralinguistic features), as well as facial expression, eye contact, gesture, posture, physical proximity, clothes and appearance (Argyle 1978). The way we respond within the interaction provides a further level of behaviour: how we prompt, cut in, and listen.

Assertiveness

We also define ourselves by our readiness to be assertive or not. Assertiveness involves knowing how to advance our life goals while respecting the interests of other people. Put another way, it means insisting on having our interests respected while other people advance *their* goals. For example, are we able to refuse a request which we feel is unreasonable?

Do you find it easy to say 'No' to a request in a situation where saying 'Yes' makes you feel you are being taken advantage of? Can you think of an occasion when this occurred? How did you react? Were you happy with the outcome? If not, how did you feel? In your imagination, go back to the occasion. Re-create the scene and re-script your part with you saying 'No'. What effect does this have on the other person? What effect does it have on you? Now ask yourself why

you said 'Yes' in the first place? How would you deal with a similar request in the future?

Promoting a relationship while retaining a feeling of self, is one of the social skills. This feeling of self is tied up with our self-esteem, i.e. the degree to which we feel we have worth. Low self-esteem is linked with nonassertive behaviour; high self-esteem with assertive behaviour. To raise her self-esteem, the individual needs to recognize her personal strengths and qualities.

Bond (1986) illustrates these points in her models of nonassertive and assertive behaviour. In the first, the individual is locked in a negative cyclic pattern of behaviour, while in the second, she has established herself in a positive cyclic pattern (Fig. 16.2). In order to break out of the first and move to the second, she has to intervene at some point in the negative cycle. She has to question the appropriateness of the role she is playing and explore new possibilities. This intervention gradually takes her from a less assertive pose to a more assertive one.

A script for an individual assessing her own assertiveness (or nonassertiveness) might run as follows:

Allow yourself to feel relaxed before you begin. Run through a relaxing procedure until you feel very calm and tuned in to yourself. Let your thoughts focus on a person you know . . . someone you are not close to . . . someone with whom you have had difficulties but are obliged to see from time to time . . .

Let your mind gently focus on this person . . . let her take shape . . . notice how she looks: her expression . . . what she is wearing . . . spend a little time re-creating her presence . . . then see yourself also,

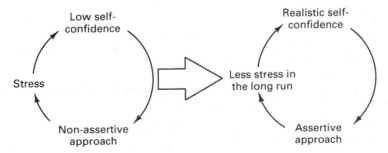

Figure 16.2 Breaking out of the stress/low confidence trap. From Bond 1986, with permission from Butterworth-Heinemann Ltd.

including expression and clothes, as you, in your mind's eye, greet this person.

Observe your nonverbal behaviour . . . does it strike the right note? . . . is the conversation balanced in the sense that neither person is acting aggressively to the other's submissive behaviour? . . . if it is unbalanced what, if anything, do you think you should do about it? . . . it may be that you feel your behaviour is appropriate . . . on the other hand, you may wish to modify your style, to make it more assertive . . . you will know best what is needed in the situation . . .

If you decide to modify your style, consider ways in which you might begin . . . test these out in your imagination . . . notice how your new behaviour feels . . . spend a few minutes mentally experiencing the scene . . .

BENEFITS AND PITFALLS OF SELF-AWARENESS EXERCISES

Exercises such as those described can heighten our awareness of the way we relate to other people. We also in the process, deepen our self-knowledge.

Awareness exercises in general bring us to a closer understanding of who we are: we learn to 'listen' to the self in all its aspects, and to tune in to its nuances. Self-awareness exercises, by their emphasis on 'exploring, experimenting, experiencing', thus lead us to a better understanding of ourselves (Stevens 1971).

The pitfalls of self-awareness include the following:

1. Regularly engaging in introspection may lead to a tendency to become self-centred.

2. The determined pursuit of self-understanding may lead some people to take themselves too seriously, even to the point of losing their sense of humour. This is misuse of the self-awareness concept.

3. Getting to know oneself can be a painful process, while changing oneself is difficult. Our efforts are however, rewarded by the discovery that we have more power than we realized to control our lives: a thought which itself engenders a sense of calm.

As a relaxation technique, self-awareness might be said to be at the other end of the scale from distraction (the diversion of attention away from the self). Each is effective on its own, but together they complement one another: self-awareness protecting the individual from the hazards of denial, while distraction protects her from too much introspection.

FURTHER READING

Bond M 1986 Stress and self-awareness: a guide for nurses. Butterworth Heinemann, London
Burnard P 1992 Know yourself: self-awareness activities for nurses. Scutari Press, London

Tschudin V 1991 Beginning with awareness: a learner's handbook. Churchill Livingstone, Edinburgh

CHAPTER CONTENTS

**Physiological and psychological aspects of imagery
134**
Laterality 134
The unconscious 134
Consciousness 135

Therapeutic effects of imagery 135

Procedure of a therapeutic imagery session 136
Relaxation 136
Introductory remarks to participants 136
Termination 136

Exploring single senses 136

Symbolic imagery 137

The use of metaphor 138
Transformations 139
Distancing 139

Colour 139
Chakras 140
White light 141

Guided imagery 141

A summarized evaluation of imagery 142

Pitfalls 142

17

Imagery

Imagery has already been mentioned during discussion of passive relaxation, breathing, the Alexander technique and self-awareness. Here imagery is considered in its own right.

Achterberg (1985) defines imagery as 'the thought process that invokes and uses the senses'. Sight, sound, smell, taste, and touch modalities can all be involved in this activity, which may take place in the absence of any external stimulus. It could be said that imagery is thinking in pictures as opposed to thinking with words.

The importance of the image was underlined by Aristotle who said that without it, thought is impossible. Einstein also, found imagery an essential component of thought. It is particularly associated with the creative function of thinking. However, we are forming images all the time, whether making plans for the future, remembering items from the past or creating fantasy in realms beyond our experience.

Although the precise mechanism of imagery is unknown, it is believed to involve the right cerebral hemisphere. Consequently, in this chapter there is a short discussion of the concept of laterality. Psychological aspects of imagery are then considered, followed by sections on its therapeutic effects and the procedure of an imagery session. Exercises which use different kinds of imagery are then presented, such as:

- single sense imagery
- imagery as symbol
- imagery as metaphor
- colour imagery
- guided imagery.

PHYSIOLOGICAL AND PSYCHOLOGICAL ASPECTS OF IMAGERY

Laterality

The cerebral cortex is divided into two hemispheres, each of which has four lobes: frontal, parietal, temporal and occipital. Research indicates that the hemispheres have specialized roles. One side, usually the left, is believed to process logical thought and language. It is involved in linear, analytic and rational thinking, reading, writing and mathematical activity. The right hemisphere is seen as dealing with information of a nonrational nature, being concerned with creative thinking, fantasy, metaphor, imagery, dreams, analogies, intuition and emotion, including feelings of stress. Also processed on this side is the viewing of objects in space, the recognition of patterns and the interpretation of sensory impressions (Fig. 17.1).

Lyman et al (1980) claim to have found a connection between images and emotions, having shown experimentally that emotionally charged situations are more likely than neutral ones to be accompanied by imagery. They posit a direct relationship between the right hemisphere (which is associated with imagery) and the autonomic system (which governs the physiological responses associated with emotion).

The link between imagery and physiological processes can be demonstrated by imagining a lemon (Barber et al 1964):

Visualize its exterior shape, colour, scent and texture; then slice it across the middle, look at the pale, glistening flesh, squeeze it gently and watch the juice dripping from it; take the cut end to your mouth and lick

it. Notice your mouth watering.

Electromyographic recordings also demonstrate associations between visualization and physiological activity: positive imagery has been shown to lower muscle tension levels and negative imagery to raise them (Jacobson 1938, McGuigan 1971).

In applying these findings, it is suggested that a useful approach to stress relief and relaxation is through methods which involve the right hemisphere (Davis et al 1988).

The unconscious

Freud (1973) viewed the unconscious as a repository of repressed fears and unresolved emotions. It thus represented aspects of ourselves which we wished to forget. Its contents were only available in certain states such as dreaming, when the conscious mind was less dominant. A Jungian view of the unconscious however, saw it as also containing the seed of infinite new possibilities deriving from insight, intuition and inspiration (Fordham 1966, Jung 1963). Thus, while Freud viewed it in negative terms, Jung's view was primarily positive.

Whatever their theoretical position, writers in general agree that the unconscious operates not with the language of logic, but through pictures, emotions, senses, symbols and imagery, i.e. the concerns of the right hemisphere. Hidden and elusive, the unconscious does not lend itself to direct investigation, either from the scientist or from the self-analysing individual. It is this quality of elusiveness that moves Jung to speak of the difficulty of penetrating one's own being. His archetypal figures (earth mother, wise man, per-

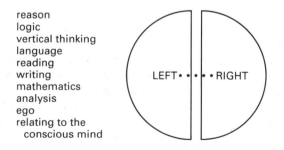

reason
logic
vertical thinking
language
reading
writing
mathematics
analysis
ego
relating to the
  conscious mind

LEFT • • • • • RIGHT

imagery
creativity
lateral thinking
recognition
rhythm
emotions
dreams
symbols
synthesis
id
relating to the
  unconscious mind

Figure 17.1 Left and right hemisphere activities. Adapted from Shone (1982).

sona, shadow, anima and animus) are the expression of attempts to find new ways of gaining access to the unconscious.

The inner guide

Arising out of these ideas is the concept of the 'inner guide': a mental construct that links the individual with her inner self. Capable of channelling information from the unconscious, the inner guide may be seen as the personification of the intuitive self. It can take forms other than those of archetypal figures and may appear as any person or animal whose attributes have appealed to the individual's imagination.

Typically the inner guide evolves in the mind during a session of deep relaxation, using an imagined setting of rich sensory quality. Oyle (1976b) suggests a place of peace and beauty such as a mountain lake or a natural grotto, while Ferrucci (1982) prefers an Alpine peak reached after an arduous climb. A figure is conjured up; it advances slowly. The visualizer welcomes the approaching figure, noticing everything about it: what it looks like, how it is dressed, who it resembles. A dialogue ensues. Ferrucci warns against the possibility of the guide being no more than a self-deceiving fantasy and suggests criteria for testing its authenticity:

- Does it bring answers which come from the self?
- Does it bring understanding?
- Does it carry a sense of rightness?
- Does its message make sense in the light of reason and morality?
- Will its advice stand up in real life situations?

Even after acceptance of the guide as authentic, its advice should always be scrutinized and not blindly accepted. Although the guide is an aspect of the inner self, it may not be working in the individual's best interests. On the other hand, too sceptical an attitude will tend to generate fewer ideas than a trusting one.

The individual need not feel restricted to one guide, and may find it useful to have one male and one female, each supplying complementary wisdom. A hazard of working with a number of inner guides however, is that the personality may come to be seen as a collection of separate entities when the aim of the exercise is to achieve maximum integration.

Any meeting with an inner guide should be rounded off with words of gratitude, respect and appreciation as this helps to strengthen the individual's respect for her inner self. Continuity also, is important and may be established by an agreement to meet on another occasion.

Consciousness

The normal waking state can be seen as occupying one pole of a continuum whose other pole is represented by sleep. Phenomena such as dreaming, drug-induced states, hypnosis, meditation, daydreaming, deep relaxation and guided imagery are thought to lie somewhere between the two poles. Their position in relation to the continuum is unknown since research has not yet determined their precise nature. They are seen as states of consciousness which are altered in some way. During altered states it is believed that the influence of the left brain is reduced, allowing the right brain to become dominant (p. 162). This allows material which is normally hidden to become accessible. Thus the altered state is seen as having the potential to clear a path to the interior of the self.

THERAPEUTIC EFFECTS OF IMAGERY

Imagery can be used in a therapeutic sense to promote the following:

1. Self-development and psychological change. These effects are expanded in Chapter 18.

2. Relaxation. Zahourek (1988), working in a nursing context, sees imagery as a therapeutic tool which can reinforce the message to relax.

3. Diversion. This strategy is employed to distract the mind from stressful thoughts.

4. Healing. This is an area not covered in the present work.

PROCEDURE OF A THERAPEUTIC IMAGERY SESSION

Relaxation

For the imagery to be effective, the individual should first be in a state of relaxation. Fanning (1988) regards relaxation as 'an absolute prerequisite' of effective imagery. The individual may use any method she finds helpful, but passive approaches are seen as being the most appropriate (Achterberg 1985). Thus relaxation is a precondition as well as a result of therapeutic imagery.

Introductory remarks to participants

As with other approaches, a short passage of explanation is appropriate.

Imagery is about building pictures in the mind. The pictures can be pleasant or unpleasant. The first kind induce a feeling of calm, the second, of unease.

The relaxing effect of pleasant imagery is partly due to the distraction it creates from stressful thoughts. Daydreaming is an example of this kind of imagery. However, the imagination can also bring us nearer to our inner selves, and this aspect of it is used to help people discover new possibilities in themselves, thereby enriching their lives. This kind of imagery is more structured than daydreaming.

You'll find it helpful to make yourself relaxed before you begin.

Termination

A session of imagery should be gradually brought to an end. First, the image is deliberately allowed to fade. Then the visualizer slowly brings her attention back to the room in which she is lying, and in her own time, opens her eyes. In the next few minutes she gives her limbs a gentle stretch and then resumes normal activity.

EXPLORING SINGLE SENSES

It seems that people differ in the vividness and clarity of the images they create, and also in the ability to control the image once formed (Finke 1989). Imaging ability is thus not a unitary skill. Again, some people find it easier to conjure up images than others.

There is some evidence to suggest that image-forming can be improved with practice, although the extent of any such improvement has not been determined (Kosslyn 1983, Lichstein 1988). Nevertheless, exercises are often used in the belief that they help to develop innate potential. A difficulty in imaging should not, however, be seen as a deficit but rather, as a manifestation of the many ways in which human beings differ from one another. People who report difficulty in forming images, may also describe a sensation which fulfils the same function in their thought processes.

For those who wish to explore their capacity to create images however, the following exercises are presented. They use the modalities of sight, sound, smell, taste, touch, temperature and kinaesthetic sense. A total of 15–20 seconds can be spent on each item.

Sight

Visualize:

- a shape: circle, triangle, square
- an oak tree
- a snail
- a sailing boat
- a button
- a strand of hair.

Sound

Since visual images tend to be more dominant than auditory ones, it can be useful, when evoking the latter, to surround oneself with an imaginary mist or darkness which swallows up any visual images and releases sounds in isolation. Imaging:

- the wind blowing through the trees, through river sedges, through sheets on a clothes line
- the ring of your telephone
- different people calling your name
- horses' hooves on different surfaces: cobblestone, tarmac, hard sand, deep mud

- scales played on the piano
- traffic starting off
- water flowing along a rocky stream bed, lapping on a lake shore or cascading from a height.

Smell

Slowly conjure up one by one, the following smells:

- thyme trodden underfoot
- petrol fumes
- newly baked bread
- hyacinth scent
- chlorine
- new mown grass
- vanilla.

Taste

Imagine the taste of:

- sprouts
- figs
- banana
- mayonnaise
- grapefruit
- toothpaste.

Touch

Let other sensory images fade as you turn your attention to those of touch. Evoke the following tactile images:

- shaking hands
- standing barefoot on loose, dry sand
- running your fingers over satin, velvet, sacking
- brushing past fur
- holding a smooth pebble
- threading a needle.

Temperature

Image sensations of heat and cold:

- drinking a hot liquid
- sunlight falling on your arm
- moving from a warm room to a cool one
- holding an ice-cube

- stepping into a warm bath.

Kinaesthetic sense

This sense is the perception of body movement. Feel yourself engaged in a form of activity:

- swimming
- running on grass
- sawing wood
- throwing a ball
- climbing a sand dune
- hanging a coat on a peg
- stirring syrup.

Imagery drawn from all sense modalities

Fanning (1988) suggests an exercise which draws on all the above sense modalities:

Take a fruit that you like, say an orange. Feel its texture . . . weight . . . size . . . notice its shape . . . colour and surface markings . . . is it firm or soft? . . . smell it . . . then dig your nail into the peel and begin to tear it off. Listen to the faint sound of the tearing. As you peel the orange, notice how the flesh gets exposed here and there, releasing a new smell. Separate the segments and put one in your mouth . . . bite through its juicy flesh . . . feel the sensation of the juice running over your tongue . . . recognize the taste of orange . . .

From the above exercise it can be seen that variety of sensory detail helps to build a vivid mental image. When we visualize a scene we usually draw on more than one sense modality, and we can make the scene still more vivid by adding further sensory information. Images of sight, sound, smell, texture, temperature and the sensation of body movement can all be used to enrich the mental picture. Guided imagery (p. 141) employs these ideas.

SYMBOLIC IMAGERY

Jung (1963) writes that symbols serve to connect us with the unconscious; they are keys which can unlock the deeper parts of the psyche. Symbols also feature in the writings of Assagioli where he notes the tendency for people to project meaningful ideas onto them. One of Assagioli's best known examples is his visualization of a rose (1965), paraphrased below:

Picture in your mind a rose bush . . . see its roots . . . its stem . . . its leaves. Crowning the stem is a rose in tight bud. See it folded inside its protective sepals. As you watch, the sepals begin to roll back revealing the closed flower, firmly and intricately packed . . . gradually, the petals begin to unfold and as they do, you feel a blossoming also taking place within you . . . the rose continues to open and as you gaze at it, and smell its perfume, you feel its rhythm resonating with your own rhythm . . . stay with the rose and as it opens further revealing its centre, allow an image to take shape – one that represents whatever is creative and meaningful within you . . . focus on the image . . . and let it speak to you . . .

The symbol is seen here as a phenomenon to be experienced rather than decoded. It is suggested that by identifying with the symbol, the individual can achieve self-discovery and healing. This idea has been developed by Ferrucci, a student of Assagioli's. Two examples of Ferrucci's visualizations (1982) are presented below (in slightly altered form).

The fount

Imagine a rocky cleft in which a natural spring rises. It is a warm summer day. See the bubbling jet of water sparkling in the sunlight . . . listen to its gurgling and splashing . . . the water is clear and pure . . . cup your hands and drink from it . . . feel the liquid travelling down your throat and into your body . . . step into the spring and feel the water flowing over you . . . your feet, legs and the whole of your body . . . imagine it also flowing through your thoughts . . . and through your emotions . . . feel the water cleansing you . . . let its purity unite with your purity . . . let its energy become your energy . . . and as the fount continues to renew itself, feel life within you also renewing itself . . .

The bell

Picture a meadow on a warm day. You are lying in the soft grass, surrounded by scented wild flowers. In a nearby village church, a bell begins to peal. The sound it makes is pure and clear and as it reaches you, it

arouses within you a deep, hidden joy . . . the sound fades for a moment as the wind changes . . . then . . . it returns . . . carried back to you, this time with renewed force . . . filling the air and echoing through the valley . . . and as you listen, the sound seems to vibrate inside you . . . resonating with your own melody . . . and awakening new possibilities within you . . .

THE USE OF METAPHOR

Imagery lies at the heart of metaphor. Metaphor itself, by describing one thing in terms of another, offers a fresh approach; a new and more telling interpretation.

Three items which illustrate the use of metaphor in relaxation imagery follow. In each one, the individual identifies with the image.

The ragdoll

Sit in an armchair. Close your eyes. Take one deep breath low down in your chest. Then let your breathing set its own rhythm . . . listen to it . . . and as you listen to it, imagine a ragdoll . . . see its soft floppy arms and legs . . . its lolling head . . . its slumped body . . . inert . . . immobile.

Now, try seeing yourself as that ragdoll. Conjure up a feeling of being slumped . . . the weight of your arms dragging your shoulders down . . . your head rolling into the chairback . . . your face expressionless . . . your jaw relaxed . . . feel the passive quality of the ragdoll . . . and as you continue to sit there . . . enjoy the feeling of being passive . . .

The fragment of seaweed

Lie down in a quiet place. Close your eyes. Breathe in deeply once . . . then relax into the rhythm of your natural breathing . . .

Picture a length of seaweed, rich, dark green, leafy seaweed, floating in the shallows. Air pockets keep it buoyant and allow it to bob up and down. As it floats, it changes shape, drawn this way and that as the currents swirl beneath it . . . pulling it . . . twisting it . . . stretching it . . . bunching it . . .

Now, picture yourself as that piece of seaweed . . . notice how limp your body feels . . . your outstretched arms and legs gently swept to and fro . . . feel the wave passing underneath you . . . lifting you up as it rises, and lowering you as it dips, but always buoying you up . . . feel your body giving to the movement of the water . . .

The jelly

Settle yourself in a peaceful place. Close your eyes and listen to your breathing . . . listen to it getting calmer with every moment that passes . . .

Imagine a jelly not quite set. It has been turned out of its mould and stands, holding itself together but not yet firm. Every time the plate is moved, it wobbles.

Now, think of yourself as that jelly. You are standing on a dish, and every time someone knocks the table, a ripple runs through you. You yourself, are not able to initiate the movement; only others can do that by bumping into your table or moving your dish . . . and, every time this happens, you wobble. One bump, and you wobble several times . . . imagine you are about to be bumped into . . . feel your body limp . . . let all the tension go out of it . . . let yourself become a wobby jelly . . .

Transformations

Images can also undergo transformations: harsh images can give way to smooth ones. Fanning (1988) shows how negative emotions, represented by harsh images, can be influenced to move in a more positive direction, when the harsh images are transformed into smooth ones.

Imagine the sound of discordant music . . . listen to its harsh tones . . . and as you do, let your painful thought express itself in terms of the dissonant notes . . . feel the mood of your difficulty resonating with the sound. Then gradually allow the image to undergo a transformation . . . follow the music as it slowly resolves into harmonies . . . and, as the harmonies fill the air, experience the beginnings of a change in your feelings . . .

Other examples of negative imagery resolving into pleasanter forms are:

- sour lemon juice into sweet lemon sorbet
- sandpaper into silky fabric.

Both come from Fanning (1988). The next two are drawn from Davis et al (1988):

- a screaming siren into a woodwind melody

- the glare of a searchlight into the soft glow of a lamp.

Four of the sense modalities (taste, touch, sound and sight) are represented in these examples. The fifth, smell, is illustrated below in the transformation from:

- burning rubber into smouldering pine logs.

The above are simply examples. The most effective imagery is that which the individual creates for herself, choosing the context to which she can best relate.

Distancing

Distressing events can be overwhelming. Moreover, the intensity of the emotion aroused by them may cloud the individual's judgement. In order to gain a more objective view, she may find it useful to draw back from the scene mentally: in effect, to distance herself. Certain images promote the feeling of being able to put a distance between herself and the situation:

- a leaf floating downstream
- clouds moving across the sky
- helium-filled balloons rising
- bubbles being blown away
- a train receding along a straight track.

COLOUR

People say they have favourite colours. Is this because colours are associated with pleasant events in their experience? Or is it simply because certain colours make them feel good? It is generally believed that red is a stimulating colour and blue a soothing one but to what extent is the preference for one over the other tied up with the mood of the moment? Such notions might help to explain why a person does not always choose the same colour. Or does she simply become sated with one colour and feel the need to replace it with another (as in decorations, clothes etc.)? These are psychological considerations, though the aesthetic aspects of colour give the topic a further dimension.

However, in the present context we are concerned with psychological aspects. Certainly colours can have strong effects. Some of these can be explored through exercises in colour imagery. The following example is adapted from the work of an autogenic therapist, Kai Kermani (1990).

With your eyes closed let the word 'colour' float into your mind. The word may first evoke one particular colour although others will quickly follow. Take the one that first appears. Stay with it. Let it develop in any way it wants to: flooding your field of vision, appearing in patches, little flecks or any other arrangement. Concentrate on the colour in a passive way, letting it speak to you. Does it remind you of anything? Does it trigger any special feelings or memories? If it has no effect on you, try 'stepping into' it and allowing it to surround you . . .

After a few minutes, or when you are ready, allow the colour to draw itself away from you. In your mind's eye, watch it resuming the form it had in the beginning.

If colour can indeed influence our mood, then colour visualization could have particular value. We could surround ourselves with single colours to gain specific effects, soothing our feelings when we are anxious and raising our mood when we are depressed. Single colours are again explored in the following two exercises.

Imagine finding yourself in a room decorated exclusively in a colour of your choice. See the entire room in this one colour, the walls, ceiling, paintwork, carpet, upholstery. If you have difficulty, try going through the motions of painting the walls and hanging the curtains. Totally immerse yourself in this colour and notice the effect it has on you . . . does it relax you or give you a lift? . . . why did you pick it? . . . what associations does it have for you? . . . stay with it long enough to absorb its full effect . . . then let it fade.

Now picture yourself in a room decorated in a colour you don't like. Surround yourself with this colour, let it permeate your consciousness (so long as it doesn't disturb you, in which case stop the exercise). Ask yourself why you dislike this colour and what effect it is having on you. When you are ready, let the colour fade and be replaced by the colour of your choice before ending the visualization.

(It is preferable to end colour imagery sessions with a colour that the visualizer feels comfortable with, in order to carry away a rewarding sensation.)

Ernst & Goodison (1981) present a sequence in which colour flows to and from the visualizer. It is reproduced here in modified form:

First relax yourself using any method you find works for you. Close your eyes if they are not already closed. Let your mind be as still as possible. Pick a colour that feels right for you. Pick it spontaneously and see it before your eyes. You can picture it as brushstrokes of paint, coloured cloth, tinted smoke or coloured atmosphere. Let it extend all round you. Notice its quality, its tone and be aware of any associations it has for you. Feel yourself relating to this colour, harmonizing with it, becoming infused with it. Imagine yourself absorbing the colour through every pore of your skin until your body is filled with it . . .

Now . . . let the colour begin to radiate from you . . . feel yourself releasing it . . . making it expand all round you until it gradually comes to fill the room you are in. As you continue to generate more colour, see if you can fill the building you are in . . . pause for a moment . . . then slowly begin to draw the colour back, first from the building . . . then from the room . . . watching it get more condensed . . . until it gathers in a cloud around you . . . feel yourself bathed in this colour . . . now . . . absorb it back into your being . . . into the very organs of your body . . . pause again . . . then watch it drawing itself away from all parts of you . . . feel yourself being emptied of the colour. Convert it back to the paint, cloth or smoke in which it started. Be aware of how you feel after doing the exercise. Notice any effect it had on you.

Chakras

In Hatha Yoga vital energy is seen as being focused in specified areas of the body known as 'chakras'. These are situated at:

- the base of the spine
- the lower abdomen
- the navel
- the heart
- the throat
- the brow
- the crown of the head.

Each chakra is associated with one of the colours of the spectrum: the base of the spine with red, the lower abdomen with orange, the navel with yellow, the heart with green, the throat with blue, the brow with indigo and the crown of the head with violet.

Kermani (1990) presents a passage of healing imagery based on the chakras, which is reproduced here in slightly altered form:

See yourself lying in a natural setting of your choice. The sun is shining and it is warm and pleasant. Look around you . . . build the scene. What plants are growing? Do they have a scent? What sounds can you hear? Feel the sun on your body. Imagine its rays bringing warmth to all parts of you. Imagine also, the light broken up into its component parts so that it falls in a coloured spectrum across your body: warm red rays falling on your legs and hips, relaxing and warming them; orange rays casting a gentle light over your lower trunk; a soft yellow light glowing across your stomach; green rays casting a soothing light over your heart; blue light bathing your throat and lower face, a cool indigo light falling on your brow and violet light around your head.

Picture, a ray of blue light travelling from each eye . . . allow these twin rays to carry away any tension . . . carrying it into the vastness of space . . . as it recedes, feel yourself relaxing . . . finally, a silver light appears . . . let it gather up all the colours and . . . as it does, let it draw away any remaining tension from your body, dissolving it and leaving you in a state of great calmness . . . imagine the silver light spreading around you to form a circle . . . allow the circle to include others who also wish to share this peace. They stay for a few moments and as they leave, you notice they have left a gift for you . . . it is a gift which you will recognize . . .

When you are ready, gently allow the scene to fade . . . slowly, bring your attention back to the room in which you are lying. Feel the floor beneath you as you open your eyes.

White light

The Rosicrucians, a brotherhood formed during the Renaissance, regarded white light as a symbol of guidance, inspiration and healing. The idea has been developed by Samuels & Samuels (1975):

Take yourself in your mind's eye to a place that is special for you. Imagine it filled with brilliant white light . . . let that light flow through you . . . filling your body and your mind . . . healing you . . . strengthening you . . . renewing you

GUIDED IMAGERY

Guided imagery can be used for different purposes ranging from relaxation to psychotherapy. The purpose here is restricted to the promotion of relaxation. The visualizer conjures up a naturalistic scene, often of her own choosing, and moves around within it, noticing particularly, its sensory content. A meadow, forest, beach or garden makes a suitable setting. A path is a useful feature since it can suggest a goal, carry the visualizer through the scene or provide a passage for the inner guide.

Where imagery is being presented to a group, it is convenient for the instructor to decide on a particular scene and to suggest its basic structure. For example, if a meadow is decided on, the instructor can suggest other features such as a stream and a backdrop of distant hills. The time of year and the weather can make the scene more vivid. The visualizer is asked to notice the scents and sounds as well as the appearance of the scene. It is left to the instructor as to how much information is offered. The participant fills in the detail.

If a forest is chosen, the visualizer might be asked to notice the trees, how tall they are, how dense they are; to notice bird calls and sounds of water; to experience the cool shade and smell the dank undergrowth.

If it is a beach, the individual can be asked to imagine a stretch of shoreline, to feel the sand under her feet, to smell the salty air, feel the hot sun, hear the waves breaking and the sea-birds calling.

Or, if it is a garden, the individual can be asked to notice the layout of shrubs and open spaces, the cool grass, the scented herbs and flowers, the warm, moist air, and to experience tactile images such as the smooth bark of the beech tree or the soft bark of the redwood.

The following paragraphs (adapted from Lichstein 1988) give the flavour of guided imagery:

Please get comfortable and close your eyes. As your mind becomes more peaceful, your body will also lose some of its tension. I am going to ask you to imagine a scene which you find pleasant and relaxing. Take a moment to choose the setting . . .

Let your scene take shape . . . create its visual detail, making it as vivid as you can . . . imagine the sounds that accompany it . . . the scents that float in the air . . . the textures that surround you . . . feel the warmth of the sun on your skin . . . find a path and experience the sensation of moving through the scene . . . feel the tension leaving your body and enjoy the peace and calm of the scene you've created . . .

This kind of imagery is widely practised in the clinical field for inducing relaxation.

A SUMMARIZED EVALUATION OF IMAGERY

Imagery is a safe and noninvasive technique which does not require elaborate equipment. As a coping tool for reducing anxiety and stress, it has been found successful (Donovan 1980, Hamm & O'Flynn 1984, King 1988). Some researchers have speculated on the mechanism by which this might occur, Dossey (1988) suggesting that imagery brings about a change in the individual's perceptions.

PITFALLS

A list of the pitfalls relating to imagery can be found at the end of Chapter 18 (p. 151).

FURTHER READING

Ernst S, Goodison L 1981 In our own hands: a book of self-help therapy. Women's Press, London
Ferrucci P 1982 What we may be. Mandala, London
Jung C G (ed) 1978a Man and his symbols. Pan Books, London
Samuels M, Samuels N 1975 Seeing with the mind's eye: thehistory, technique and uses of visualization. Random House, Toronto
Zahourek R P 1988 Relaxation and imagery: tools for therapeutic communication and intervention. W B Saunders, Philadelphia

CHAPTER CONTENTS

Introduction 143

The method of goal-directed visualization 144
Position 144
Preparatory relaxation 144
Special place 144
Receptive visualization 145
Positive self-statements or affirmations 145
Programmed visualization 145
Termination 146
Additional technique 146

Relaxation and goal-directed visualization 146

Applying the method of goal-directed visualization 146
Visualizations for people who want to give up smoking 148
Evaluation of the use of imagery in changing smoking behaviour 150

Other applications of goal-directed behaviour 150

Pitfalls of imagery and goal-directed visualization 151

18

Goal-directed visualization

INTRODUCTION

In their book *Seeing with the Mind's Eye*, Samuels & Samuels (1975) describe a technique using imagery which has two phases, receptive and programmed. In the receptive phase which is passive, the individual listens to her inner self, drawing on her own wisdom. In the programmed phase, she engages in an active and deliberate thought process for the purpose of improving a situation or resolving a problem in her life. The Samuels' work has been developed by Achterberg (1985), Simonton et al (1986) and others in areas of medicine and healing; and by Shone (1984) and Fanning (1988) among others in areas of self-development and relaxation. Since in this book we are concerned with the latter area, the definitions of Fanning and Shone are appropriate. Fanning describes this kind of imagery as 'the conscious, volitional creation of mental sense impressions for the purpose of changing oneself'; Shone refers to it as a mental experience which helps to bring about desired outcomes. Implicit in both definitions is the notion of a goal.

How does this form of imagery differ from other forms? One answer is that it is more explicit than techniques which rely on metaphor and symbolism; it is also more purposeful than reverie states such as daydreaming. How is it different from talking to yourself, reflecting, and giving yourself advice? This approach may not be very different, but it does seek to offer a structured, step-by-step approach.

143

Among its advantages are the following:

1. New possibilities can be explored without the need to commit oneself to their effects.

2. Tasks perceived to be difficult can lose some of their threat after being visualized with a successful outcome. This is mental rehearsal, where the individual familiarizes herself with the feared situation and, in her imagination, achieves her goal. This raises her belief in her own powers. As a secondary effect, she feels more at peace with herself.

The method uses a variety of techniques such as progressive relaxation, guided imagery and internal dialogue, which have been previously discussed (Chs 4, 17 and 1 respectively). In this chapter goal-directed visualization is described. An example of how it might be used to help people give up smoking is presented. Other possible applications are considered and, finally, there is a section devoted to the pitfalls of imagery in general.

THE METHOD OF GOAL-DIRECTED VISUALIZATION

The aspects of goal-directed visualization discussed here are:

- position
- preparatory relaxation
- special place
- receptive visualization
- positive self-statements or affirmations
- programmed visualization
- termination
- an additional technique.

Position

The visualizer lies down in a comfortable position in a dimly lit, warm room, free from noise and interruption. She closes her eyes.

Preparatory relaxation

Imagery is preceded by a short session of relaxation, since relaxation is generally regarded as a precondition as well as an effect of visualization. The technique employed can be chosen by the individual, although Achterberg (1985) suggests that passive forms of muscle relaxation are more appropriate than tense–release which she claims is ineffective for imagery work. Slow, gentle, abdominal breathing will also help to induce deep relaxation. The visualizer may recite appropriate phrases such as 'My mind is calm and clear', 'I am open to images that will help me'.

Although this preliminary relaxation is common practice, there is little evidence to support its value as a facilitator of imagery (Lichstein 1988). Indeed, there are, those who claim the opposite i.e. that a totally relaxed body is accompanied by a mind devoid of images (Jacobson 1938). If muscular relaxation clears the mind of images, how can it also promote them? Lichstein (1988) refers to this as a matter yet to be resolved. Perhaps the answer lies in finding a level of relaxation which is deep enough to release tension but not so deep that images cannot form.

Special place

Lying quietly, the visualizer builds an imaginary scene or 'special place' as a retreat for relaxation and guidance (Davis et al 1988). The scene is rich in sensory images, of sight, sound, smell, taste, texture, temperature and gives her a feeling of peace and tranquillity. A beach, meadow, lake, or forest all offer possibilities. The visualizer is encouraged to imagine how the body would feel in the special place, emphasizing sensations like sinking into springy turf or soft sand. Some time is spent initially setting the scene so that it can easily be re-created in subsequent visualizations. Since imagery is a right hemisphere activity, the constraints of logic do not apply. Thus, the special place may contain any figment of the imagination which the visualizer finds useful, as for example, a permanent sunset in the background, a viewing screen in a forest clearing or a crystal ball in a mountain spring. It is in such a scene that the inner guide could appear (p. 135), and so, there should be a clearly defined way in.

Some people prefer an indoor special place like an attic room or a garden shed; others like to have both, using them on different occasions. There is no right or wrong way: whatever works for the individual is right.

Receptive visualization

The visualizer pictures herself in her special place. This is where she can feel in tune with herself and where she will be likely to gain insights. She is in a state of mind that allows her to listen to herself. It is a passive state of mind which, in some ways resembles daydreaming, but differs from the latter in that the visualizer is asking specific questions of herself (Samuels & Samuels 1975). Whether she is making a choice, sorting out a conflict, uncovering motivations or exposing automatic thoughts, the receptive visualization is a way of allowing intuitive insights to be released and inner wisdom to be revealed.

The visualizer should be advised that if uncontrollable or unpleasant feelings which she is not ready to deal with, arise, she can walk away or distance herself in some other manner. She can also end the visualization. Otherwise she quietly tunes in to her unconscious. If ideas do not flow, the inner guide can be called and asked for advice (p. 135).

An example of a receptive visualization script is given below. (Allow 10 or 15 minutes for it.)

Lie down. Get yourself comfortable and close your eyes. Run through a relaxing procedure until you feel very calm. Visualize yourself lying in your special place. Evoke its atmosphere by mentally experiencing its sights, sounds, smells and textures. Feel at home there. Let your attention gently focus on the item that preoccupies you . . . just keep an open mind . . . quietly listen to the thoughts that flow through it . . . if you are stuck, call on your inner guide . . . listen to the wisdom your inner guide brings . . . realize that it is your own wisdom, coming from your deeper self . . . spend a few minutes listening to yourself . . .

When you are ready, end your visualization and gently bring your attention back to the room.

Write down any ideas that came to you. Consider them. Have you gained any insights? Do you want to change your way of handling this situation? Are there more positive ways of handling it?

Receptive visualizations can be repeated as often as they continue to provide insights.

Positive self-statements or affirmations

The positive self-statement, often referred to as an affirmation, helps the visualizer to see herself as being capable of realizing her aspiration and achieving her goal. Inherent in the affirmation is the suspension of self-doubt. Examples include the following:

- I believe in myself.
- I am in control of my life.
- I can achieve my aim.

While the above statements are of a general nature, additional affirmations relevant to the matter in question, can also be composed. Thus, for a person wishing to become more relaxed, the following statements may be included:

- I feel calm.
- I am at peace.
- I can cope in stressful situations.

Positive self-statements need to be short, in the first person and the present tense; the best ones are those composed by the individual herself (Fanning 1988). When repeated, they act like self-hypnotic suggestions, influencing the individual's view of herself in a positive direction, and adding force to the positive images of the programmed visualization (described below).

Programmed visualization

General comments

In this phase, the individual may work on images that emerged during the receptive phase, turning them over and trying them out in different forms in her imagination. When she finds the most effective solution to her problems, she visualizes herself as instrumental in achieving it. Actions are imagined which allow her to feel herself displaying the qualities she wants to possess. Goals are mentally reached with the individual operating as their successful agent. By daily repetition, the new images of herself start to blend with her self-image, tending to generate still more positive internal dialogue, and, in the manner of a self-fulfilling prophecy, increasing the likelihood of the desired outcome in real life.

Sometimes, while in the programmed stage, the visualizer gets 'stuck'. In this case, returning to the receptive stage may help to clear the block.

On other occasions, the receptive and programmed phases may not be clearly separated. Not all visualization work falls neatly into receptive and programmed categories, and individuals should not feel under pressure to create them separately if one continuous visualization seems more appropriate. There is no set pattern for the programmed visualization: the topic itself will determine the style.

Procedure for programmed visualization

The preliminaries are similar to those for receptive visualization, that is, the person relaxes herself using cue-controlled relaxation (p. 65) or passive muscular relaxation (Ch. 7).

She then evokes the scene of the situation she wants to resolve, whatever it might be. (This is not the special place but a real-life situation.) Again, rich sensory detail is essential to bring it to life. Time spent building the scene enables her to experience it more keenly. She then works on the item, experimenting with it until she finds a good solution which she then enacts in her imagination. She plays a role which succeeds.

The tone of the programmed visualization is demonstrated in the following passage:

Let your thoughts become quiet and bring your attention to focus on your goal. Believe in your capacity to reach it . . . don't dwell on the difficulties; just think of the result. If there are problems, see them as a challenge . . . feel an eagerness to achieve . . . to be a person who has reached that goal . . . feel yourself in the part . . . imagine yourself as having arrived . . . congratulate yourself for getting there . . . enjoy it . . .

Termination

When the visualization is over, the procedure is brought to an end with a termination on the following lines:

If you are ready, gradually bring your attention back to the room you are in . . . slowly count one . . . two

. . . three . . . and, as you open your eyes, feel yourself alert and refreshed.

Goal-directed visualization thus consists of the individual opening herself to her own wisdom (receptive phase), and then using it in her imagination to bring about the desired outcome (programmed phase).

Additional technique

'Distancing', i.e. drawing back from the scene to examine her actions, is a technique which allows the visualizer to gain a more objective view. In an imaginary viewing screen or crystal ball she watches her behaviour patterns; how she copes with situations and relates to other people.

This approach may highlight maladaptive responses she might be making. She then modifies those responses and reruns the film in a way which leads to a successful outcome. The next move is for her to step into the scene in her imagination, in order to experience the skills she observed herself displaying on the screen.

RELAXATION AND GOAL-DIRECTED VISUALIZATION

It can be seen that relaxation is related to goal-directed visualization in a variety of ways.

• It is used as a preparatory measure to induce a state of mind conducive to visualization. Before the individual begins her visualization, she should first become relaxed.

• It may be experienced as a secondary effect following mental rehearsal in which the individual sees herself successfully coping with an activity which has hitherto been associated with stress.

• Certain problems may create a need for relaxation while the goal is being achieved, such as withdrawal from cigarettes or tranquillizers.

Goal-directed visualization is thus not a primary method of inducing relaxation, but it does have close links with it.

APPLYING THE METHOD OF GOAL-DIRECTED VISUALIZATION

Unlike most other methods described in this

book, goal-directed visualization addresses the specific problems of a person. This feature is seen in both the receptive and the programmed components. Thus it is not possible to present a model script without a clear understanding of the background.

A key factor is the motivation of the visualizer. While for some individuals this is not a problem, others may need encouragement. One way of fostering motivation is to make the goals specific. For example, having a timescale for a smoking abstinence programme defines it more clearly. Creating subgoals or intermediate stages is another useful strategy, since they act as stepping stones along the way. This has the effect of making the ultimate goal seem easier to reach, as well as providing rewards at intervals. Smoking one less cigarette a day can constitute a subgoal; so can taking one more step to a person recovering from injury. Difficulties can be considered in advance and ways of solving them worked out (Fig. 18.1).

Samuels & Samuels (1975) advise the individual not to confide her visualization to anyone who may not share her faith in the wisdom of the goal and in her capacity to reach it. Unshaken belief is vital for her success.

Of course, participants in some groups may be too demoralized to begin; they may feel they have little future; they may be angry or depressed. These are valid reactions which call for modification of the method and perhaps referral to a specialist agency. In general however, the approach can be a useful one.

Although it is difficult to construct a model script without specific knowledge of the problem concerned, an attempt is made here to provide an example.

The reader is reminded of the principal items in the method.

Receptive visualization. The individual tunes into her own wisdom

Self-statements. She reaffirms herself through positive internal dialogue.

Programmed visualization. She works on a plan for the future in which she sees herself surmounting obstacles, realizing possibilities and achieving goals. The keynote of this stage is seeing the self as succeeding.

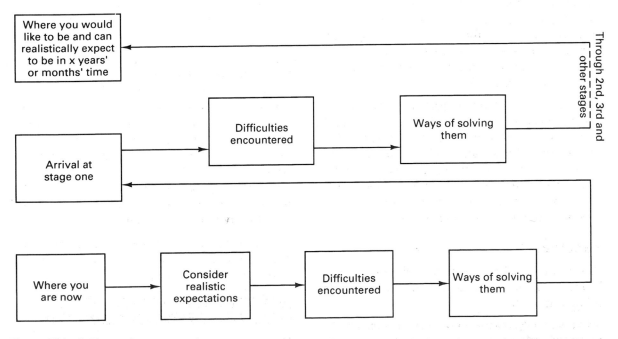

Figure 18.1 Setting goals.

Visualizations for people who want to give up smoking

It could be argued that smoking has more to do with relaxation than smoking abstinence has, and many people become smokers because they perceive cigarettes as being a source of mental calm. However, many such people then wish to quit smoking. Quitting is associated with stress, which means that the same people may be seeking relaxation training. Health care professional increasingly find themselves faced with groups of people who are struggling to give up cigarettes and for whom relaxation training has been prescribed. Although any of the methods in this book might help, a method which directly addresses the problem would seem to have particular advantages.

Within a single group of people who wish to reduce their smoking habits, there may be a wide variety of aspirations: one person may want to cut down from 40 cigarettes a day to 20, another may want to give up altogether. They may also have different ideas as to how to go about it: one may want to reduce by one cigarette a day, another may want to make a more abrupt change. On the other hand, the group may consist of people who are looking for ways of avoiding relapse after having successfully given up smoking. The following visualization (adapted from Fanning 1988) is designed for people who have decided to give up altogether.

Receptive visualization

Lie or sit in a position which you find comfortable. Close your eyes. Allow yourself to unwind. (The instructor presents either passive relaxation or slow breathing.) As your body and mind become calm, let your special place take shape in your imagination. Notice the sights, sounds and smell of the place. Put out your hand and feel the textures: the grass, the rug, the pine needles, etc . . . feel that you are there . . . lying peacefully . . . tuned into yourself.

Gently bring your mind to focus on your smoking habit. Explore your feelings about it. Why do you smoke? Perhaps you hadn't thought about it before, just taken it for granted. In your mind's eye, take out a cigarette and light up . . . what does it do for you? . . .

Run through different situations during the day when you feel the need of a cigarette . . . start with breakfast time . . . what prompts you to reach for the first cigarette? . . . then follow yourself to work . . . smoking on the journey . . . at work in your coffee break . . . after the midday meal . . . again in the afternoon . . . on the way home . . . to round off the evening meal . . . last thing at night . . . do you notice that you smoke for different reasons? . . . do you get different rewards from smoking? . . . when do you find you particularly want a cigarette? . . .

Bring your visualization to an end when you are ready . . .

The visualizer may feel she smokes for different reasons at different times. Some of the reasons why people smoke are:

- to feel reassured
- to relieve boredom
- to feel soothed
- to feel relaxed
- to give her hands something to do
- to get a lift
- to reward herself
- to keep her weight down.

She decides which of these apply to her and is then urged to think of alternative ways of meeting these needs:

- For reassurance, she tells herself 'She does not need a crutch'.
- To relieve boredom, she gets out a crossword puzzle.
- To feel soothed, she reminds herself of the love of her partner.
- To feel relaxed, she runs through a relaxation sequence.
- To give her hands something to do, she carries a small, rounded pebble which she rolls in her hand.
- To get a lift, she remembers the prize she won for cookery/essay-writing/athletics last year.
- To reward herself, she buys the salmon roll instead of the cheese roll.
- To keep her weight down, she eats an orange instead of a second helping of potatoes, or goes for a walk/workout etc.

Positive self-statements or affirmations

The individual cultivates a view of herself as a healthy, nonsmoker by composing a few positive self-statements which she recites regularly to herself:

- I am healthy
- I am a nonsmoker
- I have the strength to control my habits
- I value the time when I am not smoking.

Additionally, she is gentle with herself for occasionally breaking her resolve:

- I can forgive myself for occasionally breaking my resolution.

Some people find it helpful to have one strong reason for changing their behaviour and to focus on this one idea whenever they feel in danger of weakening.

Programmed visualization

This takes the form of a mental rehearsal of coping activities.

At the start of the session the instructor can offer passive relaxation or relaxation through abdominal breathing.

Lie down and spend a few minutes relaxing quietly. Imagine yourself at the beginning of a normal day. Run through every moment when you think you might want to light up. Have an alternative way of dealing with every urge to smoke. Start with the moment when you would have the first cigarette of the day . . . evoke the scene using sensory detail to bring it to life . . . really live the moment in your imagination . . . feel yourself craving a cigarette, then promptly use your alternative strategy . . . and as you do so, encourage yourself with your positive self-statements . . .

Move on to the next moment when you would want to light up . . . and the next and so on . . . making each moment come alive by re-creating the scene as vividly as you can . . . experiencing alternative strategies and encouraging yourself with positive self-statements . . . remind yourself of the beneficial effects of giving up smoking: clear lungs, no cough, extra change in your pocket . . . and if you feel your resolution weakening, remind yourself why you made it in the first place.

Continue through the day, appreciating the experiences that not smoking opens up to you: the taste of your food . . . the garden scents . . . the fresh smell of your clothes . . . and the easy way you climb the hill. See yourself as someone who doesn't smoke . . .

At some point, feel your stress levels rising as something goes wrong at work . . . you weaken and take out a cigarette . . . but after a couple of puffs you stub it out . . . allow yourself to feel pleased that you could have a slight relapse and still remain determined to conquer your habit . . . see yourself continuing to carry out your resolution . . . see yourself as someone who can cope without resorting to cigarettes . . .

When you are ready, bring your visualization to an end with count of one . . . two . . . three . . . open your eyes . . . look around you . . . stretch your arms and legs . . . and in your own time prepare to resume normal activity.

Some visualization therapists include an aversion component as a further incentive to give up smoking. This could take the form of dirty ash trays, blackened lungs, stained fingers or smoky atmospheres. Aversive measures work for some people; other people simply switch off if the image becomes too unpleasant.

The benefits of programmed visualization come from daily practice: the constant repetition of a routine in which the individual sees herself as successful in the task she has set herself. The above example is offered as a guideline or starting point from which the health care professional may wish to develop her own script. Alternatively, participants can be encouraged to compose their own visualizations since the most effective ones are those designed by individuals for their own use (Fanning 1988).

Where motivation needs strengthening, the following additional visualization may be found useful:

Find a quiet moment. Relax yourself and close your eyes. Imagine the house in which you expect to be living ten/five/two years from now. Go inside . . . explore it . . . what does it tell you about the occupant: yourself? . . . who else lives there? . . . try identifying with your older self . . . notice how it feels to be that older self . . . at work . . . at her hobby . . . with her family . . . then, try looking back at yourself as you are now . . . do you have anything to say to yourself? . . .

When you are ready, allow your visualization to fade . . . slowly, bring yourself back to the present . . . counting one . . . two . . . three . . . as you open your eyes . . .

Evaluation of the use of imagery in changing smoking behaviour

Some formal smoking cessation programmes have been shown to have high success rates (Feldmann & Richard 1986, Schwartz 1987). Success, when it has occurred, has been attributed to different components of the programmes: education, stress reduction, cognitive-behavioural strategies and relaxation imagery.

The relapse rate however, also tends to be high. Shiffman (1985) believes that relapse occurs when individuals lack the coping skills to continue their abstinence. Such coping skills include:

- behavioural strategies:
  a. removing oneself from a scene in which others are smoking
  b. practising relaxation
- cognitive strategies:
  a. using pleasant imagery to divert oneself from the thought of smoking
  b. creating images of improved health.

Because relaxation imagery has been successfully used for smoking cessation, Wynd (1992) employed it in the prevention of relapse. Her controlled study covered a post-cessation period of 3 months. At the end of that period, 72% of subjects were still abstaining from smoking.

OTHER APPLICATIONS OF GOAL-DIRECTED VISUALIZATION

Goal-directed visualization can be used in a wide range of situations and conditions associated with stress, for example:

1. performance fear
2. anger
3. problem solving and decision making
4. eating disorders
5. agoraphobia and panic
6. alcohol and drug dependence.

From insights gained during the receptive phase, a realistic solution can be worked out. This solution can then be mentally rehearsed during the programmed visualization, and a successful outcome experienced in the imagination.

Performance fear

The programmed visualization can be used to take the individual through every moment of the event. The scene becomes familiar to her. She mentally experiences all possible occurrences and develops coping strategies for dealing with them. Above all she experiences the successful achievement of her goal. This has the effect of building and maintaining her confidence.

Anger

For an individual who wishes to reduce her tendency to become angry, alternative and preferred courses of action can be mapped out. The programmed visualization is employed to familiarize the individual with her capacity to respond in these preferred ways. Relaxation and positive self-talk play a prominent part (Fanning 1988).

Problem solving and decision making

A receptive visualization can be used to collect ideas for solutions. After weighing them up, the unrealistic ideas are discarded and the realistic ones retained. Possible results are then predicted both in the short term and in the longer term. These are then considered for their merits and disadvantages which together form the basis of the individual's final choice. Having picked what she considers to be the best solution, the individual mentally puts it into effect, experiencing its successful outcome in a programmed visualization. Figure 18.2 illustrates the process of problem solving in the case of two alternative courses of action.

Vissing & Burke (1984) found that individuals who regularly practised visualization when faced with problems, had more success at solving them than those who did not.

Eating disorders

In the case of people wishing to lose weight,

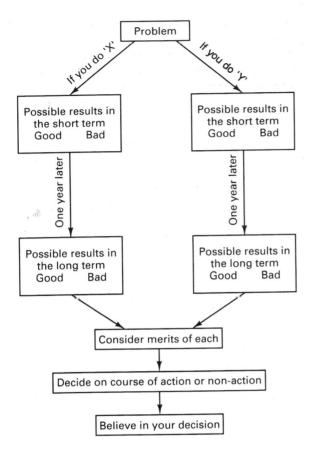

Figure 18.2 Problem solving.

alternative strategies may be found to take the place of eating. These are incorporated into daily programmed visualizations in which the individual sees herself successfully carrying out her plan (Fanning 1988). In the course of it she builds an image of herself as someone who looks nice whatever size she is, but has chosen to lose some weight. Any diet she is following should be medically approved.

Anorexia calls for more specialized treatment.

Agoraphobia and panic

Programmed visualization takes the form of mental rehearsal and is often performed in a hierarchical fashion, i.e. a list of situations from low to high threat is drawn up. The individual starts with the lowest, and taking each one in turn, mentally goes through the experience of over-

coming her fear, using slowed breathing, relaxation techniques and positive self-talk. This method is known as desensitization and was first introduced by Wolpe in 1958.

Alcohol and drug dependence

In programmed visualization the individual mentally rehearses the successful achievement of her goal using positive self-talk and alternative strategies. She also finds ways of relaxing herself during the period of dose-tapering and beyond.

Although it is not known to what extent the effects of this kind of visualization transfer to real life, it is believed that the individual's performance is enhanced by having mentally viewed herself in a successful role. A similar idea inspires Maltz (1966) when he writes of the mechanism within us which needs to be presented with unqualified success goals in order to function as a success mechanism.

Imagery is used as a therapeutic aid in some types of pain, although it should never be viewed as a substitute for medical attention. It can however, be a useful coping device for minor ailments, such as aches in different parts of the body. Its use as adjunctive therapy in some forms of intractable pain (Achterberg 1985, Simonton et al 1986) is a specialized area not covered in the present work.

PITFALLS OF IMAGERY AND GOAL-DIRECTED VISUALIZATION

A cautious attitude is advised when using imagery. Pitfalls include the following:

1. Visualization should never be allowed to take the place of medical help. People suffering from mental or physical symptoms should consult their doctor, and those already receiving medication should let their doctor know of their intention to use relaxation and imagery techniques.

2. Imagery and visualization methods are not suitable for people suffering from severe mental disorders. Imagery is particularly inadvisable for

people who have difficulty in separating fantasy from reality and for those who experience hallucinations.

3. Some people have difficulty in creating images. For them, a muscular approach might be more useful.

4. Goals, which must be set by the individual herself, need to be attainable. To set goals that are out of the individual's reach will only create additional stress.

Goals may also be set too low to be constructive, as occurs in individuals whose self-esteem has crumbled. Exceptionally low self-esteem can make a person feel she does not deserve success and joy. A first step would be to help her to value herself.

Working towards a goal often entails the need to change. The individual, however, may not want to change, and although she would like to reach the goal, she places obstacles in its path.

5. Since imagery tends to put people in touch with deeper parts of themselves, strong emotional reactions such as anger, resentment, guilt and frustration may be experienced. Weeping is fairly common. If it occurs, the instructor can reassure the distressed participant on the following lines:

It's all right to weep here . . . it often happens . . . it shows how deeply relaxed you are . . . and how truly in touch with yourself.

Insofar as the participant is working through previously suppressed material, weeping may have positive value for her. The instructor on the other hand, may find the reaction difficult to handle. Such an incident would be a matter for discussion with the supervisor (p. 16).

Zahourek (1988) likes to warn participants at the outset that deep-seated emotions may be released during imagery. Larkin (1988) suggests to participants that they need acknowledge only those emotions they feel comfortable with. This is not to disclaim responsibility for their feelings, but rather, to allow time for them to be accepted.

Mildly disturbing thoughts can be reduced in intensity by blurring the image, letting it recede or dissolving it in white light. For severely disturbing thoughts, the image should be can-

celled and the visualization terminated.

In a study that rated the occurrence of different negative reactions, it was found that intrusive thoughts had the highest frequency, followed by disturbing sensory experiences and the fear of losing control. The frequency of such effects bore no relation to the therapist's experience (Edinger & Jacobsen 1982).

6. By contrast, intruding images can be so attractive that the visualizer is lured in their direction, away from the original goal. This is daydreaming; it differs from therapeutic forms of imagery in that it is unstructured and tends to be remote from reality. (This is not to say that daydreaming is without psychological benefit, since it is essentially a self-affirming strategy (Singer 1975). Some people however, daydream to the extent of having difficulty in relating to the real world.)

7. A participant may be so depressed that he or she is harbouring thoughts of suicide. Any mention of taking his or her life must be viewed seriously and the trainee urged to seek professional help.

8. Occasionally, an individual may experience feelings of unreality. These can be dealt with by a grounding technique such as feeling the floor underneath her (p. 164). If however, the feeling is strong, the image should be allowed to fade, and the visualization brought to an end.

9. It is not the object of the exercise to create a hypnotic trance. Neither is it likely that one will occur. However, since some individuals are more susceptible than others, the possibility exists that the instructor may inadvertently create one. When a person is in an hypnotic trance, the power of suggestion becomes greater. That being so, the instructor needs to be aware of the phenomenon of posthypnotic suggestion.

Posthypnotic suggestion results in the individual blindly carrying out injunctions outside the trance situation. For example, a statement such as: 'When you go home you will assert yourself' would be indiscriminately applied. This would leave no room for reassessment of the situation which might, in changing circumstances call for a modified approach.

Any suggestion which could be applied inappropriately outside the relaxation session should be avoided. Generally speaking however, post-hypnotic suggestion is not a problem since the individual tends to resist any exhortation that runs counter to her personal goals and moral principles (Lynn & Rhue 1977).

However, if the instructor is in doubt as to the effect of her words, she can terminate the session with a cancelling statement (Shone 1982) on the lines of:

Before you bring your visualization to an end, cancel any suggestion you do not wish to take effect in your waking life.

As mentioned earlier, it is unlikely that unintentional hypnosis will occur.

10. As part of the visualization procedure, the individual constructs new self-statements. One of these may be ill-conceived. The visualizer needs to be alerted to this possibility and to the need to cancel any such self-statement.

11. Certain colours can have a powerful and unexpected effect on a person. The antidote for such an experience is to substitute white light for the offending colour, while at the same time, attaching a message of calmness to the white light. If however, the effect of the colour is very strong, the visualization should be brought to an end.

12. Jung felt that too much emphasis on the inner world could take a person away from everyday happenings, and that it was important to ground oneself in something solid such as work or family.

13. Occasionally, a participant has difficulty returning from his visualization. Repeating the termination procedure usually resolves the problem. Another device is to include in the termination procedure some reference to feeling alert and refreshed.

When techniques are being learned and applied, one cannot count on instant success. As with any other new skill, the most that may be expected is a trend in the desired direction. Frequent practice however, strengthens this trend.

FURTHER READING

Fanning P 1988 Visualization for change. New Harbinger, Oakland, California

Gawain S 1978 Creative visualization. Whatever Publishing, Mill Valley, California

Korn E R, Johnson K 1983 Visualization: the use of imagery in the health professions. Dow Jones-Irwin, Holmwood, Illinois

Shone R 1984 Creative visualization. Thorsons, Wellingborough

Zahourek R P (ed) 1988 Relaxation and imagery: tools for therapeutic communication and intervention. W B Saunders, Philadephia

CHAPTER CONTENTS

Introduction: altered states of consciousness 155

Principles of autogenic training 157

The autogenic technique 157
    Introductory talk to trainees 157
    Conditions 157
    Induction 157
    The exercises 158
    Termination 159
    Home practice 159
    Other AT exercises 160

Evaluation of autogenic training 160

Pitfalls of autogenic training 160

19

Autogenic training

INTRODUCTION: ALTERED STATES OF CONSCIOUSNESS

An altered state of consciousness is often referred to as a 'trance'. It has been described as a condition in which critical faculties are suspended and the 'limits of a person's usual frame of reference and beliefs temporarily altered making her receptive to other patterns of association and modes of mental functioning' (Erickson & Rossi 1979).

The classic trance is the hypnotic trance, induced by procedures which create intense focal awareness, such as concentrating on a swinging pendulum. The individual becomes highly responsive to suggestion: 'the process whereby the individual accepts a proposition put to her by another, without having the slightest logical reason for doing so' (Hartland 1971). Outwardly, the trance resembles drowsiness and dozing and is accompanied by a general reduction of muscle tone and a dilatation of the capillaries; the person is however, awake and highly focused although she may lose awareness of her surroundings.

Hypnosis may also be self-induced, in which case the individual herself governs the trance and plants the suggestions. The attention is again turned inwards although this trance is described as a light one in which the individual retains awareness of her surroundings, being conscious of herself in all her senses (Rosa 1976). She does not however, reflect on herself (Rosa 1976), which is to say that she does not distinguish between the self as subject (the 'I') and the self as object (the 'me') (Mead 1934).

Incomplete understanding of the mechanism of trance makes it difficult to draw further distinctions between trance states of differing depth. Some writers see altered states of consciousness as separate entities, different in kind from each other, while others view them as lying on a continuum between sleep at one end, and wakefulness at the other. The latter view suggests that the altered states represent varying grades of trance, different only in degree and all part of the same entity (Barber 1969, 1970).

Autogenic training is an approach derived from self-hypnosis. It dates from the 1930s, when Johannes Schultz, a psychiatrist attending the Berlin Neurobiological Institute, discovered that some patients had learned to put themselves into a light trance by concentrating on images of heaviness and warmth. Even more interesting was the fact that they had seemed to benefit in terms of their mental health. Schultz called this self-generated trance state 'autogenic', and proceeded to develop a therapy based on it.

The goal of the procedure was attainment of this autogenic state, achieved by means of given phrases recited by the pupil. These phrases, by their imagery and autosuggestion, created what was called the 'autogenic shift'; a shift of the participant away from a stressed state towards the autogenic state. Exactly what however, was the autogenic state? And where did it lie in relation to other states such as sleep and wakefulness?

A prominent exponent of the method has described the autogenic state as one of drowsiness (Luthe 1965). His work has led to the current view which favours the continuum theory, and places the autogenic state at a point near the sleep end of the continuum, as shown in Figure 19.1.

Today autogenic training (AT) is an established approach, but since the trainee is active in her own treatment, it is generally regarded as a relaxation technique rather than a form of hypnosis.

What however, is the difference between hypnosis and relaxation? Zahourek (1985) answers the question by pointing out that hyp-

Figure 19.1 Hypothetical position of the autogenic state on a continuum between sleep and the waking state.

nosis purposely aims at producing a trance and emphasizes therapeutic suggestion. In relaxation by contrast, there is no striving for a state of trance, and any suggestion made is under the control of the individual herself who, as a human being, is constantly making suggestions to herself anyway. Certainly, some of the devices used in relaxation, i.e. passive concentration, self-suggestion and imagery, are closely related to hypnosis, but they are not confined to that practice; and their effective use does not require the full knowledge of a formal hypnosis training (Zahourek 1985). To ensure that they are used responsibly however, it is necessary for the health care professional to have clear goals, to use techniques designed to promote those goals and to be aware of the hazards involved.

The following sections do not provide the information and training needed to set up as a teacher of autogenic training. They are included in order to demonstrate the use of component techniques such as imagery and autosuggestion, which, as mentioned above, are part of most relaxation approaches (Larkin 1988). So much are they part of relaxation that Barber (1984) finds elements of suggestion in all stress reduction methods.

Davis et al (1988), addressing their book particularly to those who 'work with people who are in stress' (itemizing doctors, nurses, therapists, teachers and supervisors) present step-by-step directions for mastery of different approaches, one of which is self-hypnosis. They claim that no cases have been reported, even among the most inexperienced practitioners, of harm resulting from self-hypnosis (Davis et al 1988). This is an important point because, although self-hypnosis is not one of the methods contained in this book, there is no strict demarcation between self-hypnosis and relaxation.

PRINCIPLES OF AUTOGENIC TRAINING

Autogenic training teaches the body and the mind to relax. It is based on four requirements.

1. Reduced external stimulation, i.e. an absence of loud noise, bright light or other invasive stimulus.

2. An attitude of passive concentration, described, in the booklet advertising the autogenic training course, as a state of mind which is relaxed, nonstriving and unconcerned with the end product. This means not forcing any change, rather, just letting the exercise work (Achterberg 1985); an 'allowing' rather than a 'doing' (Rosa 1976). If, while engaged in passive concentration, distracting thoughts enter the mind, they can be ignored or gently dismissed. Thoughts which carry insightful images however, can be seen as a valuable product of the exercise. Passive concentration may be said to exist in other approaches such as meditation and some forms of progressive relaxation.

3. The repetition of relaxation-inducing phrases based on six central themes:
   - heaviness in the arms and legs
   - warmth in the arms and legs
   - calm and regular heartbeat
   - calm breathing
   - warm solar plexus
   - cool forehead.

These phrases are repeated to emphasize their effect. Suggestions of heaviness can be intensified by images of lead, while those of warmth can be deepened by images of sunshine or warm water (Rosa 1976). The first two themes are frequently presented on their own (by clinicians and researchers alike), although it is not known at what cost to the overall relaxation effect (Lichstein 1988).

4. Mental contact with the body part to which the phrase refers.

THE AUTOGENIC TECHNIQUE

Central to AT is the principle of client control: the trainer describes the method, but it is the trainee who carries it out. To reinforce this notion, the phrases are styled in the first person. The instructor reads them out and the trainee repeats them. Schultz & Luthe (1969) worked slowly through the schedule, taking 6 months to complete the instruction. The need to save time and money has, however, led to reductions in length, and now the full programme is often presented in a single session. Either way, daily practice periods are necessary to obtain mastery.

The phrases themselves may be interspersed with relevant messages such as 'I feel at peace' or 'I am relaxed', as in the following version (adapted from Lichstein 1988).

Introductory talk to trainees

A short description prepares the trainees:

The method you are going to learn consists of short phrases describing sensations of heaviness and warmth in the limbs. I'll be reading them out and as I do I'd like you to focus your attention on each in turn, repeating the phrase under your breath.

An important feature of this approach is that you should feel passive and casual about it, and that you shouldn't try to force any response to occur.

Conditions

Setting. The room should be quiet and the lighting dim.

The trainer's voice. A slow, calm and soothing tone is appropriate (Lichstein 1988).

Position of trainee. A lying posture is preferable to a sitting one. If however, the trainee is sitting, her head should be supported.

Induction

The trainer proceeds with the induction:

Please close your eyes. Imagine yourself in a place that makes you feel relaxed . . . perhaps a warm, sunny meadow. Picture yourself lying there.

(Pause).

In a moment I am going to ask you to focus your attention on different parts of your body, but first I want to remind you how important it is for you to adopt a passive and casual attitude towards the procedure.

This means letting the sensations of heaviness and warmth arise on their own rather than making an effort to bring them about. Spend a few moments settling yourself . . .

The exercises

The session begins as above with a few minutes of quiet relaxation. This is followed by 18 exercises, each composed of a group of phrases. Each phrase is recited by the instructor and repeated, mentally or vocally, by the learner. About 30 seconds are allotted for each exercise and a further 30–45 seconds for continued focusing of attention by the trainee.

Exercise 1

Begin with the dominant arm.

I feel at peace.
My right arm is heavy.
My right arm is heavy.
I feel at peace.
My right arm is heavy.
My right arm is heavy.

Please continue to think about the heaviness in your arm as you lie in the sunny meadow.

Exercise 2

I feel at peace.
My left arm is heavy.
My left arm is heavy.
I feet at peace.
My left arm is heavy.
My left arm is heavy.

Think of your arm being heavy as lead.

Exercise 3

I feel at peace.
Both my arms are heavy.
Both my arms are heavy.
I feel at peace.
Both my arms are heavy.
Both my arms are heavy.

See yourself lying in the meadow, with your arms resting heavily on the lush grass.

Exercise 4

I feel at peace.
My right leg is heavy.
My right leg is heavy.
I feel at peace.
My right leg is heavy.
My right leg is heavy.

Think of your leg being heavy as lead.

Exercise 5

I feel at peace.
My left leg is heavy.
My left leg is heavy.
I feel at peace.
My left leg is heavy.
My left leg is heavy.

Exercise 6

I feel at peace.
Both my legs are heavy.
Both my legs are heavy.
I feel at peace.
Both my legs are heavy.
Both my legs are heavy.

Feel your legs sinking into the ground.

Exercise 7

I feel at peace.
My arms and legs are heavy.
My arms and legs are heavy.
I feel at peace.
My arms and legs are heavy.
My arms and legs are heavy.

Continue to imagine yourself with heaviness in your arms and legs, lying in a sunny meadow.

Exercises 8–14

These are similar to Exercises 1–7, but warmth is substituted for heaviness. The effect can be augmented by images of the sun's warmth.

Exercise 15

I feel at peace.
My arms and legs are heavy and warm.

My heartbeat is calm and regular.
My heartbeat is calm and regular.
I feel at peace.
My heartbeat is calm and regular.
My heartbeat is calm and regular.

Exercise 16

I feel at peace.
My arms and legs are heavy and warm.
My heartbeat is calm and regular.
My breathing is calm.
My breathing is calm.
I feel at peace.
My breathing is calm.
My breathing is calm.

Exercise 17

The abdomen phrases are omitted for people with stomach inflammation.

I feel at peace.
My arms and legs are heavy and warm.
My heartbeat is calm and regular.
My breathing is calm.
My abdomen is warm.
My abdomen is warm.
I feel at peace.
My abdomen is warm.
My abdomen is warm.

Exercise 18

I feel at peace.
My arms and legs are heavy and warm.
My heartbeat is calm and regular.
My breathing is calm.
My abdomen is warm.
My forehead is cool.
My forehead is cool.
I feel at peace.
My forehead is cool.
My forehead is cool.

Images of cool air streams may be created to reinforce the feeling of a cool forehead (Samuels & Samuels 1975).

Termination

This allows the individual to make a gradual return to normal activity.

When you are ready, slowly allow yourself to become aware of the room you are in. Open your eyes. Let them scan the interior of the room. Tell yourself you are going to feel refreshed and alert. Make a few weak fists with your hands. Bend and stretch your elbows a few times. Then your knees. Gently stretch your body. Roll on to your side and slowly get up.

Home practice

Written handouts enable trainees to practise at home. This home practice is essential and builds up the skill of being able to respond readily to the phrases. Eventually, a single key phrase will have the capacity to switch on total relaxation.

Exponents insist that the basic phrases remain unchanged. The choice of imagery however, is left to the participant; a sunny beach, a heated bath, or a favourite chair in front of a log fire may be used as alternatives to the warm meadow scene. Having chosen her scene however, the participant should remain with it throughout the training period.

The phrase 'I feel at peace' could be replaced by 'I am relaxed' or 'I feel calm' as alternative self-suggestions for reducing tension. Such phrases, additional to the basic autogenic phrases, are examples of what Schultz called 'intentional formulae': personal maxims for life-enhancement. Other examples adapted from Davis et al (1988), are:

- I believe in myself (for those lacking in confidence).
- I have control over what I eat (for compulsive eaters).
- Smoking is an unhealthy habit (for people who wish to quit smoking).
- My mind is quiet and serene (for anxious individuals).

Certain physiological problems can be addressed through 'organ-specific formulae' such as:

- My throat is cool (for a troublesome cough).
- My feet are warm (for a tendency to blush).

The trainee will incorporate particular phrases according to her personal requirements. AT should not however, be viewed as a substitute for medical attention.

Other AT exercises

AT also includes meditative exercises which involve colours, objects, concepts and people.

Other exercises known as 'advanced' belong to an area described as therapy rather than training, and are beyond the scope of this book.

EVALUATION OF AUTOGENIC TRAINING

Research indicates that AT successfully induces relaxation in most people. Of the 2400 case histories meticulously documented by Schultz & Luthe (1969), most support the effectiveness of AT. Until recently however, there have been few controlled studies, but this picture is gradually changing. Spinhoven et al (1992) demonstrated a significant positive change in the incidence of tension headache in subjects receiving AT and self-hypnosis, compared with subjects on a waiting list. This result could not have been due to the greater effectiveness of self-hypnosis, since the same researchers compared AT with self-hypnosis and found them to be of equal efficacy.

When AT was compared with supportive group psychotherapy in asthma sufferers, significantly greater benefit was seen to occur in the AT group (Henry et al 1993).

Not all results however, are positive, and many are equivocal. Lichstein, reviewing studies in 1988, was unable to find conclusive evidence that AT phrases carry more power as relaxants than phrases employed in other relaxation approaches.

Because of its focus on warmth, AT is thought to exert a direct influence on the autonomic system, reducing levels of physiological arousal. Henry et al (1993) suggest, by way of explanation, that AT might be re-establishing a balance between the sympathetic and the parasympathetic nervous systems.

In conclusion, it can be said that AT is a genuine method of relaxation training (Lichstein 1988). Researchers suggest that AT may also be useful as an adjunctive treatment in some medical conditions where aetiological factors include psychosocial stress (Henry et al 1993).

PITFALLS OF AUTOGENIC TRAINING

1. The phrase inducing abdominal warmth should be deleted for people suffering from gastric inflammation (Rosa 1976).

2. AT is not suitable for children under five years of age nor for people lacking motivation.

3. Trainees should be advised to keep their personal formulae realistic. Creating unattainable goals will only lead to disappointment.

4. In the unlikely event of the phrases causing distress, the messages of heaviness and warmth can be reversed, i.e. the limbs can be made to feel light and cool; alternatively, the procedure can be stopped.

The pitfalls of visualization are also relevant (p. 151); points 1, 2 and 9 particularly, should be noted.

FURTHER READING

Kermani K S 1990 Autogenic training. Souvenir Press, London
Lichstein K L 1988 Clinical relaxation strategies. John Wiley, New York

Rosa K R 1976 Autogenic training. Victor Gollancz, London

CHAPTER CONTENTS

Introduction 161
Benefits of meditation 162

A procedure for meditation 163
Introductory remarks to the novice meditator 163
A meditation session 163
Practice 164

Focal points for meditation 164
The breath 164
Visual object 165
Parts of the body 167
Mantras 168

Evaluation of meditation 169

Pitfalls of meditation 169

20

Meditation

INTRODUCTION

The word 'meditation' is used to describe varied states of inner stillness. It is also used to describe different methods of attaining those states. Again, the many schools of meditation, all have their own interpretation. Thus with no universally agreed meaning, attempts to define the word founder. Common to all interpretations however, is the concept of emptying the mind of thought, that is, letting go the preoccupations that make up the mind's chatter.

If there is a general aim in meditation, it might be described as nonattachment although some writers such as Fontana (1991) feel that to have an aim at all tends to destroy the result since any kind of goal-setting calls on rational powers.

Meditation could therefore be said to be an opening of the self to reveal its inner world, while at the same time conveying no hint of determination since that would be alien to the meditative state.

People come to meditation for many reasons:

- to find peace
- to achieve awareness
- to gain enlightenment
- to find themselves
- to empty the mind
- to experience true reality.

Since relaxation is one of the effects of all these pursuits, meditation is a relevant topic for inclusion in a book such as this.

Originating in the East, meditation is an integral part of the Hindu, Taoist and Buddhist religions. In the West, versions have been created which are simpler to master, and these have for the most part, evolved from Zen and Yoga. The material presented here is of a nonreligious form and comes from a variety of modern sources, notably the work of Fontana (1991, 1992).

It has been pointed out that meditation is both a state and a method. As a state, it is one in which the mind is stilled and listening to itself. The meditator is relaxed but at the same time alert.

As a method, it consists of focusing attention on a chosen stimulus. This concentration is sustained but effortless and has the effect of detaching the meditator from external life events on the one hand and from her own mental activity on the other. Thoughts may enter her head, but instead of examining their content, she allows them to drift away.

This attitude has been described as one of passive concentration, and it implies that the meditator has a relaxed attitude while at the same time giving attention of the kind that is without criticism or judgement. Mental functions such as searching and knowing are inappropriate since they are processed by the left brain (p. 134); rather the meditator should cultivate what in Zen is called a 'don't know mind', that is, a mind which is open and receptive to new, undreamed-of possibilities. Past and future associations are shed. The mind is emptied of all thought save awareness of the stimulus.

In common with hypnosis and daydreaming, meditation is an altered state of consciousness. Fontana (1991) distinguishes it from other altered states, seeing it rather as a rediscovery of normal consciousness since it takes the individual to the heart of the self.

The meditator does not fall into a trance, become drowsy or surrender control; on the contrary, she is in a state of heightened awareness, alert, aware of her surroundings and securely focused on the present moment.

Passive concentration is also a feature of autogenic training and receptive visualization, although not of programmed visualization which, as it is involved with the achievement of goals, is essentially a left brain thinking activity and therefore, remote from meditation. However, to say that meditation excludes the analytical thinking process does not imply that such thinking is of lesser value: analytical thinking is an essential human activity. But its tendency to dominate mental activity has the effect of devaluing its counterpart, the imagination. Meditation enables the individual to redress the balance.

What is the mechanism underlying the state of meditation?

A number of theories have been put forward to account for the effect of meditation on the individual. Of these, Banquet's (1973) shift in hemispheric dominance is widely accepted. Research suggests that during meditation the left cerebral hemisphere loses its dominance, resulting in a more influential right hemisphere than occurs in everyday life. As a result, linear, verbal thinking plays a less prominent part, allowing intuitive, wordless thinking to express itself.

Benefits of meditation

Devotees of meditation claim that they benefit greatly from its practice. These are some of the advantages they mention.

- A better understanding of the self is achieved through meditation. That is, through meditation the individual becomes more aware of herself and more receptive to the insights that arise from her deeper being.
- A new sense of relaxation and inner peace can be derived from meditation.
- The process itself promotes a clearer mind and improved powers of concentration. These extend outside the meditation session.
- The individual, by discovering her inner self, is able to live more in harmony with herself.
- By developing a sense of detachment, the individual comes to accept that many of her unpleasant emotional reactions are no more than short-lived bodily sensations created by her thoughts.
- The emphasis on self-awareness helps the individual to live in the present and to value the here-and-now. When the mind is concentrated in the moment, it becomes keenly alert.

A PROCEDURE FOR MEDITATION

Introductory remarks to the novice meditator

A few words describing the procedure are required before starting the first session.

Meditation is an ancient method of quietening the mind. The method you are about to experience is a nonreligious form. It is concerned with focusing the attention on different phenomena such as the breath, a visual object or a repeated phrase. The effect of the meditation will be to make you feel very peaceful. At no time will you lose consciousness or be controlled by any outside force. The state you reach will be entirely created by you. It is best to come to meditation without expectations; rather, to have an attitude which makes you content to be in tune with yourself.

A meditation session

A session may be seen to have four components:

1. attention to position
2. a winding-down procedure
3. concentration on a chosen stimulus
4. return to everyday activity.

Attention to position

In an environment that is quiet and warm, the meditator takes up a sitting or a lying position. Sitting is preferred since some people tend to fall asleep when lying down. The individual may sit in a straightbacked chair, sit cross-legged on a cushion on the floor, or take up the lotus position (cross-legged with each foot resting on the opposite thigh). This position can be very uncomfortable for people who are not used to it; even in the East it has never been obligatory if the novice found it unbearable.

Whichever sitting position is chosen, the hands rest on the thighs, with the fingers gently curled or arranged in traditional symbolic postures. The head should be held in a relaxed position directly above the spinal column to release the neck muscles from strain while the eyes may be closed or slightly open.

Winding-down procedure

Participants are asked to direct their thoughts inwards.

The meditation session is preceded by a check for muscle tension, i.e. each participant checks all her muscle groups to make sure they are as relaxed as possible. It is often referred to as scanning and may be introduced in the following way:

I am going to ask you to check that your muscles are as relaxed as possible. Starting with your feet, notice any tension . . . then move up to your ankles, shifting them slightly if they are not relaxed . . . now your legs . . . and your hips . . . settle them into the chair or the floor. Continue up through your body to your shoulders, letting them drop down. Allow your arms to fall comfortably, with your fingers free of tension. And now your head: relax your jaw and let your tongue rest in your mouth . . . let all the muscles in your face feel smoothed out. Allow yourself to unwind, and as you unwind, feel in tune with yourself . . . listening to yourself . . . just being you . . . experiencing what it is to be you . . . being aware how it feels, without delving into reasons, explanations or even words . . .

Irritating sounds or bodily discomfort may interrupt the meditation. Davis et al (1988) suggest 'softening' them by purposely giving them attention for a few moments instead of pretending that they do not exist.

Concentrating on a chosen stimulus

'All meditations are built upon . . . concentration and tranquillity' (Fontana 1992). The individual quietly focuses attention on the chosen stimulus which may take the form of breath watching, gazing at a visual object or chanting a mantra. The purpose of the stimulus is to hold the attention of the participant.

This may be difficult at first since the mind is used to being engaged in a constant stream of images, memories and associations, all competing with one another. It will not help the individual to fight these distractions, but if she can accept their presence and continue her concentration on the stimulus, they will become weaker. This approach will also help to foster the passive attitude which promotes meditation. Some people find it useful to regard intruding thoughts as clouds drifting by, or leaves floating down a stream. The attention is then gently brought back to the item under focus.

The result of this meditation may be nothing more than a respite from stress for the individual. On the other hand, as the focused mind enters a state of clarity and tranquillity, a deeper part of the self may be reached whereby new insight is gained (Fontana 1991).

Any hint of depersonalization may be counteracted by a process known as 'grounding' or bringing the individual back to the here-and-now. It involves encouraging the meditator to return her attention to some form of body awareness. Fontana (1991) suggests concentrating on the breathing, while Titlebaum (1988) emphasizes the value of feeling the ground. The following passage is adapted from Titlebaum (1988):

Be aware of the ground beneath you. Feel it taking the weight of your body. Feel it supporting you. Notice the parts of your body which touch the ground or are in contact with the chair, if you are sitting. Concentrate on the sensations you are getting from these contact points and feel safely tethered to the ground.

The duration of the session should depend on the experience of the meditator; 5 minutes is considered enough for the novice, 15–20 minutes for the experienced practitioner.

Return to everyday activity

The return to everyday activity, also known as arousal or termination, is a sequence which brings the meditation to a close:

When you are ready, let your meditation come to an end. If your eyes are open, remove your gaze from the point of focus. If your eyes are closed, allow the point of focus to fade until it disappears. Let it go with a feeling of gratitude towards it. Then turn your attention to your breathing, slowly counting 10 natural breaths.

To help your muscles regain their tone, try slowly moving the body round in small circles before you get up. A few gentle stretches will also enliven the muscles.

Practice

Regular practice enhances the benefits of meditation. Lichstein (1988), reviewing the evidence, refers to numerous studies which indicate a direct association between the number of hours spent practising and the beneficial effects of meditation.

FOCAL POINTS FOR MEDITATION

Items on which the attention may be focused cover a wide range of objects, sounds and other phenomena. Included in this section are the following:

- the breath
- visual objects, i.e. circle, mandala, candle, china bowl
- parts of the body, i.e. space between the eyes, crown of the head, big toe
- mantras.

Concentration on the breath is mentioned first for a number of reasons (Fontana 1991):

- it is constantly available
- it has a rhythmical quality
- it is directly linked to the autonomic system
- it symbolizes the life force.

The breath

The practice of counting the breaths, with one count for every outbreath, is commonly used as a stimulus to hold the attention. On reaching the count of 10, the meditator reverts to 'one' again, and continues the process for 5 minutes. The breaths should be natural and unhurried. Other forms of breathing meditation consist of focusing the attention on parts of the body involved in respiration such as the tip of the nose or the moving abdomen.

The tip of the nose

In the passage below the meditator concentrates on the tip of her nose. It is assumed that she has already gone through a winding-down procedure (see above). Plenty of time should be allowed between the sentences.

Let your attention focus on your breathing and in particular, on the tip of your nose, that curved piece of cartilage that separates your nostrils. If you like, touch it with your fingertips to increase your awareness of it. Then concentrate on the feeling of air passing from the outside into your nostrils . . . notice how cool it is. Notice also the warmth and moistness of the air that leaves your nostrils. Allow your breathing rhythm to be completely natural as you focus your attention on the tip of your nose. Feel the sensation of air being drawn in . . . sweeping into your nostrils and, in its own time, passing out again. If outside thoughts intrude, gently return to the sensation at the tip of the nose. Continue to focus your attention on that point . . . feel your senses converging on that one spot.

On another occasion the meditator might wish to adopt a different focus as in the next passage.

The moving abdomen

Here, a counting procedure is combined with focusing attention on the abdomen.

Gently turn your attention to your breathing. Begin by noticing it in a general kind of way, then slowly bring your mind to focus on the movement of your abdomen. Keep your attention fixed on the movement of your abdomen . . . swelling as the air is breathed in and sinking as it is breathed out. Allow the air to pass in and out quite naturally while you are concentrating on the abdominal movement. Do not try to influence the breathing rhythm but let yourself flow with it. If your mind wanders, gently bring it back to the swelling and sinking abdomen. Counting the breaths helps to hold the attention . . . one count for every breath out . . . and when you get to 10 or lose count, start again. Please continue on your own.

Visual object

Visual concentration on an object, sometimes referred to as gaze meditation, offers varied possibilities. Almost any object can become the focus of attention but typically the object is chosen for its symbolic value or its neutral associations: a geometric shape, a candle or a flower all have these characteristics.

The circle

A circle has the following symbolic qualities:

- It has substance in that it may be solid.
- It has emptiness in that there may be nothing inside it.
- It has motion in that it can roll and spin.
- It has stillness in that it may come to rest.
- It has wholeness by virtue of enclosing all its parts within it.
- It has continuity in that any point along its circumference is both the end and the beginning.

If a circle is chosen as an object for meditation, the instructing meditator should draw a thick-edged ring about 30 cm (1 foot) in diameter, emphasize the centre with a dot, and hang it on the wall. It should be level with the eyes of the seated participant, who positions herself at a comfortable distance from it (Fontana 1991).

The following script can then be used.

Let your gaze fall on the centre of the circle and then remain there. Consider the circle simply as a shape and let it speak to you in intuitive terms rather than in words. Try to keep your gaze focused on the centre while at the same time absorbing the whole image. Do not examine it, but feel yourself experiencing it. Maintain the visual experience without reacting to it. Feel the image extending around your point of focus. Be aware of its extremities as your mind flows from the centre to the edges and from the edges to the centre. If your attention should wander, gently bring it back to the centre point. Spend several minutes gazing at the image.

The mandala and the yantra

These serve a sacred purpose in the Buddhist religion. Their complexity, beauty and harmony enrich their symbolic quality and make them the supreme focal object for visual meditation. Although created for use by devotees, they can be meditated on at any philosophical level, and examples are shown in Figures 20.1 and 20.2. The mandala generally contains representations of living things while the yantra is predominantly geometric.

Both enclose symbolic motifs arranged in con-

Figure 20.1 A mandala. Reproduced from The Stream of Consciousness by Pope & Singer (1978) with permission from Plenum Publications.

centric rings around a clearly defined central point. This point symbolizes the inner self on the one hand and divine consciousness on the other, while the enclosing circles represent the cycle of life and the notion of Nature forever renewing herself. Thus the mandala/yantra stands for the personal as well as the transpersonal, for change within permanence, for life both in the present and in eternity, while affirming the fundamental unity of all things.

The candle

As mentioned above, the visual image can be used in different ways to clear the mind of thought. For instance, while the individual is gazing at the object, she can intermittently close her eyes and allow the image to re-create itself in her mind, as in the following meditation on a candle flame in a darkened room:

Let the candle flame hold your attention. Sit without moving while you gaze at it. Focus on the flame in a relaxed but constant way, letting the image fill your mind. (If the flame is too bright, focus on the top rim of the candle.) Continue for at least a minute. Now abruptly close your eyes. Notice that the image of the candle prints itself in the darkness . . . hold the shape in your mind's eye . . . accepting any change of colour . . . if it slips to one side, gently bring it back . . . continue to focus on it until it fades . . . then open your eyes and resume your gaze on the candle. Continue repeating the sequence in silence for several minutes.

The image that appears behind the closed eyes is known as the 'after-image'.

Figure 20.2 A yantra. Reproduced from The Elements of Meditation by Fontana (1991) with permission from Element Books.

The after-image. When the gaze is fixed on a particular point for about a minute and the eyes subsequently closed, the phenomenon of the after-image occurs. This is the negative representation of the object stared at. It immediately begins to fade and after about 20 seconds or so, has disappeared. It is a physiological reaction which occurs when the retinal cells get fatigued. Experiencing the after-image is quite different from re-creating forms in the imagination, a practice which belongs more to visualization than to meditation.

If the meditator is in doubt as to what he is seeing behind his closed lids, there are two questions he can ask himself:

1. Does the image fade, or disappear within 20 seconds? If so, it is likely to be an after-image.
2. Can he scan the image, i.e. trace its outlines? If every time he moves his eyes to trace the outline the image moves too, it is behaving like an after-image (Samuels & Samuels 1975).

A china bowl

Certain objects lend themselves to a more exploratory approach. A flower or a piece of porcelain fall into this category. For instance, Davis et al (1988) suggest a china bowl:

Settle your gaze on the object. Take it all in . . . then, after a few moments, allow your eyes to travel over the object, tracing its lines . . . noticing its colours . . . its decoration . . . and the way it glistens . . . do not dwell on who made it, how or for what purpose, but see it simply as a shape. Experience its visual qualities as if you were seeing it for the first time. If your mind wanders, gently bring it back to the object.

Parts of the body

Other body parts as well as the breathing organs can be used to provide a focus of attention. This kind of meditation is a feature of yoga, where energy centres (chakras) are represented by the base of the spine, the lower abdomen, the navel, the heart, the throat, the space between the eyebrows and the crown of the head. After meditating on the sites in this order, the physical energies are said to be transformed into spiritual energies.

Yoga is a separate subject, and no attempt is made here to present it. However, the symbolic nature of the chakras makes them suitable sites for meditations outside yoga. Two examples are given here: the space between the eyebrows and the crown of the head.

On a simpler level, any part of the body can serve as the stimulus, for instance the big toe, as shown below.

The space between the eyebrows

Behind closed lids, let your eyes turn upwards and settle on the space between your eyebrows. Relate to it . . . recognize its closeness to your brain . . . feel its central position . . . imagine viewing it from the outside . . . then, imagine viewing it from the inside . . . let your attention come to focus on that one spot . . . feel drawn to it . . . as the space between your eyebrows is part of your, so you are part of that space.

Pause.

If outside thoughts drift into your mind, mentally blow them away and return to your point of focus . . . to the space between your eyebrows.

The crown of the head

With your eyes closed, focus your attention on the crown of your head, concentrating on it in a passive way. Let your awareness be drawn to it and held there. See it from the outside, noticing how it appears . . . then imagine it from the inside, from under the dome of your head.

(Pause.)

Symbolically as well as literally, it represents the highest part of you. If thoughts intrude, let them blow away . . . let them drift away from you as you gently return your attention to the crown of your head . . . feel yourself identifying with it . . . experiencing it . . . feel yourself uniting with all that is highest within you.

The big toe

With your eyes closed, your legs uncrossed and your muscles relaxed, draw your attention to your right big toe. See it in your mind's eye . . . move it gently to make its presence felt . . . notice how it feels when you move it . . . focus on the sensations you get from bending and stretching it . . . be aware of the feel of the sock or stocking over it, or of the shoe restricting it . . . think of it carrying the full weight of the body . . . think of its strength and its mobility . . . if unwanted thoughts intrude, gently bring your attention back to the toe . . . focusing on the toe . . .

Mantras

A mantra is a verbal stimulus which can be used to concentrate the attention. Traditionally it embodies an ancient, sacred truth whose meaning reveals itself to the meditator during the process of concentration. A well-known example is the Sanskrit word 'om' which is said to represent the primal sound. Pronounced like 'home' without the 'h' (Smith & Wilks 1988), the sound can be intensified by stretching the syllable to form a . . . oo . . . mmmm (Fontana 1991). It is the *sound* of the mantra that has particular value for the novice meditator, although its meaning may also be contemplated at a later stage. The following piece is adapted from a passage in Fontana (1991):

Breathe in gently and as you let the air out, recite the word om: a . . . . .oo . . . . .mmmm. Feel the sounds vibrating within your body: feel the 'a' ringing in your belly, feel the 'oo' resonating in your chest and the 'mmmm' resounding in the bones of your skull. Let these sounds provide a focus for your attention. Link them into your natural breathing rhythm. Keep the breathing calm and slow and avoid any inclination to deepen it. After 10 breaths, gradually reduce the volume of the sound until the word is spoken under your breath. Lower it further. Keep your attention focused on the mantra. Eventually, you will come to a point where your lips cease to move and the syllables lose their form so that you are left with just an idea. Feel it clinging to your mind, united with it. If thoughts intrude, turn them into puffs of smoke and watch them being blown away.

Many other sounds or words can act as mantras i.e. 'peace', 'harmony', 'calmness', or phrases such as 'God is love' and 'here-and-now'. It does not matter if the word has a meaning, since constantly reciting it will tend to divest it of that meaning, although the word may still retain its aura. It is advisable however, to choose a word that has no emotional associations for the user, and one that is unlikely to stir up her thoughts. While the main purpose of the mantra is to hold the meditator's attention, its rhythmic repetition also has a soothing effect.

On the other hand, a mantra may be picked expressly for its meaning, in which case, it is not reflected on philosophically so much as experienced; it is identified with rather than analysed.

Lichstein (1988) compares mantra chanting with dwelling on the muscles in progressive relaxation (Ch. 4) and to the silent recitation of phrases in autogenic training (Ch. 19) and points out that in addition to their inherent relaxation properties, they all share the capacity to divert the attention from stressful thoughts.

Transcendental meditation

Transcendental meditation (TM) is an approach which sets great store by the mantra. Its central feature is the contemplation and repetition of a Sanskrit mantra bestowed by Maharishi Mahesh Yogi who brought the movement to the West in 1959. As well as gathering many disciples, TM attracted a great deal of research: from several hundred studies it emerged that TM created significant physiological changes associated with relaxation. However, lack of controls and the use of self-selected (volunteer) subjects weakened the validity of some of these findings.

Proponents of TM insist on the mantra being chosen with ceremony and in secrecy by a master teacher, although this practice has not been shown to be any more effective than one which uses simple words (Benson 1976).

EVALUATION OF MEDITATION

There is no doubt that meditation is an effective way of reducing tension, and one which often leads to deep states of physiological and phenomenological relaxation (Lichstein 1988). However, it is uncertain how much more effective it is than any other relaxation practice. Research findings are inconsistent; some point to the superior benefit of meditation, while others such as that of Holmes et al (1983) are unable to show that meditation is any more effective at lowering physiological arousal than ordinary rest.

Lichstein suggests two reasons for these contradictory findings: one is the varying amount of practice carried out by subjects in different studies, while the other concerns personality factors which result in some individuals being unable to benefit from meditation.

Weighing the evidence, much of which has compared TM with progressive relaxation, Lichstein (1988) concludes that neither method shows any marked advantage over the other.

A number of studies have investigated the proposition that meditation produces a unique state of consciousness, but the evidence for this is weak.

PITFALLS OF MEDITATION

These can be found at the end of the following chapter.

FURTHER READING

Fontana D 1991 The elements of meditation. Element, Shaftesbury
Fontana D 1992 The meditator's handbook: a comprehensive guide to eastern and western meditation techniques. Element, Shaftesbury

Smith E, Wilks N 1988 Meditation, Optima, London
West M A (ed) 1987 The psychology of meditation. Oxford Science Publications, Oxford

CHAPTER CONTENTS

Origins of the relaxation response approach 171

Benson's method 172
  The key elements 172
  Introductory remarks to participants 172
  Induction 172

Features of Benson's method 173

Evaluation of the relaxation response method 173

Pitfalls of meditation 173

21

The relaxation response

ORIGINS OF THE RELAXATION RESPONSE APPROACH

In the 1970s, the physiologist Herbert Benson, who was studying aspects of high blood pressure at Harvard's Thorndike Laboratory, was approached by a group of transcendental meditators who believed that their meditations could lower their blood pressure. Unconvinced, Benson at first discouraged their idea but he later changed his mind. He and his colleagues then began to carry out a series of investigations which revealed that transcendental meditation (TM) was accompanied by marked physiological changes: there were reductions in the heart rate, breathing rate, oxygen consumption, blood lactate levels and, of particular interest to Benson, blood pressure. These changes reflected diminished activity in the sympathetic nervous system.

One study demonstrated drops in systolic and diastolic pressures from group averages of 146 and 93.5 mmHg respectively (borderline high pressure) to 137 and 88.9 mmHg (within normal range), following several weeks of practising TM. Oxygen consumption was found to be reduced by 10–20% within the first 3 minutes of meditation. (It is interesting to compare this result with work on the sleeping state where the oxygen consumption was found to be reduced by only 8% and not before the subject had been sleeping for 4 or 5 hours.) These were impressive findings, particularly so, given that the recordings were not made during periods of meditation. The subjects however, were volunteers who had already applied to join a transcendental meditation course to reduce their blood pressure. This would suggest that their motivation was high.

Extensive study of other meditation practices led Benson to the belief that the above effects were not confined to the practice of TM, but were the result of certain key elements common to all meditation practices. He set out to identify these elements, seeing them as responsible for eliciting what he called 'the relaxation response', or a state of reduced metabolic activity. To Benson (1976), this was 'a natural and innate protective mechanism' that opposed the effects of the stress response. Viewed in these terms, the relaxation response appeared synonymous with parasympathetic nervous activity.

The key elements that Benson (1976) identified were:

- a quiet environment
- a comfortable position
- a mental device word or object to focus on
- a passive attitude.

BENSON'S METHOD

The key elements

Quiet environment. In the ideal setting there is an absence of any background stimulus, pleasant or unpleasant.

Comfortable position. Benson does not insist on any particular position since he feels that discomfort might draw the attention away from the mental device. The meditator should be allowed to choose her own position. She can however, be too comfortable; the orthodox lotus position (p. 163) is thought to have been introduced to prevent the meditator falling asleep. For the same reason Benson does not recommend a lying position.

Mental device. Since his studies had shown that TM was not unique in its ability to lower physiological arousal, Benson concluded that any repetitive, monotonous stimulus capable of holding the attention, could fulfil the function of the Sanskrit mantra, i.e. that any emotionally neutral object, sound or other phenomenon could be

used as a focal point of attention. Benson chose the word 'one', which has similar qualities of resonance to the primal sound 'om', but he felt the choice of word or words was best made by the individual herself. He refuted the idea that the mantra's meaning added to its effect.

Passive attitude. Passive acceptance is an essential feature of the approach. A 'let it happen' attitude should be adopted. Benson regards the passive attitude as 'perhaps the most important element in eliciting the relaxation response'. If distracting thoughts intervene, they should be ignored and the meditator's attention returned to the recited mantra.

Introductory remarks to participants

A few words explaining the method are addressed to novices.

The relaxation method you are about to learn is a nonreligious version of meditation. It has a very simple form, requiring that you sit comfortably in a quiet place; that you focus your attention on the word 'one' and that you adopt an attitude which is accepting and unconcerned.

These conditions will help you to experience what is called the relaxation response; a state which research shows, is associated with reduced physiological activity. That means the heart rate will become slower and the blood pressure will fall. You'll notice that you feel calmer than usual and the whole sensation will be a pleasant one.

At no time will you lose consciousness or be controlled by an outside force. The state you reach is one which you will have induced in yourself.

Induction

When participants are ready, the induction sequence itself is carried out. The following version is adapted from Benson (1976). The '10 minutes' mentioned can be extended to 20 as the meditator becomes more experienced.

Settle comfortably in whatever position you have chosen, and close your eyes. Relax all your muscles, starting with your feet and ending with your face. Feel yourself deeply relaxed.

Notice the rhythm of your breathing. Let the air in through your nose, allowing the breaths to take place quite naturally. Each time you exhale, recite the word 'one' under your breath. Repeat the word slowly every time you breathe out. If thoughts intrude, try to ignore them, and continue repeating the word 'one'.

Avoid any inclination to judge how successful you are being. Keep your attitude passive, and allow relaxation to occur in its own time. Please continue for 10 minutes . . .

When you are ready to end your meditation, continue to sit quietly for a few minutes with your eyes closed, then for a few minutes longer with them open.

FEATURES OF BENSON'S METHOD

As shown above, the induction is short and simple. Benson writes that his method carries little embellishment. Perhaps he made it too simple; in excluding all but the essentials, he may have overlooked the value of ceremony and ritual, which are important factors for some individuals (Carrington 1984, Lichstein 1988).

The emphasis placed on 'passive attitude' recalls the 'passive concentration' of autogenic training (Ch. 19). It is also not far removed from the quiet observation that characterizes progressive relaxation. It would seem that, underneath their varying procedures, the approaches are saying much the same thing (Lichstein, 988).

Along with other practitioners, Benson stressed the importance of regular practice, to be carried out once or twice a day. When practising at home, people are urged not to use an alarm, but to guess when it is time to end the meditation.

In identifying what he considered to be key factors, Benson's purpose was not to create a rival approach, but to devise a standardized technique which could be used in scientific investigation. In many ways his technique resembles transcendental meditation except that the word 'one' replaces the Sanskrit mantra and the process is entirely secularized (Lichstein 1988).

EVALUATION OF THE RELAXATION RESPONSE METHOD

It has not so far been possible to replicate the marked relaxation effects produced by Benson in his early studies (Lichstein 1988). However, compared to transcendental meditation, little research has been carried out on the relaxation response. What results are available are inconsistent. Where the relaxation response approach has been compared with simple rest however, it has on the whole, emerged as equal or superior (Lichstein 1988). Benson's method is widely used in the clinical field.

Lichstein is persuaded that, in his concept of key elements, Benson did in fact discover a truth, but one whose mechanism is far from being understood.

PITFALLS OF MEDITATION

1. Meditation is not suitable for people in acute psychotic states. People suffering from milder forms of mental illness, who wish to practise meditation, should first discuss it with their doctor or psychologist.

2. Meditation should not be used as a substitute for medical treatment. Individuals who may be already receiving medication should inform their doctor of their wish to study meditation since the effects of one may influence the other (McCormack 1992).

3. Although the central idea of meditation is to keep the mind focused and aware, it does occasionally happen that an individual loses the sense of who and where she is, or develops the feeling of being 'outside her body'. These are trance-like states of disorientation and depersonalization. In this event, a grounding strategy similar to the one referred to in Chapter 20 (p. 164) may provide a remedy. Altered states associated with a sound stimulus, e.g. a mantra, are more likely to lead to trance than those associated with other stimuli such as breathing. The instructor can safeguard against disorientation and depersonalization by regularly reminding participants to keep their attention focused on the stimulus (Fontana 1991).

4. Meditation creates an altered state of consciousness. The novice will not know in advance how he will respond. It is therefore recommended that, to begin with, sessions be kept short, that is, 5 minutes in length. This can be

increased to 15 or 20 minutes for those with experience but not exceeded, as it possible to meditate too much and run the risk of getting out of touch with day-to-day life. Benson (1976) reports that none of the subjects in his studies displayed ill effects after meditating for 20 minutes twice a day.

5. The breathing meditations in Chapter 20 do not seek to interfere with the natural breathing rate or rhythm. However, the mere request to become aware of the breathing can result in a slight alteration of its rhythm. It is therefore suggested that before attempting breathing meditations, the reader become familiar with the section of hyperventilation in Chapter 15 (p. 119).

6. Benson (1976) believed that it was better to practise meditation before a meal than directly after it. He considered that the process of digestion, by drawing the blood to the viscera, interfered with the physiological changes associated with meditation, and advised waiting for at least 2 hours after eating. Recent research investigating the distribution of blood during meditation, supports Benson's view: Bricklin (1990) found that the blood flow to the brain during meditation increased dramatically, rising on average by 65% of its normal volume. It would not therefore be constructive to practise meditation at a time when other demands were being made on the vascular system.

7. The lotus position has been referred to as the posture traditionally adopted in the East. This posture however, was never obligatory even in its country of origin. In the West it may be inadvisable for novices even to attempt it because of the excessive stretching of the joint structures which accompanies it. Sitting cross-legged on a cushion is no less conducive to meditation, and many people practise meditation sitting in a chair.

8. Some meditation may be disturbing if the stimulus object has unpleasant associations. A change of stimulus is therefore indicated.

9. The outcome should not be judged in terms of success or usefulness because these are rational dimensions. Progress is seen in terms of self-discovery rather than achievement (Fontana 1991).

10. Those who expect meditation to be a ready remedy for life's problems may become disillusioned. Meditation should be seen as a way of life, not as a panacea.

11. It is possible for an individual to experience euphoric states in which she believes she has made a profound spiritual discovery. Fontana (1992) advises a cautious approach to the interpretation of material from the inner self.

12. For those who have undergone psychoanalysis, the idea of ignoring their flow of thoughts may not come naturally. Benson (1976) reminds us that psychoanalysis trains people to regard their thoughts as a vital link with the inner self. People who have experienced this form of therapy may have some initial difficulty in learning meditation.

13. Because of individual variation, there will always be some people who gain very little from meditation.

Guidance should be sought from an experienced teacher by those wishing to pursue more advanced forms of meditation since they are beyond the scope of this book.

FURTHER READING

Benson H 1976 The relaxation response. Collins, London

Miscellaneous topics

SECTION CONTENTS

22. 'On-the-spot' techniques 177

23. Relaxation in pregnancy and childbirth 183

24. Assessment and research 187

25. Drawing the threads together 195

CHAPTER CONTENTS

Introduction 177
Characteristics of on-the-spot techniques 178
Factors affecting the success of on-the-spot
techniques 178

The exercises 178
Physical actions 178
Scanning 179
Breathing 180
Cognitive strategies 181

'On-the-spot' techniques

INTRODUCTION

The goal of most methods described in previous chapters has been the induction of deep relaxation: a slowly induced state which allows the individual to lose all tension. In order to achieve this, she must detach herself from environmental stimuli and focus all her attention on the method. This approach is appropriate where total relaxation is required and where the environment is making no current demands on her.

The individual may however, be looking for a more superficial technique which works fast: a strategy to lighten the effect of a stressor suddenly imposed upon her. The aim here is not to release all tension but to lose superfluous tension. Far from being detached from the environment, the individual wants to be fully alert to deal with its challenges. Instead of eliminating stressors, she wants to increase her tolerance of them. What she needs is a technique which can be implemented at a moment's notice, and still allow her to carry on with the task, whatever it might be.

Such an approach goes under a variety of names: instant, emergency, immediate, rapid, quick, all of which carry an appropriate hint of urgency. 'Brief' which sounds more neutral, is used by some practitioners. In the present work, the phrase 'on-the-spot' has been chosen, since, while acknowledging the need of the moment, it also conveys a sense of being equal to the occasion.

Contracted forms of relaxation have already been referred to. The rapid relaxation of Öst (1987) is one example (p. 67), where the individual recites a cue word on exhalation while scanning the body for tension. Mitchell's (1987) 'key movements', which are capable of unlocking the body from tense postures (p. 82), are another example.

Although the aim of on-the-spot techniques is to lose excess tension, retaining only what is necessary for the task, these techniques are not the same as differential relaxation. Differential relaxation is a principle to be applied throughout the day, regardless of activity. By contrast, on-the-spot techniques are designed to exert a momentary effect in the face of sudden threat.

A variety of methods for inducing relaxation at short notice are presented in this chapter. They are derived from methods already described, being, for the most part, compacted versions of them. They work best in individuals who have given the parent method many hours of practice. It is practice that enables the individual to turn on the full effect at short notice. Thus, on-the-spot techniques are shorthand versions of lengthier methods previously learned.

Characteristics of on-the-spot techniques

Lichstein (1988) lists the essentials of such techniques. They need to be:

- Portable: short enough and convenient enough to be used in most situations.
- Unobtrusive: not attracting attention or interrupting ongoing work.
- Capable of inducing moderate levels of relaxation. The object is not to induce deep relaxation but to enable the individual to carry on with the task, in as relaxed a state as possible.

Factors affecting the success of on-the-spot techniques

Not every strategy is going to succeed every time. A number of factors may influence the outcome.

1. Situation. The degree of inherent threat in a situation may vary. Situations of high threat tend to reduce the effectiveness of the technique.

2. Sensitivity to internal cues. A person's ability to recognize her own physiological and psychological cues is important. As stress levels rise, the cues become more pronounced. The earlier she is able to pick them up, the more effective will be the relaxation device that she applies.

3. Level of skill attained by previous practice. The capacity to 'switch on' relaxation whenever the individual feels under stress depends to a great extent on the level of skill attained in any one technique. This in turn depends on the amount of home practice that has been carried out.

4. Personal preference in choice of technique. Individuals have preferences for some methods over others (Woolfolk & Lehrer 1984, Payne 1989). The method in which a person feels most at ease will be likely to induce greater relaxation than a method which feels alien to her.

5. Diversionary content of the technique. Diversion, such as the reciting of a mantra is said to contribute to the effect of a relaxation device. The stronger the diversionary element, the greater the power of the technique (Lichstein 1988). It is a useful feature where all that is required is a reduction in stress levels, as in the condition of panic. Where successful coping relies on intellectual and verbal skills, distraction is less useful, and a technique which leaves the mind free to focus on the issue is more appropriate.

THE EXERCISES

A technique may be picked from any of the following approaches:

- Physical actions
- Scanning
- Breathing
- Cognitive strategies.

Physical actions

When under stress the individual tends to close up physically. It is an unconscious reaction to any kind of threat and has the effect of making her feel less exposed. Although the action may not be observable, the muscles involved may nevertheless be minutely contracting. To help release that tension, one of the following manoeuvres could be adopted:

1. key changes
2. posture
3. shaking a sleeve down
4. stretchings.

Key changes

Certain physical actions may serve as keys to unlock body patterns of tension. Mitchell (1987) (p. 82). The individual may find her personal key in one of the following four actions.

1. Spreading the fingers. The order is:

Fingers and thumbs long . . . hold them there for a moment . . . then stop . . . let them recoil into a gently curved position.

2. Separating your teeth. The order is:

Drag your jaw downwards . . . feel your jaw hanging down inside your mouth . . . then stop . . . feel your throat slack, your tongue loose and your lips gently touching.

3. Pulling the shoulders towards the feet.

Feel a distance growing between your shoulders and your ears . . . and, stop pulling . . . let your shoulders rest where they are.

4. Pushing the head back.

With your shoulders pulled down, lift your head; carry it up and back, keeping your chin pointing towards your feet. Stop. The resulting position should feel comfortable.

Posture

A mental impression of being one's full height promotes a sense of ease and confidence. Reminders are contained in phrases such as:

- think 'tall'
- think 'up'.

The second item is drawn from the Alexander technique (p. 89).

Shaking a sleeve down

This action loosens the muscles in the arm and shoulder and has the added advantage of appearing a quite natural thing to do.

Stretchings

Musculoskeletal benefit is derived from stretchings (Ch. 13). In the context of on-the-spot relaxation, they are aimed at structures which have been held in one position for some length of time, such as the spinal joints during long-distance motoring. A few examples appear below:

- trunk twisting (Fig. 13.14)
- back arching (Fig. 13.15)
- crouching (Fig. 13.16).

Other stretching exercises may be found in Chapter 13.

Scanning

Scanning is a shortened version of passive relaxation. It involves a brief tour of the body during which the individual checks for unnecessary tension. Four approaches are described:

1. relaxation by recall with counting
2. behavioural relaxation checklist
3. sweeping the body
4. the ripple.

Relaxation by recall with counting

Bernstein & Borkovec (1973) contracted their progressive relaxation training programme into a release-only format for four groups of muscles: the arms, head and neck, the trunk and the legs. In its most summarized form it consists of a counting procedure: two counts are allotted to each body part as attention is focused on it and tension released.

One . . . two, (arms relax) . . . three . . . four, (head and neck relax) . . . five . . . six, (trunk relax) . . . seven . . . eight, (legs relax) . . . nine . . . ten, (whole body relax) . . .

Behavioural relaxation checklist

This is based on the assumption that if an individual looks relaxed, to some extent he will feel relaxed. A checklist (Table 9.1), which can be memorized, covers 10 postures characteristic of relaxation (Poppen 1988):

Feet . . . resting with toes lying free
Hands . . . fingers gently curled
Body . . . without movement
Shoulders . . . dropped and level
Head . . . still, and facing forwards
Mouth . . . teeth separated, lips unpursed
Throat . . . loose
Breathing . . . slow and gentle
Voice . . . no sound
Eyes . . . lightly closed behind smooth eyelids.

Sweeping the body

Kermani (1990) describes a routine used for releasing body tension. It involves sweeping the surface of the body with an imaginary large, soft paintbrush (p. 59)

Starting at your feet, sweep the brush in your mind's eye, up your legs and the front of your body as far as your shoulders . . . then down your arms to your fingertips . . . then, a long sweep up the full length of the back . . . continuing into the neck and scalp . . . over the brow . . . and down to the face and jaw.

The ripple

This is a single wave of relaxation which begins at the head and rolls down the body to the feet (Priest & Schott 1991) (p. 56):

Starting at the top of your head, feel the relaxation rolling down your body in one continuous wave . . . feel it releasing tension as it descends . . . relaxing each part of your body in turn . . . until it reaches the tips of your toes. Try synchronizing the ripple with a slow breath out.

Breathing

Stress is associated with physiological arousal. This arousal is brought about by the action of the sympathetic nervous system, and includes an increase in the respiratory rate. Slowed breathing is associated with parasympathetic activity. Thus, by consciously slowing the breathing rate, it may be possible to counteract the effects of the sympathetic nervous system and generally check the symptoms of arousal.

Three techniques are described. Each one has a greater chance of success if it is introduced before the state of stress becomes established.

1. abdominal breathing
2. using words as cues
3. a breathing cycle.

Abdominal breathing

Since sudden stress is associated with apical (upper costal) respiratory movements, and relaxation with abdominal respiratory movements, breathing which focuses attention on the abdomen will tend to have a quietening effect (p. 118).

Let your attention focus on your abdomen. Feel it swelling as you breathe in and sinking as you breathe out. Keep the breathing as gentle and as slow as you can.

Using words as cues (cue-controlled relaxation)

Repeated past associations of a word such as 'relax' with the relaxed state give the word the status of a cue. When subsequently recited on the outbreath, this word tends to bring about a state of relaxation (Öst 1987) (p. 65).

Let your breathing be as natural as possible . . . just before you begin to breathe out, think the word 'relax' . . . slowly release the air as you focus on the word . . . breathe in . . . and, repeat the sequence . . . keep the rhythm as gentle as you can . . . avoid deliberately deepening the breaths . . . continue for a few moments . . .

A short version might run:

In . . . relax and out slowly . . . in . . . relax and out slowly . . .

or simply:

Relax

A breathing cycle

Lichstein (1988) presents a breathing technique for helping to relieve stress in a crisis situation. It consists of a deeper than usual breath in, which is held for a few seconds before being slowly exhaled. Lichstein points out how each component of the exercise has value: the inbreath diverts attention from the distressing thoughts; the breath-retention raises the P_{CO_2} level inducing mild lethargy, and the slow outbreath helps to reduce muscle tension. The cycle begins with the outbreath in the exercise below:

Breathe out a little more fully than usual. Let the air flow in to fill your lungs. Hold it for 5 seconds. Then exhale slowly. As you let the air out, feel the tension going with it. Then, let your breathing recover its normal rhythm.

Since deep breathing can increase the possibility of hyperventilation, immediate repetition of this exercise is not recommended.

Cognitive strategies

These are methods which deal with stress by changing our thoughts. They include the following approaches:

1. self-talk
2. autogenic phrases
3. imagery
4. thinking of a smile
5. additional strategies
6. environmental markers.

Self-talk

Since thoughts influence feelings, positive thoughts will tend to generate positive feelings (Beck 1976, Ellis 1962). Phrases affirming the value of the self, repeated often, colour our view of ourselves, and in a positive direction (p. 7). Feeling in control and feeling relaxed will tend to increase coping powers whatever the source of the stress.

Phrases tending to promote a sense of control over the situation include:

• I am competent

• I can deal with this
• I am in control
• My coping powers are good.

Phrases tending to induce a relaxed state of mind include:

• I feel at peace
• I am relaxed
• I am calm and composed
• My thoughts are peaceful ones.

The above phrases provide examples of positive self-talk; however the most effective phrases are those which the individual has composed for herself.

Autogenic phrases

Training in autogenics (Ch. 19) can result in relaxation occurring after recitation of a single phrase. It could be a heaviness phrase, a warmth phrase or one relating to feelings of peace. When recited it can act as a key to switch on autogenic effects.

Imagery

Both single images and transformations can promote relaxation. Two examples of the former are (p. 138):

• the rag doll
• the piece of seaweed.

Identifying with the characteristics of an inert image can help to mitigate feelings of stress. Anger, panic and frustration may all respond to this kind of imagery.

Transformations refer to the mutation of one substance into another (p. 139). The first substance is harsh, the second smooth and they are linked by some sensory quality as in the following (Fanning 1988):

• sandpaper . . . to . . . silk
• chalk squeaking on the blackboard . . . to . . . high musical notes
• burnt toast fumes . . . to . . . baking bread
• fluorescent orange . . . to . . . soft peach
• sour gooseberries . . . to . . . sweet raspberries.

The individual focuses attention on the harsh image which she then resolves into the smooth one. The transformation becomes a metaphor for her own feelings which are thereby helped to undergo a change from negative to positive.

Thinking of a smile

Facial expression has been found to influence emotions. A positive expression tends to induce a positive feeling in that individual (p. 138). Thus, if a person smiles, her feelings of stress will tend to be diminished. However, as it is not always appropriate to smile, it is enough to stay with the thought of it and simply to imagine the smile.

Additional strategies

Since diversion tends to reduce the experience of stress (p. 178), techniques which distract the attention can sometimes be useful. Images of strong light or invented telephone numbers are suggested:

Strong light

Imagine an intensely bright light such as that from a powerful torch. Imagine it beamed into your eyes from a distance of 45 cm (18 in). Let it blot out all images.

Telephone number

Invent a telephone number. Make it a long one, so that you will have to concentrate hard. Hold it in your head for one to three minutes, depending on the situation.

The environmental marker

Several writers suggest marking appliances which are potential sources of stress (Öst 1987, Mitchell 1987) (Chs 8 and 10). Coloured dots stuck, for instance, on to the telephone, wristwatch or steering wheel, serve to remind the individual to maintain low levels of tension. Öst suggests changing the colour of the markers frequently since their effect dwindles as the eye gets habituated to the dot.

CHAPTER CONTENTS

Breathing and antenatal training 183
Awareness of breathing 184

Other forms of relaxation 185
Muscle relaxation 185
Massage 185
Visualization 185
For relaxing during discomfort 186

23

Relaxation in pregnancy and childbirth

This chapter differs from the rest of this book in that it focuses on a condition for which relaxation training is offered, rather than the description of particular technique. It has been included because of the widespread use of relaxation in the field of obstetrics where the aim has been to achieve an altered response to physical pain through acquired skills (Culverwell & McKenna 1988).

Relaxation has been taught antenatally since the 1930s when Grantly Dick-Read saw it as a means of breaking the cycle of pain–fear–tension–pain in childbirth. His particular concern was to reduce the fear many women have of labour (Dick-Read 1942). Others followed, teaching a variety of methods, most of which were concerned in different ways with the control of breathing. The purpose of these methods was to provide a distraction from the discomfort of strong uterine contractions (Noble 1988), and also to ensure that the fetus received an adequate supply of oxygen.

BREATHING AND ANTENATAL TRAINING

Breathing using contrived techniques has lost credibility over the years. Research has shown that a pregnant or labouring mother whose natural breathing is artificially augmented is more likely to suffer from the ill-effects of lowered carbon dioxide levels than to gain from increased levels of oxygen (Buxton 1973). Buxton's study included a group who had been taught controlled breathing. It was found that this group, compared with subjects who had been given other forms of antenatal training, exhibited marked hyperventilation with resulting adverse effects (p. 119). Stradling (1983) has since reaffirmed the dangers of overbreathing during labour.

Some hyperventilation may occur physiologically in labour without affecting the normal fetus (Polden & Mantle 1990). It is not however, in the interests of the fetus to increase the degree of hyperventilation, because the resulting low carbon dioxide levels could theoretically lead to both vasoconstriction of uterine blood vessels, and interference in the transfer of oxygen to the tissues and fetus (see p. 120). Moreover, hyperventilation can be followed by apnoea (temporary cessation of breathing) which could also reduce the availability of oxygen. A compromised fetus would be more vulnerable to these effects than a normal fetus (Polden & Mantle 1990).

In the light of such findings, antenatal teachers no longer use controlled breathing exercises but instead, encourage women to breathe freely, naturally and easily, seeing the interests of the fetus best served by breathing rates and rhythms determined by the mother's own physiology. (Stradling 1983, Noble 1988). Breathing exercises, if they are taught at all, are designed primarily to protect against hyperventilation. *Awareness* of breathing however, is widely taught. It is seen as a means of helping the mother to understand her body.

Awareness of breathing

While emphasizing that breathing should be effortless, mothers are invited to explore the different aspects of the expanding chest (Priest & Schott 1991). (Plenty of time should be allowed for this exercise.)

Sit quietly. Allow your breathing to settle to a resting rhythm. Place your hands over your lower ribs, (fingers almost touching), and become aware of the movements that occur underneath them. Think of the air gently flowing in and down towards your hands . . . and then flowing out along the same route . . . make sure the rate is a natural one and that you don't overbreath. Let your body tell you when to breathe in and out . . . Move your hands down a bit lower and feel the whole abdomen gently rising and falling in synchrony with your breaths.

Take a little rest, then lean forwards with your arms resting on a table. This position gives full play to chest movement in the back. Don't be in a hurry. It's important to keep the breathing natural . . .

Finally, sit back and lay one hand over your upper abdomen and the other over your chest just below your collar bones. Take plenty of time. Notice movement taking place under both hands. Perhaps you also notice that the more relaxed you feel, the more movement there is under your lower hand. Conversely, a slow, abdominal breathing rhythm helps to induce relaxation. It is useful to remember this in moments of emotional unease, since calming the breathing can help to settle the emotions. Otherwise, your body takes care of your respirations, giving you more air when you need it and reducing the supply when you don't.

The connection between respiration and the experiences of exertion, pain and emotion can be made by asking the women to consider what happens to their breathing when they run for a bus, bang their skin or get angry. The women will understand how effort, discomfort and emotion can temporarily disrupt the breathing pattern (Priest & Schott 1991). Since disrupted breathing can take the form of increased ventilation, this is an opportunity for discussing hyperventilation: its causes, how to recognise it, and how to relieve its symptoms.

Breathing awareness exercises for inducing relaxation

Many women find breathing awareness exercises have a relaxing effect. Two examples follow.

Sit, lie or stand comfortably. Turn your thoughts towards your breathing and watch it settling down to a resting pattern. Become aware of the movement occurring in your upper abdomen and lower chest. Without doing anything to change the rhythm, focus your attention on these areas. Perhaps your breathing is also getting slower. Above all it is gentle. Notice how calm you feel, breathing in this way. Feel the soothing nature of this quiet breathing.

Settle down in any position you find comfortable. Let your body decide when to breathe in and out. Enjoy the feeling of being in tune with your body's needs. Notice how the rate slows down, reflecting your resting state. Notice also, the gentle rhythm. Next time you breathe out, let the breath carry your tensions away. Next time you breathe in, let the breath bring calmness . . . breathe out tension . . . breathe in calm . . .

OTHER FORMS OF RELAXATION

Other forms of relaxation as well as breathing awareness are widely taught in pregnancy, their object being to help the mother through the birth experience.

Muscle relaxation

Muscle relaxation is the best known of the other methods mentioned above. The tense–release version practised in the early days has, since 1963, given way to Mitchell's method (Ch. 10), for the following reasons:

1. Mitchell's method does not activate the muscles typically associated with tension, i.e. the clenching and hunching muscles. Instead, by a simple change of joint position, it creates a reciprocal state of ease and comfort.

2. Joint change, when applied to a 'key' area in a trained individual, can relax the whole body in the space of a few seconds. Thus, Mitchell's method can have a general and very immediate effect.

3. Mitchell discourages any kind of interference with the natural breathing pattern.

Relaxation can be taught in a variety of positions: lying, sitting, kneeling on all fours, kneeling with arms supported on a chair seat, standing with raised arms resting on the wall or any other position which the woman finds comfortable. This equips her with a range of positions to choose from, both in pregnancy and in labour.

Massage

Kitzinger (1987) suggests massage in the form of gentle, stroking movements directed from the centre to the periphery. As the hand moves down the extremity, the woman imagines her tensions flowing out.

Visualization

Imagery can be used to enhance relaxation during both pregnancy and labour.

Getting in touch with the baby

The following script is based on a passage by Priest & Schott (1991).

Let your thoughts focus on the baby growing inside the uterus. Imagine him or her lying safe and warm and comfortable, lulled by your heartbeat and rocked by your movements. Your baby can move his or her limbs, can swallow and can hear sounds. He or she is familiar with your voice and the voice of the father and will recognize them after birth. Think of your baby growing inside you, getting ready to be born, while you are waiting to receive him or her . . .

Slowly, in your own time, bring your attention back to the room, but do not be in a hurry to get up.

Some women like to sing to their unborn baby, soothing it and welcoming it to the family.

Comparing labour to the sea

Polden & Mantle (1990) offer several examples of imagery for use during the first stage of labour. Ocean waves and mountain peaks are used as metaphors, to help women withstand the intensity of the contractions. The following is adapted from one of their suggestions:

Imagine a beautiful day out at sea . . . with blue sky, still air and calm water. As the day wears on, the surface of the water begins to show the odd ripple. These ripples are small and you hardly notice them. Gradually the tiny ripples turn into small waves; waves which you ride quite easily. After a while, the waves get higher, and as they get higher, they get closer together. You continue to ride them. Still higher and closer together . . . the waves seem almost to overwhelm you, but as they dip you notice that they are carrying you nearer to the shore . . . nearer to the shore where your baby will be born.

For relaxing during discomfort

Some teachers prepare women for the birth by simulating the discomfort of a contraction. They do this by getting the woman's partner or another member of the group to apply an uncomfortable pinch or squeeze to her arm or thigh. The woman is asked to relax towards the pressure in an effort to reduce the sensation. The aim is to help the woman feel she can raise her pain threshold. The pinch or squeeze should last about a minute. It starts with a light touch and gradually builds up in intensity over the first 30 seconds; in the second half-minute it is gradually released. Slow, gentle breathing should accompany the exercise (Williams & Booth 1985, Polden and Mantle 1990).

Before using the techniques contained in this chapter, the pitfalls relating to each should be read in the corresponding sections of the book. The chapters on breathing (Ch. 15) and visualization (Ch. 18) both contain lists of relevant pitfalls (p. 122 and p. 151 respectively).

This chapter does not cover all the relaxation strategies for helping women through labour. For further information in this highly specialized field, readers are referred to the Further Reading section below.

FURTHER READING

McKenna J (ed) 1988 Obstetrics and gynaecology. Churchill Livingstone, Edinburgh
Polden M, Mantle J 1990 Physiotherapy in obstetrics and gynaecology. Butterworth Heinemann, Oxford
Priest J, Schott J 1991 Leading antenatal classes: a practical guide. Butterworth Heinemann, Oxford
Williams M, Booth D 1985 Antenatal education: guidelines for teachers, 2nd edn. Churchill Livingstone, Edinburgh

CHAPTER CONTENTS

Assessment 187
Ways of measuring relaxation 188
Questionnaires 188
Self-rating 189
Physiological measurement 191
Observation 192
Counting the training sessions 192
A practical approach to assessment 192
The placebo effect 192

Research into relaxation 192
General remarks 192
Some research on relaxation and specific
conditions 193

24

Assessment and research

This chapter is devoted to the topic of assessment and considers some of the ways in which it may be achieved. It ends with a short discussion of the problems and results of research.

ASSESSMENT

Assessment means 'estimating' or 'judging' (Kirkpatrick 1983), in this case estimating the degree of stress or relaxation present in an individual. With regard to relaxation training, assessment is needed for the following reasons.

1. To obtain a profile of the individual's problems. It is likely that the relaxation training will be part of a wider programme of anxiety management, in which case the activities of the professionals concerned will be integrated.

2. To measure existing tension levels. Such a measure provides a baseline when evaluating progress. It should be carried out after a short period of rest in order to allow for the relaxation effects which occur, in the absence of any relaxation technique, as part of the process of adapting to a restful environment (Lichstein et al 1981).

3. To choose the most appropriate method of relaxation. The results of the first assessment may reveal information which suggests that a particular approach is indicated.

4. To measure the benefit from the relaxation training in terms of reduced tension levels. Alternatively, assessment may focus on symptoms such as tension headache or hypertension and the degree to which these have been relieved by the relaxation training.

5. To provide feedback for the participant. Positive feedback acts as a reinforcer, negative feedback provides useful corrective information.

6. To collect quantifiable data for research. Therapy can be designed in a way which lends itself to the development of a research project. Research methods themselves however, are not covered in this book.

Thus, assessment covers questions such as:

- What is the problem?
- What is the best way of approaching it, i.e. which relaxation method or methods are indicated?
- How tense is the individual before training?
- How relaxed is the individual as a result of the relaxation training?
- Is her tension headache/hypertension relieved?
- Is she aware of her progress?
- Can this work contribute to research?

Although assessment is time-consuming, its benefits are clear and every effort should be made to carry it out in some form.

Ways of measuring relaxation

Relaxation has psychological, physiological and behavioural components, so a test which is restricted to only one of these cannot claim to be comprehensive. To give an accurate measure of the degree of relaxation present, assessment should cover all three components. Only an assessment which takes account of these multiple dimensions can reflect the complexity of the relaxation state.

Since there is no test which covers all three, the components must be measured separately. Possible forms of measurement include the following:

1. questionnaires
2. self-rating
3. physiological measurement
4. observation
5. counting the training sessions.

Questionnaires

A questionnaire is a list of questions requiring 'yes/no' or similar answers, which can be converted into numerical scores. Its purpose is to obtain information about a specific topic. A standardized questionnaire is the instrument of choice as it will have been tested on different groups of people and average scores will have been established, against which the individuals' scores can be compared. This kind of questionnaire is the only kind that can be used for quantitative assessment and research. In the case of relaxation, such a questionnaire could be used to obtain information both at the start and at the end of a course of treatment, in order to see how people progress and to compare them with groups diagnosed as 'anxious' or 'normal', for example.

The advantages of questionnaires are that they are quick, cheap and easy to complete. It is also easy to collate the results. Their disadvantages include the possibility of inaccuracy if the questions are misunderstood, or of missing out information, should forcing responses into yes/no categories fail to express the complexity of a person's position.

The interview schedule

An alternative and more sensitive approach is to use an interview schedule. Here, the interviewer guides the individual through a list of questions, making sure those questions have been understood and drawing fuller answers than are possible in a questionnaire. Thus, the interview schedule provides more detailed and more complete information than the questionnaire. Quantifying the results however, is more difficult and the interview schedule is subject to variability between interviewers, each of whom may have different ways of interviewing people.

Examples of questionnaires

There is available a wide range of standardized questionnaires, each designed to measure a particular aspect of mental distress. The following are examples.

The Hospital Anxiety and Depression Scale (HAD) (Zigmond & Snaith 1983). This contains 14 items, 7 relating to anxiety and 7 to depression. The score gives an indication of the degree to which the individual is suffering from either condition. The Scale is also able to pick up alterations over time.

The General Hospital Questionnaire (Goldberg & Williams 1988). This consists of 12 items and is designed to detect feelings of distress in the individual. As a simple screening device it is used for much the same purposes as the HAD.

The Beck Depression Inventory (Beck et al 1961). Measures of the level of depression can be obtained from this questionnaire which can be used at different stages of illness and recovery.

The Cognitive Anxiety Questionnaire (Lindsay & Hood 1982).

This contains 12 items and reflects some of the commonest thoughts associated with anxiety. The Scale measures the tendency of the individual to engage in such thoughts.

These are all simple screening devices for use with individuals. The results, when obtained at the beginning and at the end of a training course, give an indication of change over time in the individual concerned.

The results can also be used to assess the effectiveness of relaxation training on groups of people. In this case, means and standard deviation are calculated so that the data can be used for statistical purposes and employed, for instance in building a case for funding.

The Hospital Anxiety and Depression Scale is shown in Figure 24.1. It has been picked as an example because of its widespread use and general applicability. Questions 1, 4, 5, 8, 9, 12 and 13 relate to anxiety, and questions 2, 3, 6, 7, 10, 11 and 14 relate to depression. Scoring instructions are attached to the assessment sheet but not included here. A score of 8–10 in either section indicates a mild degree of the condition, while a score of 11 or above suggests the advisability of referral to a specialist agency. Although the Scale is seen as a screening tool, it is, in the present context, used primarily to measure tendencies to mental distress which may change over the period in which relaxation is practised. Any resulting change should not however, be totally attributed to relaxation, since other factors such as changing environmental circumstances may be contributing to alterations in scores.

Specific questions for participants

To make the assessment information more specific to the group whose problems are being measured, additional questions could be put to the participants, for example:

- In the case of a smoking cessation group, 'How many cigarettes are you now smoking a day?'
- In the case of a person suffering from agoraphobia, 'How many times have you been out of the house in the past week?'

Each person could select two or three personally meaningful targets like these and keep a record of their progress in relation to them. Precise targets, such as the above examples, are measurable and therefore preferable to vague aspirations such as 'I'd like to feel better'.

Self-rating

Related to the questionnaire is the self-rating scale, i.e. the rating an individual gives herself. It often takes the form of a visual analogue. Though it is a highly subjective assessment, it is nevertheless considered valuable since relaxation is regarded as an internal state with a strong subjective component. Self-rating may take different forms, for use before, during and after the relaxation session, and for homework use.

Before the session. As a pretreatment measure one of the following is picked:

- A self-rating scale in the form of a line calibrated from 0 to 10 where 0 represents total relaxation, and 10 maximum tension. The intervening numbers refer to intermediate states. The trainee rings the appropriate number.
- A rating scale which consists of numbered descriptors signifying different degrees of relaxation and tension, as in Poppen's (1988) self-rating scale (p. 74). Again, the trainee rings the appropriate number.

In each case the measure is taken after a short period of rest.

During the session. It is arranged with trainees

SECTION 1

NAME: DATE: AGE:

This section is designed to help identify how you feel. Read each item and place a tick in the box opposite the reply which come closest to how you have been feeling in the past few weeks. Don't take too long over your replies: your mmediate reaction to each item will probably be more accurate than a long thought out response.

Tick only one box in each section

(1) I feel tense or 'wound up':
Most of the time ....
A lot of the time ....
Time to time, Occasionally ....
Not at all ....

(2) I feel as if I am slowed down:
Nearly all the time ....
Very often ....
Sometimes ....
Not at all ....

(3) I still enjoy the things I used to enjoy:
Definitely as much ....
Not quite so much ....
Only a little ....
Hardly at all ....

(4) I get a sort of Frightened feeling like 'butterflies' in the somach:
Not at all ....
Occasionally ....
Quite often ....
Very often ....

(5) I get a sort of frightened feeling as if simething awful is about to happen:.
Very definitely and quite badly ...
Yes, but not too badly ....
A little, but it doesn't worry me ..
Not at all ....

(6) I have lost interest in my appearance:
Definitely ....
I don't take so much care as I should
I may not take quite as much care
I take just as much as ever ....

(7) I can laugh and see the funny side of things:
As much as I always could ....
Not quite so much now ....
Definitely not so much now ....
Not at all ....

(8) I feel restless as if I have to be on the move:
Very much indeed ....
Quite a lot ....
Not very much ....
Not at all ....

(9) Worrying thoughts go through my mind:
A graet deal of the time ....
A lot of the time ....
From time to time but not too often
Only occasionally ....

(10) I look forward with enjoyment to Things:
As much as ever I did ....
Rather less than I used to ....
Definitely less than I used to ....
Hardly at all ....

(11) I feel Cheerful:
Not at all ....
Not often ....
Sometimes ....
Most of the time ....

(12) I get Sudden feelings of panic:
Very often indeed ....
Quite often ....
Not very often ....
Not at all ....

(13) I can sit at ease and feel relaxed:
Definitely ....
Usually ....
Not often ....
Not at all ....

(14) I can enjoy a good book or radio or TV programme:
Often ....
Sometimes ....
not often ....
Very seldom ....

Figure 24.1 The Hospital Anxiety and Depression Scale. Adapted from Zigmond & Snaith (1983) Acta Psychiatrica Scandinavica 67: 361–370 with permission from Munksgaard, Copenhagen, and reproduced from *Anxiety and Stress Management* by Powell & Enright (1990) with permission from Routledge, London.

that they should raise one finger if and when they feel completely relaxed.

After the session. The same self-rating scale that was used before the treatment is now presented again.

Marking scales before and after treatment gives a measure of the effect of the treatment.

During homework periods. A form, such as the one illustrated in Figure 8.3 (p. 65), may be completed. This helps to ensure that practice is carried out as well as providing an indication of the degree of benefit obtained.

A diary, when used to record instances of high stress, is another form of self-report; so is the record sheet (Fig. 8.2, p. 63) in which the occurrence and intensity of anxious feelings are recorded on a numbered scale together with details of the particular coping strategy adopted. The advantages of the self-report method are that it is quick, easy, cheap and nonthreatening to the trainee. It does however, have limitations.

1. Responses may be influenced by social concerns which enter into the individual's judgement, for example:
   - people tend to say what they feel is expected of them
   - they may say what they think the trainer wants to hear
   - they may present a view which shows them in a favourable light.
2. A placebo effect may be operating, whereby belief in the approach leads some people to report more benefit than has in fact occurred (see below, p. 192).

These factors result in a tendency for the responses to be unduly positive.

In his discussion of the verbal aspects of multimodal assessment, Poppen (1988) suggests remedies for this tendency. The individual can be reminded that questions of any sort tend to be answered differently, depending on who is asking the question for instance a friend, a newspaper reporter or a doctor. This highlights the fact that there are many ways in which a question may be answered. The individual can then be asked to distinguish between the answer she feels is expected of her and the answer that reflects what she really feels. The second interpretation is, of course, the one that is required.

Self-rating can only provide a rough guide as to the effects of training. Its value lies particularly on an intrapersonal level, that is, where measurements are taken in the same individual before and after training sessions. Interpersonally, i.e. when comparing one individual with another, self-rating is less useful because of the varying standards of the reporters (Lichstein 1988).

Physiological measurement

Assessing the effect of relaxation training on body systems provides an objective measurement. A variety of indicators are in current use, including pulse rate, blood pressure, respiratory rate, muscle tension, blood flow, skin conductance and electrical activity in the brain. Some are more invasive than others. The results indicate the level of physiological arousal in an individual, and the test or tests are carried out before and after relaxation sessions. The baseline is established before training begins and, in common with all pretreatment measures, should be recorded after a short period of rest (see above).

It might be supposed that this approach offered the perfect solution. The field of physiological assessment however, is not as straightforward as it appears. Keable (1989) discusses these points:

- Physiological measures can be distorted by circumstances. The individual may, prior to a relaxation session, have eaten, which would result in artificially low arousal scores; she may have taken exercise immediately before which would raise her scores; emotional distress would also raise them and drugs would distort them. Tests therefore need to be conducted under controlled conditions.
- Since the physiological response of individuals is to some extent idiosyncratic, a single measure may not include relevant information. To gain an accurate picture therefore, a system which provides multiple measurements is needed.

Poppen (1988) adds the following point.

- Even in the case of specific symptoms, it is not always clear how their measurement should be approached. In tension headache for example, it might be thought that electromyography of the surrounding muscles would be appropriate; however, exactly which muscles should be measured is less clear. Or again, instead of measuring the electrical activity, it might be more constructive to measure the bloodflow through the surrounding muscles (Olton & Noonberg 1980). Researchers hold different views.

Furthermore, while measuring the pulse and the breathing rate are simple procedures, most other physiological measures require equipment and expertise, neither of which may be available.

In spite of these difficulties however, physiological measurement is an important aspect of general assessment.

Observation

Informal unstructured observation is practised by most trainers and used to corroborate information collected from other sources. A structured form of observation such as role play may also be employed. However, since the presence of the observer tends to affect the outcome, it is sometimes carried out in her physical absence but with the use of videos, tape recorders and two-way mirrors. (Ethical considerations demand that the individual's consent must first be obtained.)

It was in an attempt to structure the observation process that Schilling & Poppen (1983) devised the Behavioural Relaxation Scale as an assessment tool (p. 72). As mentioned in Chapter 9, the scale provides a quantified measure of the motor component of relaxation (Poppen 1988).

Counting the training sessions

In the absence of an easy and accurate method of measuring the effects of relaxation training, some clinicians may resort to counting the sessions attended on the assumption that a fixed number of sessions will create a predictable level of relaxation skill. This method can never be more than a rough guide of progress, since there is known to be a mismatch between the amount of teaching and the amount of learning that occurs in any lesson (Poppen 1988).

A practical approach to assessment

Because none of the above measures alone offers the perfect solution, and because relaxation is a multimodal state, assessment ideally includes a variety of measures, each reflecting a different dimension of relaxation. Time-consuming as it is, careful assessment is important. Its value cannot

be overemphasized if clinical practices are to have credibility.

However, it is acknowledged that overworked health care professionals may find it difficult to meet the above requirements, particularly if their groups are large. In this event, the following procedure could be set up:

- Participants are asked to state (verbally or in writing) what they hope to gain from the course. They can be asked to list three targets as described above.

While the course is in progress:

- Some kind of self-rating is carried out regularly.
- Some kind of physiological assessment is carried out regularly (pulse or breathing rate).
- The attendance rate is noted
- Home practice is monitored (Fig. 8.3).

At the end of the course:

- Participants are asked if the course satisfied the three targets they listed in the beginning.

It should be noted that this kind of assessment is minimal. A system which provides fuller information is desirable for clinical purposes, and essential for research purposes.

The placebo effect

Any measurement of relaxation will be affected to some extent by the placebo effect. This is the benefit derived by the individual as a result of her belief in the efficacy of the procedure, and it is separate from the procedure's intrinsic value. Simply believing in the treatment creates benefit, and this enhances the total effect. The placebo effect should be borne in mind in clinical work, while in research it must be controlled for.

RESEARCH INTO RELAXATION

General remarks

While assessment measures the relaxation achieved in the individual, research tests the general value of the relaxation method. Among the questions asked by the researcher are:

- Is method X useful?
- Is it more effective than method Y?
- Does it provide more benefit in condition A than in condition B?

Clinical findings testify to the effectiveness of different kinds of relaxation training. Experimental work, ranging from single case to controlled group studies has also been carried out, and repeatedly shown favourable results. With regard to the different approaches, however, no one method appears more effective than another. Lichstein (1988), reviewing studies on progressive relaxation, autogenic training and meditation, points out that this conclusion may not, for several reasons, reflect the true picture. Research in this area is complicated by a number of factors:

1. nonstandardization of procedure
2. different methods of delivery
3. variations in amount of home practice.

1. Nonstandardization of procedure. A single technique may be presented in several different ways, for example, progressive relaxation may appear in Jacobson's original form, in Wolpe's, in Bernstein & Borkovec's or in any of their derivations. This leads to confusion when making comparisons.

2. Different methods of delivery. The procedure may be 'live' or taped. Research supports the view that a live delivery is more effective than a taped one in creating minimum tension levels (Hillenberg & Collins 1982). The taped delivery, however, has the advantage of standardizing the procedure and, by this means, promoting reliability.

3. Variations in degree of home practice. It is believed that home practice is given inadequate attention (Hillenberg & Collins 1982). Many factors may account for insufficient home practice: failure of the therapist or researcher to convey its importance, misunderstanding of its nature by the participant, or disinclination of the individual to carry it out. Most writers recommend two practice periods a day, each lasting 15–20 minutes, accompanied by some kind of self-monitoring system to record their effect and to ensure that they are carried out.

Problems, however, exist in all fields of research. Their existence does not diminish the need to continue evaluating the work. Rather, it emphasizes the necessity for more research. The problems are mentioned so that the health care professional can be alerted to them. Professionals wishing to carry out research are referred to other works since the scale of the topic places it outside the scope of this book (see Further reading).

Some research on relaxation and specific conditions

A wide range of conditions have been investigated to determine the effect of relaxation therapy on them. Among those which have been found to benefit significantly are (Lichstein 1988):

- essential hypertension
- insomnia
- tension headache
- anxiety
- side-effects of chemotherapy
- phobia.

The areas to benefit least have been:

- children's problems
- haemophilia
- drug abuse.

Currently, much work is focusing on the field of immunology, where enhanced functioning of some aspects of the immune system has been shown to be associated with relaxation (Kiecolt-Glaser et al 1986). More recently, Antoni et al (1991), using Bernstein & Borkovec's version of progressive relaxation plus imagery, found a positive correlation between immune system measures and frequency of relaxation practice in people who had previously been notified of their HIV positive serostatus.

Research is also being conducted in other directions: one avenue involves isolating the components of stress management and assessing their relative values. Isolation of the relaxation component has been attempted, but has so far failed to produce a conclusive result.

FURTHER READING

For assessment and research

French S 1993 Practical research: a guide for therapists. Butterworth Heinemann, Oxford

Hicks C 1995 Research for physiotherapists, 2nd edn. Churchill Livingstone. Edinburgh

CHAPTER CONTENTS

Similarities between approaches 195

Kokoszka's general theory of relaxation 195

Combining approaches 197
  Example of a script containing a variety of
  approaches 197

Other ways of achieving relaxation 198
  Smiling and laughter therapy 198

Summary 198

25

Drawing the threads together

This chapter addresses a few topics not so far discussed. Some commonalities among methods are considered, leading into a description of a general theory of relaxation. This is followed by a consideration of the ways in which techniques can be combined, and a few additional techniques are mentioned.

SIMILARITIES BETWEEN APPROACHES

In an enterprise such as relaxation training where many approaches all lead to the same goal, there are likely to be wide areas of overlap. Some of these have already been pointed out. Lichstein (1988) has identified common threads with respect to meditation, autogenics and progressive relaxation. He finds that dwelling on the breath (as in meditation), reciting phrases (as in autogenic training) and concentrating on muscle sensations (as in progressive relaxation), are activities which resemble one another. Benson (1976) is of the same view in claiming that all three methods are characterized by a monotonous, repetitive stimulus equivalent to the mantra. Thus, the differences between the methods would seem to be more apparent than real; their similarities being concealed by their terminology.

KOKOSZKA'S GENERAL THEORY OF RELAXATION

The underlying similarities of the above three

methods are reflected in the states of consciousness they produce. All three create altered states, which are, however, only slightly altered from the waking state. Eastern meditation and hallucinatory drugs on the other hand, produce deeply altered states.

An attempt to integrate the major states of consciousness in the context of relaxation and place them on one conceptual canvas has been made by Kokoszka (1987–88). His model (Fig. 25.1) shows progressive relaxation and autogenic training to lie between the waking state and non-rapid eye movement (non-REM) sleep. Characterized by mental contact with the body, both progressive relaxation and autogenics have their roots in physiological, goal-oriented, left hemisphere concerns, such as the release of muscle tension, although autogenics in particular, relying on sensory images, reaches into the influence of the right hemisphere. Overlapping the

other two, but lying in the waking quadrants is Benson's relaxation response technique, its passive emphasis placing it predominantly among right hemisphere concerns but not entirely, since its imaginal content is weak.

Deep meditation of a kind that reaches profound spiritual levels is seen as being different in kind from Benson's meditation; Kokoszka calls it an 'ultra consciousness state' and places it firmly in the domain of the right hemisphere, far away from rational ideas and goal-oriented thought.

Moving on to the sleep zones: rapid eye movement sleep is characterized by dreaming and therefore has strong right hemisphere connections; it is distinctly remote from physical and rational concerns. Non-rapid eye movement sleep however, is far removed from imaginal concerns. The individual is of course, unaware of her surroundings but the state is accompanied by muscular (albeit weak) activity.

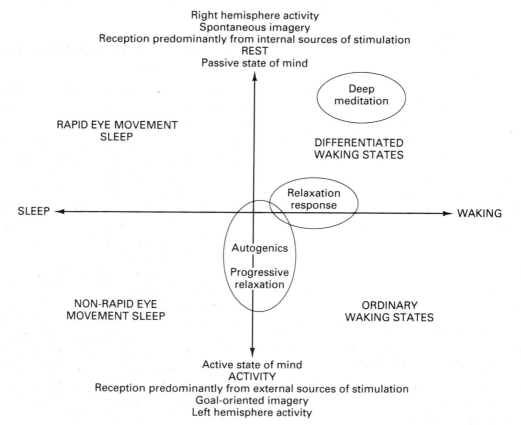

Figure 25.1 Integrated model of the main states of consciousness. Adapted from Kokoszka A 1987–1988. In: Imagination, Cognition and Personality 7: 292, with permission from Baywood, Amityville, New York, and the author.

COMBINING APPROACHES

It is not suggested in this book that attention should be systematically given to the methods in turn. The health care professional may take up any method she feels comfortable with. She may however, wish to take up more than one method and to present them in a single tuition period. This can have advantages.

1. Combinations of different relaxation and stress reduction techniques seem to be more effective than single techniques (Lehrer et al 1983, Woolfolk & Lehrer 1984, Davis et al 1988, Poppen 1988, Titlebaum 1988). Lehrer & Woolfolk (1983) found that more powerful effects were produced when techniques were used in combination than when any one technique was used alone.

2. Individuals have preferences for particular techniques. Although these preferences cannot be predicted, it is clear that they exist (Fanning 1988, Kutner & Zahourek 1988, Lichstein 1988, Payne 1989). By offering more than one technique there is a greater chance of the participant finding a method that suits her.

Ways of combining techniques may be found in *The Relaxation and Stress Reduction Workbook* (Davis et al 1988) from which the following two combinations are drawn. The first is for mental stress, the second is for physical tension.

1. 'Changing channels':
   — attention-switching (Appendix, p. 202),
   — guided imagery (Ch. 17, p. 141), and
   — coping mantra e.g. 'I am at peace' (Ch. 20, p. 168).
2. 'Stretch and relax':
   — stretchings (Ch. 13),
   — abdominal breathing (Ch. 15, p. 118), and
   — Mitchell's method (Ch. 10).

For groups of people with varied kinds of stress, more general combined programmes can be built. A few examples are given below:

1. Abdominal breathing (Ch. 15, p. 118), tense-release (Ch. 6), and guided imagery (Ch. 17, p. 141).
2. Passive relaxation (Ch. 7),

goal-directed visualizations using receptive and programmed components (Ch. 18), and self-statements (Ch. 18, p. 145).
3. Abdominal breathing (Ch. 15, p. 118), warmth and heaviness phrases (Ch. 19), and differential relaxation (Ch. 12).
4. Passive relaxation (Ch. 7), Benson's meditation (Ch. 21), and self-awareness exercises (Ch. 16).
5. Behavioural relaxation training (Ch. 9, p. 70), breathing meditation (Ch. 15, p. 119), and guided imagery (Ch. 17, p. 141).
6. Breathing pouch (Ch. 15, p. 119), eye and tongue muscle work (Ch. 4, p. 33), and meditation on a visual object (Ch. 20, p. 165).

Set patterns will not suit everyone since the needs and preferences of each person are different. Davis et al (1988) urge people to construct their own combination of techniques.

Example of a script containing a variety of approaches

As well as grouping different techniques together, several techniques can be worked into a single passage as shown here.

Please lie down. Get yourself comfortable. Allow your eyelids to grow heavy and eventually to close.

Feel the rest of your body also growing heavy . . . feel it sinking into the rug or the upholstery . . . compressing the fibres . . . sinking down so that more body area comes in contact with it . . . let your weight flow out . . . feel your body totally freed from its responsibility to hold you up . . .

Turn your attention to your breathing . . . without attempting to alter its rhythm, become aware of the movement of your chest and abdomen . . . notice the passage of the air . . . the coolness of the air entering your nostrils . . . travelling through your nose and down the back of your throat . . . notice also, the warm, moist air being exhaled . . . next time you breathe out, think the word 'relax' . . . continue slowly . . .

Now, I'd like you to scan your muscle groups one by one, checking them for tension . . . adjust your position if you are uncomfortable . . . starting with the feet, notice how they rest heavily on the floor . . . heavy as lead . . . now your legs, imagine them too heavy to lift . . . your hips too are lying heavily . . . and your shoulders, feel how they are dropped down . . . with your arms resting heavily by your sides . . .

Now, your head, let it sink back, giving its weight to the pillow, making a dent in it . . . feel your brow smoothed and your jaw relaxed . . . feel your whole body heavy, warm and relaxed . . . if tension returns, just let it go . . . let it flow out through your fingertips and toes . . .

Transfer yourself in your mind's eye to a sandy beach . . . see yourself lying in the soft sand . . . run your fingers through the dry grains . . . smell the sea air . . . feel the hot sun on your skin . . . listen to the waves breaking on the shore . . . enjoy the peace . . . if disturbing thoughts intrude, accept that they exist . . . then let them drift away like clouds passing across the sky . . . you'll attend to them later . . .

When you are ready, let the scene fade . . . gradually bring your attention back to the room in which you are lying . . . count one . . . two . . . three . . . and slowly open your eyes . . . then give your arms and legs a gentle stretch . . .

OTHER WAYS OF ACHIEVING RELAXATION

There are countless other means by which an individual may achieve relaxation: massage, aromatherapy, reflexology, T'ai Chi Chuan, Yoga, hypnosis, shiatsu, biofeedback, dance therapy, music therapy, to mention just a few. Two others are hobbies and humour. Hobbies provide a major source of relaxation since creating for sheer pleasure induces undeniable feelings of well-being and fulfilment. In her hobby the individual spontaneously expresses herself and this experience gives her a sense of being at one with herself. Feelings of peace and relaxation are the natural result. Humour also, relaxes the individual.

Smiling and laughter therapy

William James (1890/1950) remarked a century ago that the way to cheerfulness is to act and speak as if cheerfulness were already there. In

other words, smiling makes us feel happy. This idea has given rise to the facial and postural feedback hypotheses which state that feedback from facial expression and posture induces the emotion associated with that expression and posture (Izard 1977, Duclos et al 1989, Hatfield et al 1992).

Humour and laughter are related to positive moods, and few would deny that laughter releases tension. Ekman (1984) has posited the existence of neural connections between the facial muscles and the autonomic system; an idea which is supported by research. It has been shown that levels of hormones related to sympathetic activity are reduced by humour and laughter, thus suggesting an association between laughter and parasympathetic activity (Berk et al 1988). In this light, laughter can be seen as a natural tranquilliser (Hodgkinson 1987).

Smiling and laughter have been referred to as overlapping but distinct domains, the one of friendliness, the other of amusement (Van Hooff 1972). Both are effective stress relievers.

SUMMARY

This chapter has touched on a few questions that a book of this nature might raise: the way methods relate to each other; the combining of techniques and a brief reference to other methods of achieving relaxation.

In the rest of the book, selected methods of relaxation have been presented. The author has tried to convey the essence of each one, and, for most approaches, to offer enough detail to enable them to be used by someone previously unfamiliar with them.

Wherever possible, the description has been followed by some kind of evaluation which is based on the research literature. Some methods such as progressive relaxation, autogenics and meditation have received a great deal of attention by researchers, while others such as Mitchell's method and the Alexander technique have been studied very little.

In spite of the work that has already been carried out, it has not been easy to draw conclusions because of the problems which beset scientific investigation in this area. A larger body of research is necessary. This research is slowly growing, and it is hoped that data will emerge from future projects which allow firmer conclusions to be drawn.

FURTHER READING

For combinations of techniques
Davis M, Eshelman E, McKay M 1988 The relaxation and stress reduction workbook, 3rd edn. New Harbinger, Oakland, California

For other methods of achieving relaxation
Sutcliffe J 1991 The complete book of relaxation techniques. Headline, London

Appendix and References

APPENDIX

ATTENTION SWITCHING

This is a cognitive strategy which may be found useful by individuals who are plagued by disturbing thoughts. The technique consists of giving attention to particular items for specified lengths of time. The individual spends 15–20 seconds exclusively thinking about a prearranged item, then abruptly switches to another prearranged item for the same length of time. If a stopwatch is not available, she guesses the times. The items range from pleasant to neutral. The next stage is to deliberately introduce the disturbing thought, let it take shape, and as soon as it does, to replace it with a pleasant or neutral thought. The method may be described to the participant as follows:

Make a list of topics that are pleasant (such as hobbies, holidays, happy experiences) or neutral (such as the weather, telephone numbers, geometric shapes); say, 10 examples of each. Take the first one on the list and focus attention on it for 20 seconds. At the end of that time abruptly switch your attention to the next item. Concentrate on this for 20 seconds, then switch to the next item, working your way through the list. The object is to concentrate so firmly on the item that all other thoughts are excluded. It helps if the item is made as vivid as possible, and this is done by bringing out its sensory detail (the sights, sounds, smells, textures, etc.).

Work through the list every day for a week. When you feel you have built up the skill, try deliberately introducing the disturbing thought; give it a moment to take shape, then abruptly replace it with the next item on your list.

In this way you cultivate the ability to control your thoughts. You may not be able to stop uncomfortable thoughts entering your head, but you can decide how much attention you give them.

The ability to control the thoughts is present in every person. Attention switching simply helps to strengthen it. The technique is widely used. It offers most benefit, however, to people who have a facility for creating visual imagery.

REFERENCES

Abromowitz S I, Wieselberg N 1978 Reaction to relaxation and desensitization outcome: five angry treatment failures. American Journal of Psychiatry 135: 1418–1419

Achterberg J 1985 Imagery in healing: shamanism and modern medicine. New Science Library, Boston

Adams M A, Hutton W C 1985 The effect of posture on the lumbar spine. Journal of Bone and Joint Surgery 67B: 625–629

Adams M A, McNally D S, Chinn H, Dolan P 1994 Posture and the compressive strength of the lumbar spine. Clinical Biomechanics 9: 5–14

Alberti R, Emmons M 1982 Your perfect right: a guide to assertive living, 4th edn. Impact, San Luis Obispo, California

Alexander C J 1989 Relationship between the utilization profile of individual joints and their susceptibility to primary osteoarthritis. Skeletal Radiology 18: 199–205

Alexander F M 1932 The use of the self. Dutton, New York

Allied Dunbar National Fitness Survey 1992 Activity and health research: a report on activity patterns and fitness levels. Sports Council and Health Education Authority, London

American College of Sports Medicine 1991 Guidelines for exercise testing and prescription, 4th edn. Lea and Febiger, Philadelphia

Antoni M H, Baggett L, Ironson G, LaPerriere A, August S, Klimas N, Schneiderman N, Fletcher M A 1991 Cognitive-behavioural stress management intervention buffers distress responses and immunologic changes following notification of HIV-1 seropositivity. Journal of Consulting and Clinical Psychology 59: 906–915

Argyle M 1978 The psychology of interpersonal behaviour, 3rd edn. Pelican, Harmondsworth, Middlesex

Assagioli R 1965 Psychosynthesis. Turnstone Books, London

Assagioli R 1973 Act of will. Wildwood House, Aldershot, Hants

Astrand P O, Rodahl 1986 Textbook of work physiology. McGraw-Hill, New York

Bakal D A 1979 Psychology and medicine: psychobiological dimensions to health and sickness. Tavistock Publications, London

Banquet J 1973 Spectral analysis of the EEG in meditation. Electroencephalography and Clinical Neurophysiology 35: 143–151

Barber T X 1961 Psychological aspects of hypnosis. Psychological Bulletin 58: 390–419

Barber T X 1969 Hypnosis: a scientific approach. Van Nostrand-Reinhold, New York

Barber T X 1970 LSD, marijuana, yoga and hypnosis. Aldine, Chicago

Barber T X 1984 Hypnosis, deep relaxation and active relaxation: data, theory and clinical applications. In: Woolfolk R L, Lehrer P M (eds) Principles and practice of stress management. Guilford, New York

Barber T X, Chauncey H M, Winer R A 1964 The effect of hypnotic and non-hypnotic suggestion on parotid gland response to gustatory stimuli. Psychosomatic Medicine 26: 374–380

Barlow W 1975 The Alexander principle. Arrow, London

Beck A T 1976 Cognitive therapy and the emotional disorders. International Universities Press, New York

Beck A T 1984 Cognitive approaches to stress management. In: Woolfolk R L, Lehrer P M (eds) Principles and practice of stress management. Guilford, New York

Beck A T, Ward C H, Mendelson M, Mock J E, Erbaugh J K 1961 An inventory for measuring depression. Archives of General Psychiatry 4: 53–63

Beck A T, Rush A J, Shaw B F, Emery G 1979 Cognitive theory of depression. John Wiley, New York

Beiman I, Israel E, Johnson S J 1978 During-training and post-training effects of live and taped extended progressive relaxation, self-relaxation and electromyogram biofeedback. Journal of Consulting and Clinical Psychology 46: 314–321

Benson H 1976 The relaxation response. Collins, London

Benson H, Beary J F, Carol M P 1974 The relaxation response. Psychiatry 37: 37–46

Berenson S 1988 The cancer patient. In: Zahourek R P (ed) Relaxation and imagery: tools for therapeutic communication and intervention. W B Saunders, Philadelphia

Berk L S, Tan S A, Nehlsen-Cannarella S L, Napier B J, Lee J W, Lewis J E, Hubbard R W, Eby W C 1988 Mirth modulates adrenocortic-medullary activity: suppression of cortisol and epinephrine. Clinical Research 36: 121A

Bernstein D A, Borkovec T D 1973 Progressive relaxation training: a manual for the helping professions. Research Press, Champaign, Illinois

Bernstein D A, Given B A 1984 Progressive relaxation: abbreviated methods. In: Woolfolk R L, Lehrer P M (eds) Principles and practice of stress management. Guilford Press, New York.

Beverley M C, Rider T A, Evans M J, Smith R 1989 Local bone mineral response to brief exercise that stresses the skeleton. British Medical Journal 299: 233–235

Blackburn I, Davidson K M 1990 Cognitive therapy for depression and anxiety: a practitioner's guide. Blackwell Scientific, Oxford

Blair S N, Kohl H W, Paffenbarger R S, Clark D G, Cooper K H, Gibbons L W 1989 Physical fitness and all-cause mortality: a prospective study of healthy men and women. Journal of the American Medical Association 17: 2395–2401

Blair S N, Kohl H W, Gordon N F, Paffenbarger R S Jr 1992 How much physical activity is good for health? Annual Review of Public Health 13: 99–126

Blanchard E B, Young L D, 1973 Self-control of cardiac functioning: a promise as yet unfulfilled. Psychological Bulletin 79: 145–163

Bloom L J, Gonzales A M 1981 Anxiety management with schizophrenic outpatients. Journal of Clinical Psychology 38: 280–285

Bond M 1986 Stress and self-awareness: a guide for nurses. Butterworth Heinemann, Oxford, p. 98

Borkovec T D 1982 Insomnia. Journal of Consulting and Clinical Psychology 50: 880–895

Borkovec T D, Heide F 1980 Relaxation-induced anxiety: psychophysiological evidence of anxiety enhancement in tense subjects practising relaxation. Paper presented at the Annual Meeting of the Association for the Advancement of Behaviour Therapy, New York, December

Borkovec T D, Sides J K 1979 Critical procedural variables related to the physiological effects of progressive relaxation: a review. Behaviour Research and Therapy 17: 119–125

Borkovec T D, Kaloupek D G, Slama K 1975 The facilitative effect of muscle tension-release in the relaxation treatment of sleep disturbance. Behaviour Therapy 6: 301–309

Borkovec T D, Grayson J, Cooper K 1978 Treatment of general tension: subjective and physiological effects of progressive

relaxation. Journal of Consulting and Clinical Psychology 46: 518–528

Brauer A P, Horlick L, Nelson E, Farquhar J W, Agras W S 1979 Relaxation therapy for essential hypertension: a Veterans' Administration outpatient study. Journal of Behavioural Medicine 2: 21–29

Bricklin M 1990 Meditation: the healing silence. In: Bricklin M (ed) Positive living and health. Rodale Press, Emmaus, Pennsylvania

Brooke S T, Long B C 1987 Efficiency of coping with a real life stressor: a multimodal comparison of aerobic fitness. Psychophysiology 24: 173–180

Brown E B 1954 Physiological effects of hyperventilation. Physiological Review 33: 445–471

Burnard P 1991 Coping with stress in the health professions: a practical guide. Chapman and Hall, London

Burnard P 1992 Know yourself! self-awareness activities for nurses. Scutari Press, London

Buxton R St J 1973 Maternal respiration in labour. Nursing Mirror September 7th, pp 22–25

Cannon W B 1929 Bodily changes in pain, hunger, fear and rage. Appleton, New York

Cappo B M, Holmes D S 1984 The utility of prolonged respiratory exhalation for reducing physiological arousal in non-threatening and threatening situations. Journal of Psychosomatic Research 28: 265–273

Carrington P 1984 Modern forms of meditation. In: Woolfolk R L, Lehrer P M (eds) Principles and practice of stress management. Guilford Press, New York

Chow R, Harrison J E, Notarius C 1987 Effect of two randomized exercise programmes on bone mass of healthy post-menopausal women. British Medical Journal 295: 1441–1444

Clark D M 1986 A cognitive approach to panic. Behaviour Research and Therapy 24: 461–470

Clark D M 1989 Anxiety states: panic and generalized anxiety. In: Hawton K, Salkovskis P M, Kirk J, Clark D M (eds) Cognitive behaviour therapy for psychiatric problems. Oxford Medical, Oxford

Clark D M, Salkovskis P M, Chalkley A J, 1985 Respiratory control as a treatment for panic attacks. Journal of Behaviour Therapy and Experimental Psychiatry 16: 23–30

Cluff R A 1985 Chronic hyperventilation and its treatment by physiotherapy. Physiotherapy 71: 301–305

Cooper C L 1981 The stress check. Prentice-Hall, Spectrum, New Jersey

Cox T 1978 Stress. Macmillan, London

Cox T, Mackay C J 1976 A psychological model of occupational stress. A paper presented to The Medical Research Council. Mental Health in Industry, London, November

Culverwell G, McKenna J 1988 Aspects of body learning for the childbearing year. In: McKenna J (ed) Obstetrics and gynaecology. Churchill Livingstone, Edinburgh

Davidson R J, Schwartz G E 1976 The psychobiology of relaxation and related states: a multiprocess theory. In: Mostofsky D I (ed) Behaviour control and modification of physiological activity. Prentice-Hall, Englewood Cliffs, New Jersey

Davis M, Eschelman E, McKay M 1988 The relaxation and stress reduction workbook, 3rd edn. New Harbinger, Oakland, California

De Coverley Veale D M W 1987 Exercise and mental health. Acta Psychiatrica Scandanavica 76: 113–120

Deikman A J 1963 Experimental meditation. Journal of Nervous and Mental Diseases 136: 329–343

Dick-Read G D 1942 Childbirth without fear. Heinemann, Oxford

Dobson K S 1985 The relationship between anxiety and depression. Clinical Psychology Review 5: 307–324

Donovan M I 1980 Relaxation with guided imagery: a useful technique. Cancer Nursing 3: 27–32

Dossey B M 1988 Imagery: awakening the inner healer. In: Dossey B M, Keagan L, Guzzetta C E, Kolkmeier L G (eds) Holistic nursing: a handbook for practice. Aspen, Rockville, Maryland

Downie P A 1983 Cash's textbook of chest, heart and vascular disorders for physiotherapists, 3rd edn. Faber and Faber, London

Doyne E J, Bowman E D, Ossip Klein D J, Osborn K M 1983 A comparison of aerobic exercise and non-aerobic exercise in the treatment of depression. Presented at the 17th Annual Meeting, Association for the Advancement of Behaviour Therapy

Drug and Therapeutics Bulletin 1991 Hyperventilation syndrome: not to be dismissed. Consumers Association, Hertford 29: 83–84

Duclos S E, Laird J D, Schneider E, Sexter M, Stern L, Van Lighten O 1989 Emotion-specific effects of facial expressions and postures on emotional experience. Journal of Personality and Social Psychology 57: 100–108

Durham R C, Turvey A A 1987 Cognitive therapy versus behaviour therapy in the treatment of chronic general anxiety. Behaviour Research and Therapy 25: 229–234

Edinger J D, Jacobsen R 1982 Incidence and significance of relaxation treatment side-effects. The Behaviour Therapist 5: 137–138

Ekman P 1982 Emotion in the human face, 2nd edn. Cambridge University Press, Cambridge

Ekman P 1984 Expression and the nature of emotion. In: Scherer K, Ekman P (eds) Approaches to emotion. Laurance Erlbaum, Hillsdale, New Jersey

Ellis A 1962 Reason and emotion in psychotherapy. Lyle Stuart, New York

Ellis A 1973 Humanistic psychotherapy. McGraw-Hill, New York

Ellis A 1976 The biological basis of human irrationality. Journal of Individual Psychology 32: 145–168

Ellis A, Harper R A 1961 A guide to rational living. Wiltshire Books, North Hollywood

Erickson M, Rossi E 1979 Hypnotherapy: an exploratory casebook. Irvington, New York

Erickson M, Rossi E 1981 Experiencing hypnosis: therapeutic approaches to altered states. Irvington, New York

Ernst S, Goodison L 1981 In our own hands: a book of self-help therapy. The Women's Press, London

Everly G S, Rosenfeld R 1981 The nature and treatment of the stress response. Plenum Press, New York

Fahrni W H, Trueman G E 1965 Comparative radiological study of the spines of a primitive population with North Americans and northern Europeans. Journal of Bone and Joint Surgery 47-B: 552–555

Fanning P 1988 Visualization for change. New Harbinger, Oakland, California

Feldman B M, Richard E 1986 Prevalence of nurse smokers and variables identified with successful and unsuccessful smoking cessation. Research in Nursing and Health 9: 131–138

Ferrucci P 1982 What we may be. Mandala, London

Finke R A 1989 Principles of mental imagery. Massachusetts Institute of Technology, Cambridge, Massachusetts

Fontana D 1991 The elements of meditation. Element, Shaftesbury

Fontana D 1992 The meditator's handbook: a comprehensive guide to eastern and western meditation techniques. Element, Shaftesbury

Fordham F 1966 An introduction to Jung's psychology, 2nd edn. Pelican, London

Freud S 1973 Introductory lectures on psychoanalysis. Translated by James Strachey. Penguin, Harmondsworth

Friedman M, Rosenman R H 1974 Type A behaviour and your heart. Knoft, New York

Gagen J M 1984 Imagery: an overview with suggested application for nursing. Perspectives in Psychiatric Care 22: 20–23

Gallwey W T 1974 The inner game of tennis. Random House, New York

Ganster D C, Victor B 1988 The impact of social support on mental and physical health. British Journal of Medical Psychology 61: 3–17

Gardner W N 1992 Hyperventilation syndromes. Respiratory Medicine 86: 273–275

Gardner W N, Bass C 1989 Hyperventilation in clinical practice. British Journal of Hospital Medicine 41: 73–81

Gerard R 1963 Symbolic visualization: a method of psychosynthesis. Topical Problems in Psychotherapy 4: 70–80

Goldberg D P, Williams P 1988 A user's guide to the general health questionnaire. NFER-Nelson, Windsor

Goldfried M R 1971 Systematic desensitization as training in self-control. Journal of Consulting and Clinical Psychology 37: 228–234

Gray J 1990 Your guide to the Alexander technique. Gollancz, London

Green E E, Green A M, Walters E D 1970 Voluntary control of internal states: psychological and physiological. Journal of Transpersonal Psychology 9: 1–26

Griez E, Van den Hout M A 1982 Effects of carbon dioxide–oxygen inhalations on subjective anxiety and some neuro-vegetative parameters. Journal of Behaviour Therapy and Experimental Psychiatry 13: 27–32

Hamm B H, O'Flynn A I 1984 Teaching the client to cope through guided imagery. Journal of Community Health Nursing 1: 39–45

Hampson P J, Marks D F, Richardson J T E (eds) 1990 Imagery: current developments. Routledge, London

Hargie O, Saunders C, Dickson D 1981 Social skills in interpersonal communication, 2nd edn. Croom Helm, London

Harris V A, Katkin E S, Lick J R, Habberfield T 1976 Paced respiration as a technique for the modification of autonomic response to stress. Psychophysiology 13: 386–391

Hartland J 1971 Medical and dental hypnosis and its clinical applications, 2nd edn. Bailliere Tindall, London

Hatfield E, Cacioppo J T, Rapson R L 1992 Primitive emotional contagion. In: Clark M S (ed) Emotion and social behaviour. Sage, Newbury Park, California

Hawton K, Salkovskis P M, Kirk J, Clark D M (eds) 1989 Cognitive behaviour therapy for psychiatric problems. Oxford Medical, Oxford

Haynes S N, Moseley D, McGowan W T 1975 Relaxation training and biofeedback in the reduction of frontalis muscle tension. Psychophysiology 12: 547–552

Hegna T, Sveram M 1990 Psychological and psychosomatic problems. Churchill Livingstone, Edinburgh

Heide F J, Borkovec T D 1984 Relaxation-induced anxiety: mechanisms and theoretical implications. Behaviour Research and Therapy 22: 1–12

Hendler C S, Redd W H 1986 Fear of hypnosis: the role of labelling in patients' acceptance of behavioural interventions. Behaviour Therapy 17: 2–13

Henry M, De Rivera J L G, Gonzales-Martin I J, Abreu J 1993 Improvement of respiratory function in chronic asthmatic patients with autogenic therapy. Journal of Psychosomatic Research 37: 265–270

Heron J 1977 Catharsis in human development. Human Potential Research Project, University of Surrey, Guildford

Hewitt J 1977 The complete yoga book. Schocken, New York

Hicks C Research for physiotherapists, 2nd edn. Churchill Livingstone, Edinburgh, in press

Hiebert B, Fox E E 1981 Reactive effects of self-monitoring anxiety. Journal of Counselling Psychology 28: 187–193

Hillenberg J B, Collins F L 1982 A procedural analysis and review of relaxation training research. Behaviour Research and Therapy 20: 251–260

Hillenberg J B, Collins F L 1983 The importance of home practice for progressive relaxation training. Behaviour Research and Therapy 21: 633–642

Hodgkinson L 1987 Smile therapy: how smiling and laughter can change your life. Optima, London

Holmes D S 1984 Meditation and somatic arousal reduction: a review of the experimental evidence. American Psychologist 39: 1–10

Holmes D S 1987 The influence of meditation versus rest on physiological arousal: a second examination. In: West M A (ed) The psychology of meditation. Oxford Science, Oxford

Holmes D S, Solomon S, Cappo B M, Greenberg J L 1983 Effects of transcendental meditation versus resting on physiological and subjective arousal. Journal of Personality and Social Psychology 44: 1245–1252

Holmes T H, Rahe R H 1967 The social readjustment rating scale. Journal of Psychosomatic Research 11: 213–218

Horowitz M 1970 Image formation and cognition. Appleton Century Crofts, New York, p 30

Hough A 1991 Physiotherapy in respiratory care: a problem-solving approach. Chapman and Hall, London

Hughes I 1994 Personal communication

Hughes J R 1984 Psychological effects of habitual aerobic exercise: a critical review. Preventive Medicine 13: 66–78

Hutchings D F, Denney D R, Basgall J, Houston B K 1980 Anxiety management and applied relaxation in reducing general anxiety. Behaviour Research and Therapy 18: 181–190

Inglis B, West R 1983 Alternative health guide. Michael Joseph, London

Innocenti D M 1983 Chronic hyperventilation syndrome. In: Downie P A (ed) Cash's textbook of chest, heart and vascular disorders for physiotherapists, 3rd edn. Faber and Faber, London

Izard C E 1977 Human emotions. Plenum, New York

Jackson T 1991 An evaluation of the Mitchell method of simple physiological relaxation for women with rheumatoid arthritis. British Journal of Occupational Therapy 54: 105–107

Jacobson E 1934 Electrical measurements concerning muscular contraction (tonus) and the cultivation of relaxation in man: relaxation times of individuals. American Journal of Physiology 108: 573–580

Jacobson E 1938 Progressive relaxation, 2nd edn. University of Chicago Press, Chicago

Jacobson E 1942 The effect of daily rest without training to relax on muscular tonus. American Journal of Psychology 55: 248–254

Jacobson E 1964 Anxiety and tension control. J B Lippincott, Philadelphia

Jacobson E 1965 How to relax and have your baby. McGraw-Hill, New York

Jacobson E 1970 Modern treatment of tense patients including the neurotic and depressed, with case illustrations, follow-ups and EMG measurements. Charles C Thomas, Springfield, Illinois

Jacobson E 1976 You must relax. Souvenir Press, London

James W 1890/1950 The principles of psychology. Dover, New York

Janis I 1971 Stress and frustration. Harcourt Brace, New York

Jefferies W McK 1991 Cortisol and immunity. Medical Hypotheses 34: 198–208

Jung C G 1963 Memories, dreams, reflections. Vintage Books, New York

Jung C G (ed) 1978a Man and his symbols. Pan Books, London

Jung C G 1978b Selected writings. Storr A (ed). Fontana, London

Kasamatsu A, Hirai T 1966 An electroencephalographic study on the Zen meditation (Zazen). Folia Psychiatrica et Neurological Japonica 20: 315–336

Kazarian L 1975 Creep characteristics of the human spinal column. Orthopaedic Clinics of North America 6: 3–15

Kazdin A E, Wilcoxin L A 1975 Systematic desensitization and nonspecific treatment effects: a methodological evaluation. Psychological Bulletin 83:5

Keable D 1985a Relaxation training techniques – a review. Part one: what is relaxation? Occupational Therapy 48: 99–102

Keable D 1985b Relaxation training techniques – a review. Part two: how effective is relaxation? Occupational Therapy 48: 201–204

Keable D 1989 The management of anxiety: a manual for therapists. Churchill Livingstone, Edinburgh

Kelly G A 1955 The psychology of personal constructs. Norton, New York

Kelly G A 1969 The psychotherapeutic relationship. In: Maher B (ed) Clinical psychology and personality. Wiley, New York

Kermani K S 1987 Stress, emotions, autogenic training and AIDS: a holistic approach to the management of HIV infected individuals. Holistic Medicine 2:203–215

Kermani K S 1990 Autogenic training. Souvenir, London

Kiecolt-Glaser J K, Glaser R, Strain E C, Stout J C, Tarr K L, Holliday J E, Speicher C E 1986 Modulations of cellular immunity in medical students. Journal of Behavioural Medicine 9: 5–21

King J V 1988 A holistic technique to lower anxiety: relaxation with guided imagery. Journal of Holistic Nursing 6: 16–20

Kirk J 1989 Cognitive-behavioural assessment. In: Hawton K, Salkovskis P M, Kirk J, Clark D M (eds) Cognitive behaviour therapy for psychiatric problems. Oxford Medical, Oxford

Kirkpatrick E M (ed) 1983 Chambers 20th century dictionary. W & R Chambers, Edinburgh

Kitzinger S 1987 The experience of childbirth. Penguin, Harmondsworth

Kobasa S C, 1982 The hardy personality. In: Sanders G, Suls J (eds) The social psychology of health and illness.

Lawrence Erlbaum, New Jersey

Kokoszka A 1992 Relaxation as an altered state of consciousness: a rationale for a general theory of relaxation. International Journal of Psychosomatics 39: 4–9

Kosslyn S M 1983 Ghosts in the mind's machine. W W Norton, New York

Kowalski R 1987 Over the top: a self-help programme for people with panic attacks, anxiety, tension and stress. Winslow Press, London

Krall E A, Dawson-Hughes B 1993 Heritable and lifestyle determinants of bone mineral density. Journal of Bone Mineral Research 8: 1–10

Krolner B, Toft B, Nielson S P, Tondevold E 1983 Physical exercise as prophylaxis against involutional vertebral bone loss: a controlled study. Clinical Science 64: 541–546

Kutner G, Zahourek R P 1988 Relaxation/imagery with alcoholics in group treatment. In Zahourek R P (ed) Relaxation and imagery: tools for therapeutic communication and intervention. W B Saunders, Philadelphia

Lachman S J 1972 Psychosomatic disorders: a behaviouristic interpretation. John Wiley, New York

Lanphier E H, Rahn H 1963 Alveolar gas exchange during breath holding with air. Journal of Applied Physiology 18: 478–482

Larkin D M 1988 Therapeutic suggestion. In: Zahourek R P (ed) Relaxation and imagery: tools for therapeutic communication and intervention. W B Saunders, Philadelphia.

Law M R, Wald N J, Meade T W 1991 Strategies for prevention of osteoporosis and hip fracture. British Medical Journal 303: 453–459

Lazarus A A 1966 Psychological stress and the coping process. McGraw-Hill, New York

Lazarus R S 1971 Behaviour therapy and beyond. McGraw-Hill, New York

Lehrer P M 1979 Anxiety and cultivated relaxation: reflections on clinical experiences and psychophysiological research. In: McGuigan F J (ed) Tension control: proceedings of the fifth annual meeting of The American Association for the Advancement of Tension Control. AAATC, Chicago

Lehrer P M 1982 How to relax and how not to relax: a re-evaluation of the work of Edmund Jacobson. Behaviour Research and Therapy 20: 417–428

Lehrer P M, Woolfolk R L 1983a Are stress reduction techniques interchangeable or do they have specific effects? In: Woolfolk R L, Lehrer P M (eds) Stress reduction techniques. Guilford Press, New York

Lehrer P M, Woolfolk R L, Rooney A J, McCann B, Carrington P 1983b Progressive relaxation and meditation: a study of psychophysiological and therapeutic differences between two techniques. Behaviour Research and Therapy 21: 651–662

Lehrer P M, Batey D M, Woolfolk R L, Remde A, Garlick T 1988 The effect of repeated tense-release sequences on EMG and self-report of muscle tension: an evaluation of Jacobsonian and post-Jacobsonian assumptions about progressive relaxation. Psychophysiology 25: 562–567

Leibowitz J, Connington B 1990 The Alexander technique. Souvenir Press, London

Levi L 1974 Psychosocial stress and disease: a conceptual model. In: Gunderson E K, Rahe R H (eds) Life stress and illness. Charles C Thomas, Springfield, Illinois

Lewis B I 1954 Chronic hyperventilation syndrome. Journal of the American Medical Association 155: 1204–1208

Ley P 1967 Communication. Staples Press, London

Ley P, Spelman S 1967 Communicating with the patient. Staples Press, London

Ley R 1985 Agoraphobia, the panic attack and the hyperventilation syndrome. Clinical Psychology Review 5: 271–285

Ley R 1988 Panic attacks during relaxation and relaxation-induced anxiety: a hyperventilation interpretation. Journal of Behaviour Therapy and Experimental Psychiatry 19: 253–259

Lichstein K L 1983 Ocular relaxation as a treatment for insomnia. Behavioural Counselling and Community Interventions 3: 178–185

Lichstein K L 1988 Clinical relaxation strategies. John Wiley, New York

Lichstein K L, Sallis J F 1982 Ocular relaxation to reduce eye movements. Cognitive Therapy and Research 6: 113–118

Lichstein K L, Sallis J F, Hill D, Young M C 1981 Psychophysiological adaptation: an investigation of multiple parameters. Journal of Behavioural Assessment 3: 111–121

Lindsay W R, Hood E H 1982 A cognitive anxiety questionnaire. Unpublished, University of Sheffield

Looker T, Gregson O 1989 Stresswise: a practical guide for dealing with stress. Hodder and Stoughton, London

Lucic K S, Steffen J J, Harrigan J A, Stuebing R C 1991 Progressive relaxation training: muscle contractions before relaxation? Behaviour Therapy 22: 249–256

Lum L C 1977 Breathing exercises in the treatment of hyperventilation and chronic anxiety states. The Chest, Heart and Stroke Journal 2: 6–11

Lum L C 1981 Hyperventilation and anxiety state. Journal of the Royal Society of Medicine 74: 1–4

Luthe W 1962 Autogenic training: method, research and application in psychiatry. Diseases of the Nervous System 23: 383–392

Luthe W (ed) 1965 Autogenic training: psychosomatic correlations. Grune and Stratton, New York

Luthe W (ed) 1969 Autogenic therapy. Grune and Stratton, New York, Vol 1

Luthe W 1970 Research and theory. In: Luthe W (ed) Autogenic therapy. Grune and Stratton, New York, vol 4

Lyman B, Bernadin S, Thomas S 1980 Frequency of imagery in emotional experience. Perceptual and Motor Skills 50: 1159–1162

Lynn S J, Rhue J W 1977 Hypnosis, imagination and fantasy. Journal of Mental Imagery 11: 101–113

McCaffrey M 1979 Nursing management of the patient with pain, 2nd edn. J B Lippincott, Philadelphia

McCormack G L 1992 The therapeutic benefits of the relaxation response. Occupational Therapy Practice 4: 51–60

McGuigan F J 1971 Covert linguistic behaviour in deaf subjects during thinking. Journal of Comparative and Physiological Psychology 75: 417–420

McGuigan F J 1981 Calm down: a guide for stress and tension control. Prentice-Hall, Englewood Cliffs, New Jersey

McGuigan F J 1984 Progressive relaxation: origins, principles and clinical applications. In: Woolfolk R L and Lehrer P M (eds) Principles and practice of stress management. Guilford Press, New York

McKenna J (ed) 1988 Obstetrics and gynaecology. Churchill Livingstone, Edinburgh

Madders J 1981 Stress and relaxation: self-help ways to cope with stress and relieve nervous tension, ulcers, insomnia, migraine and high blood pressure, 3rd edn. Martin Dunitz, London.

Magnus R 1926 Some results of studies in the physiology of posture. Lancet 211(2): 531–536, 585–588

Maisel E (ed) 1974 The Alexander technique: essential writings of F M Alexander. Thames and Hudson, London

Maltz M 1966 Psycho-cybernetics. Pocket Books, New York

Martin C J, Ripley H, Reynolds J 1976 Chest physiotherapy and the distribution of ventilation. Chest 69: 174–178

Martinsen E W 1990 Physical fitness, anxiety and depression. British Journal of Hospital Medicine 43: 194–199

Martinsen E W, Medhus A, Sandvik L 1985 Effects of aerobic exercise on depression: a controlled study. British Medical Journal 291: 109

Mead G H 1934 Mind, self and society. Chicago University Press, Chicago

Meichenbaum D 1977 Cognitive behaviour modification: an integrative approach. Plenum Press, New York

Meichenbaum D, Cameron R 1974 Modifying what clients say to themselves. In: Mahoney M J, Thoresen C E (eds) Self-control: power to the person. Brooks/Cole, Monterey, California

Meichenbaum D, Cameron R 1983 Stress inoculation training. In: Meichenbaum D, Jaremko M E (eds) Stress reduction and prevention. Plenum Press, New York

Melzack R, Wall P D 1965 Pain mechanisms: a new theory. Science 150: 971–979

Mitchell L 1987 Simple relaxation: the Mitchell method for easing tension, 2nd edn. John Murray, London

Morris J N, Clayton D G, Everitt M G, Semmence A M, Burgess E H 1990 Exercise in leisure time: coronary attack and death rates. British Heart Journal 63: 325–334

Munk-Jensen N, Pors Nielsen S, Obel E B, Bonne Eriksen P 1988 Reversal of post-menopausal vertebral bone loss by oestrogen and progesterone: a double-blind placebo controlled study. British Medical Journal 296: 1150–1152

Neimeyer R A 1985 Personal constructs in clinical practice. In: Kendall P C (ed) Advances in cognitive-behavioural research and therapy. Volume 4. Academic Press, Orlando

Nelson L, Esler M D, Jennings G L, Korner P 1986 Effect of changing levels of physical activity on blood pressure and haemodynamics in essential hypertension. Lancet 2: 473–479

Neptune E C 1977 An investigation of the effect of meditation training in a cigarette smoking extinguishment programme. Dissertation Abstracts International 39 416B. University microfilms order number 7811433

Noble E 1980 Essential exercises for the childbearing year. John Murray, London

Noble E 1988 Maternal effort during labour and delivery. In: McKenna J (ed) Obstetrics and gynaecology. Churchill Livingstone, Edinburgh

O'Brien P 1988 Birth and our bodies. Pandora, London

Olton D S, Noonberg A R 1980 Biofeedback: clinical applications in behavioural medicine. Prentice-Hall, Englewood Cliffs, New Jersey

Onda A 1967 Zen, autogenic training and hypnotism. Psychologia 10: 133–136

Ornstein R E 1975 The Psychology of consciousness. Penguin. Hardmondsworth

Öst L G 1987 Applied relaxation: description of a coping technique and review of controlled studies. Behaviour Research and Therapy 25: 397–407

Öst L G 1988 Applied relaxation versus progressive relaxation in the treatment of panic disorder. Behaviour Research and Therapy 26: 13–22

Oyle I 1976a The healing mind. Pocket Books, New York

Oyle I 1976b Magic, mysticism and modern medicine. Celestial Arts, Millbrae, California

Paffenbarger R S, Hyde R T, Wing A L, Hsieh C C 1986 Physical activity: all causes mortality and longevity of college alumni. New England Journal of Medicine 314: 605–613

Partridge C, Barnitt R 1986 Research guidelines: a handbook for therapists. Heinemann, London

Patel C 1984 Yogic therapy. In: Woolfolk R L, Lehrer P M (eds) Principles and practice of stress management. Guilford Press, New York

Patel C, Marmot M G 1988 Can general practitioners use training in relaxation and management of stress to reduce mild hypertension? British Medical Journal 296: 21–24

Patel C, Marmot M G, Terry D Y 1981 A controlled study of biofeedback-aided behavioural methods in reducing mild hypertension. British Medical Journal 282: 2005–2008

Paul G L 1966 The specific control of anxiety: 'hypnosis' and 'conditioning'. In: Oseas L (chair) Innovations in therapeutic interactions. Symposium presented at the Meeting of the American Psychological Association, New York March

Paul G L 1969 Physiological effects of relaxation training and hypnotic suggestion. Journal of Abnormal Psychology 74: 425–437

Paul G L, Trimble R W 1970 Recorded versus live relaxation and hypnotic suggestion: comparative effectiveness for reducing physiological arousal and inhibiting stress responses. Behaviour Therapy 1: 285–302

Pavlov I P 1938 Conditioned reflexes. (Translated by Milford H.) Oxford University Press, Oxford

Payne R A 1986 Health Education for small groups, Physiotherapy 72: 56–57

Payne R A 1989 Glad to be yourself: a course of practical relaxation and health education talks. Physiotherapy 75: 8–9

Payne R A, Rowland Payne C M E, Marks R 1985 Stress does not worsen psoriasis? A controlled study of 32 patients. Clinical and Experimental Dermatology 10: 239–245

Pearce J C 1982 The bond of power: meditation and wholeness. Routledge and Kegan Paul, London

Pennebaker J W 1985 Traumatic experience and psychosomatic disease: exploring the roles of behavioural inhibition, obsession and confiding. Canadian Psychology 26: 82–95

Perls F 1969 Gestalt therapy verbatim. Real People Press, Lafayette, California

Peveler R, Johnston D W 1986 Subjective and cognitive effects of relaxation. Behaviour Research and Therapy 24: 413–420

Polden M, Mantle J 1990 Physiotherapy in obstetrics and gynaecology. Butterworth Heinemann, Oxford

Pope K S, Singer J L 1978 The stream of consciousness: scientific investigations into the flow of human experience. Plenum Press, New York

Poppen R 1988 Behavioural relaxation training and assessment. Pergamon Press, Oxford

Poppen R, Maurer J 1982 Electromyographic analysis of relaxed postures. Biofeedback and Self-regulation 7: 491–498

Porritt L 1984 Communication: choices for nurses. Churchill Livingstone, Melbourne

Powell K E, Thompson P D, Casperson C W, Kendrick J S 1987 Physical activity and the incidence of coronary heart disease. Annual Review of Public Health 8: 253–287

Powell T J 1987 Anxiety management groups in clinical

practice: a preliminary report. Behavioural Psychotherapy 15: 181–187

Powell T J, Enright S J 1990 Anxiety and stress management. Routledge, London

Priest J, Schott J 1991 Leading antenatal classes: a practical guide. Butterworth Heinemann, Oxford

Ransford C P 1982 A role for amines in the anti-depressant effect of exercise: a review. Medical Science of Sports and Exercise 14: 1–10

Read M 1984 Sports medicine: a unique guide to self-diagnosis and rehabilitation. Breslich and Foss, London

Remocker A J, Storch E T 1992 Action speaks louder: a handbook of structured group techniques, 5th edn. Churchill Livingstone, Edinburgh

Rimm D C, Masters J C 1974 Behaviour therapy: techniques and empirical findings. Academic Press, New York

Rogers A W 1992 Textbook of anatomy. Churchill Livingstone, Edinburgh

Rosa K R 1976 Autogenic training. Victor Gollancz, London

Rowbottom I 1992 The physiotherapy management of chronic hyperventilation. Journal of the Association of Chartered Physiotherapists in Respiratory Conditions 21: 9–12

Royal College of Physicians (London) 1991 Medical aspects of exercise: benefits and risks. RCP, London

Safran M R, Seaber A V, Garrett W E 1989 Warm-up and muscular prevention. Sports Medicine 8: 239–249

Salkovskis P M 1988 Hyperventilation and anxiety. Current Opinion in Psychiatry 1: 76–82

Samuels M, Samuels N 1975 Seeing with the mind's eye: the history, technique and uses of visualization. Random House, Toronto

Schilling D J, Poppen R 1983 Behavioural relaxation training and assessment. Journal of Behaviour Therapy and Experimental Psychiatry 14: 99–107

Schultz J H, Luthe W 1969 Autogenic methods. Grune and Stratton, New York

Schwartz J L 1987 Smoking cessation methods: the United States and Canada 1978–1985. National Cancer Institute, National Institutes of Health, Washington D C, NIH Publication number 87: 2940

Schwartz G E, Davidson R J, Goleman D T 1978 Patterning of cognitive and somatic processes in the self-regulation of anxiety: effects of meditation versus exercise. Psychosomatic Medicine 40: 321–328

Selye H 1956 The stress of life. McGraw-Hill, New York

Selye H 1974 Stress without distress. New American Library of Canada, Scarborough

Sheehan P W 1972 The function and nature of imagery. Academic Press, New York

Sheikh A A 1983 Imagery: current theory, research and application. Wiley, New York

Shiffman S 1982 Relapse following smoking cessation: a situational analysis. Journal of Consulting and Clinical Psychology 50: 71–86

Shiffman S 1985 Coping with temptations to smoke. In: Shiffman S, Wills T A (eds) Coping and substance use. Academic Press, New York

Shone R 1982 Autohypnosis: a step by step guide to self-hypnosis. Thorsons, Wellingborough, Northamptonshire

Shone R 1984 Creative visualization. Thorsons, Wellingborough, Northamptonshire

Sibbald B, Addington-Hall J, Brenneman D, Freeling P 1993

Counsellors in English and Welsh general practices: their nature and distribution. British Medical Journal 306: 29–33

Siegel E 1988 Stress management with staff groups. In: Zahourek R P (ed) Relaxation and imagery: tools for therapeutic communication and intervention. W B Saunders, Philadelphia

Sime W E 1990 Discussion: exercise, fitness and mental health. In: Bouchard C, Shephard R J, Stephens T, Sutton J R, McPherson B D (eds) Exercise, fitness and health: a consensus of current knowledge. Human Kinetics Books, Champaign, Illinois

Simonton O C, Matthews-Simonton S, Creighton J L 1986 Getting well again. Bantam, London

Singer J L 1975 The inner world of day-dreaming. Harper and Row, New York

Singer J L 1976 Daydreaming and fantasy. Oxford University Press, Oxford

Skinner B F 1938 The behaviour of organisms. Appleton Century Crofts, New York

Slonim N B, Hamilton L H 1976 Respiratory physiology, 3rd edn. C V Mosby, St Louis

Smith E, Wilks N 1988 Meditation. Optima, London

Snow-Harter C, Bouxsein M L, Lewis B T, Carter D, Marcus R 1992 Effects of resistance and endurance exercise on bone mineral status of young women: a randomized exercise intervention trial. Journal of Bone Mineral Research 7: 761–769

Snyder M 1985 Independent nursing interventions. John Wiley, New York

Spinhoven P, Corry A, Linssen G, Van Dyke R, Zitman F G 1992 Autogenic training and self-hypnosis in the control of tension headache. General Hospital Psychiatry 14: 408–415

Stevens J O 1971 Awareness: exploring, experimenting, experiencing. Real People Press, Moab, Utah

Stradling J 1983 Respiratory physiology in labour. Journal of the Association of Chartered Physiotherapists in Obstetrics and Gynaecology 53: 5–7

Stroebel C 1978 Quieting response training. Audio cassettes British Medical Association, London

Strongman K T 1987 The psychology of emotion. John Wiley, Chichester

Sutcliffe J 1991 The complete book of relaxation techniques. Quarto Publishing, London

Sweeney S S 1978 Relaxation. In: Carlson C, Blackwell B (eds) Behavioural concepts and nursing interventions, 2nd edn. J B Lippincott, Philadelphia

Szasz T, Hollander M H 1956 A contribution to the philosophy of medicine: basic models of doctor–patient relationship. American Medical Association Archives of Internal Medicine 97: 585–592

Talmage R V, Stinnett S S, Landwehr J T, Vincent L M, McCartney W H 1986 Age-related loss of bone mineral density in non-athletic and atheltic women. Bone Mineral 1: 115–125

Thyer B A 1983 Behaviour modification in social work practice. In: Herson M, Eisler R M, Miller P M (eds) Progress in Behaviour Modification 15: 173–216. Academic Press, New York

Titlebaum H 1988 Relaxation. In: Zahourek R P (ed) Relaxation and imagery: tools for therapeutic communication and intervention. W B Saunders, Philadelphia

Tschudin V 1991 Beginning with awareness: a learner's handbook. Churchill Livingstone, Edinburgh

Twomey L T 1993 Lumbar biomechanics and physical therapy. Journal of the Organization of Chartered Physiotherapists in Private Practice 70: 14–19

Twomey L T, Taylor J R 1987 Physical therapy of the low back. Churchill Livingstone, New York

US Preventive Services Task Force 1989 Exercise counselling. In: Guide to clinical preventive services 49: 297–303. Williams and Wilkins, Baltimore

Valentine E R 1993 The effect of lessons in the Alexander technique on music performance in high and low stress situations. Paper presented the 2nd International Conference on Psychology and the Performing Arts, Institute of Psychiatry, London, September

Van Hooff J A 1972 A comparative approach to the phylogeny of laughter and smiling. In: Hinde R A (ed) Non-verbal communication, Cambridge University Press, Cambridge

Van Montfrans G A, Karemaker J M, Wieling W, Dunning A J 1990 Relaxation therapy and continuous ambulatory blood pressure in mild hypertension: a controlled study. British Medical Journal 300: 1368–1371

Vissing Y, Burke M 1984 Visualization techniques for health care workers. Journal of Psychosocial Nursing and Mental Health Services 22: 29–32

Waddington P J 1983 Basic anatomy. In: Downie P A (ed) Cash's textbook of chest, heart and vascular disorders for physiotherapists, 3rd edn. Faber and Faber, London

Wallace A 1989 An active role for patients in stress management. The Professional Nurse 5: 65–72

Wallace J M 1980 Muscular relaxation. In: Look after yourself. Health Education Authority, London

Wallace R K, Benson H 1972 The philosophy of meditation. Scientific American 226: 84–90

Waxman D 1981 Hypnosis: a guide for patients and practitioners. Unwin Paperbacks, London

Welford A T 1973 Stress and performance. Ergonomics 16: 567

West M A 1987 The psychology of meditation. Oxford Science, Oxford

Williams M, Booth D 1985 Antenatal education: guidelines for teachers, 2nd edn. Churchill Livingstone, Edinburgh

Wilson K J W 1990 Ross and Wilson anatomy and physiology in health and illness, 7th edn. Churchill Livingstone, Edinburgh, pp. 123, 268, 269, 316

Wolpe J 1958 Psychotherapy by reciprocal inhibition. Stanford University Press, Stanford

Wolpe J 1969 The practice of behaviour therapy. Pergamon Press, Oxford

Wolpe J 1973 The practice of behaviour therapy, 2nd edn. Pergamon Press, New York

Wolpe J, Lazarus A A 1966 Behaviour therapy techniques. Pergamon Press, New York

Wood C 1984 Living in overdrive. Fontana, London

Woolfolk R L, Lehrer P M (eds) 1984 Principles and practice of stress management. Guilford Press, New York

Wynd C A 1989 The use of guided imagery to enhance power for smoking change. Dissertation Abstracts International 50 08B:3408. University microfilms order number QVM 90-02682

Wynd C A 1992 Relaxation imagery used for stress reduction in the prevention of smoking relapse. Journal of Advanced Nursing 17: 294–302

Zahourek R P (ed) 1985 Clinical hypnosis and therapeutic suggestion in nursing. Grune and Stratton, Orlando, Florida

Zahourek R P (ed) 1988 Relaxation and imagery: tools for therapeutic communication and intervention. W B Saunders, Philadelphia

Zajonc R A, Murphy S T, Inglehart M 1989 Feeling and facial efference: implications of the vascular theory of emotion. Psychological Review 96: 395–416

Zigmond A S, Snaith R P 1983 The hospital anxiety and depression scale. Acta Psychiatrica Scandanavica 67: 361–370

Index

A

Abdominal (diaphragmatic) breathing, 118–9, 122
  combined relaxation methods, 197
  hyperventilation and, 121
  in meditation, 165
  on-the-spot use, 180
Acetylcholine, role of, 6
Adrenal glands, role of, 5–6, 7
Adrenaline, role of, 5–6
Aerobic exercise, 110, 114
  bone mineral content, 112
  muscles, 112
  psychological effects, 112
Affirmations, goal-directed
    visualization, 145
  on-the-spot use, 181
  for smoking, 149
After-images, meditation, 166–7
Agoraphobia
  goal-directed visualization, 151
  physical exercise, 113
Alcohol dependency, 23–4, 151
Alexander technique, 85–93
  as differential relaxation, 97
  evaluation, 93
  on-the-spot use, 179
  principles, 86–7
  procedure, 87–93
Anaerobic exercise, 110
  psychological effects, 113
Anger
  imagery for, 148, 181–2
  physiological responses, 4
  relaxation induced, 50
  stress reduction ideas, 24
Antenatal training, breathing, 183–5
Anxiety
  Alexander technique, 93
  cognitive theories, 7–8, 62
  cognitive-behaviour theories, 9
  Hospital Anxiety and Depression
    Scale, 188–9, 190
  imagery evaluated, 142
  Öst's applied relaxation method,
    62–3, 67
  physical exercise and, 113
  progressive relaxation, 35, 36
  relaxation induced, 50
  specific effects hypothesis, 9–10
  stress management, 10, 23–4
Applied relaxation, Öst's method,
    61–8, 180
Arthritis
  Mitchell relaxation, 83
  physical exercise, 112, 114
  stress-related, 23
Assagioli, R, symbolic imagery, 137–8
Assertiveness training, 9, 131–2
Asthma, 23, 160
Attention switching, 197, 203

B

Beck, A T, cognitive theories of anxiety,
    7–8
Beck Depression Inventory, 189
Behavioural relaxation training, 69–75
  behavioural relaxation scale (BRS),
    72–4, 192
  combined methods, 72, 197
  evaluation, 75
  on-the-spot use, 180
  pitfalls, 50–1
  protocol for, 70–2
  self-report, 74–5
Behavioural theories
  anxiety, 62
  relaxation, 8–9
  see also Cognitive-behavioural
    theories
Benson's relaxation response, 4, 10,
    171–3
  combined methods, 197
  Kokoszka's general theory of
    relaxation, 196
Bernstein, D A
  differential relaxation, 96
  progressive relaxation training,
    37–41
  relaxation through recall, 54–5, 179
Blood pressure
  hypertension, 23, 50, 119
  physical exercise, 111
  progressive relaxation, 50
  relaxation response method, 171–2
Bone mineral density, physical exercise,
    111–2, 114
Borkovec, T D
  differential relaxation, 96
  progressive relaxation training,
    37–41
  relaxation through recall, 54–5, 179

Autogenic training (AT), 155–160
  altered states of consciousness,
    155–6
  with behavioural relaxation, 72
  evaluation, 160
  Kokoszka's general theory of
    relaxation, 196
  on-the-spot use, 181
  pitfalls, 160
  principles of, 157
  similarities with other approaches,
    195
  technique, 157–160
Automatic thoughts, cognitive theories,
    7–8
Autonomic nervous system, 4–5, 6
  autogenic training, 160
  breathing, 116, 117, 120, 180
  progressive relaxation, 29–30, 35
  transcendental meditation, 171

Brain, laterality of, 134, 162
Breathing, 115–22
  abdominal, 118–9, 121, 122, 165,
    180, 197
  antenatal training, 183–5
  combined methods, 118, 119, 197
  cue-controlled, 66
  hyperventilation, 23–4, 51, 116,
    118, 119–22, 181, 184
  on-the-spot relaxation, 180–1
  'out tension, in peace', 119
  pitfalls, 122
  process of, 115–6
  relaxation, 115, 117–8
  tense–release script, 44, 47
Breathing meditation, 119, 164–5, 174
Breathing pouch, 119, 197
Brief (on-the-spot) relaxation, 11,
    177–82
  see also Öst's applied relaxation
BRS (behavioural relaxation scale),
    72–4, 192
Burn-out, of trainers, 16

C

Cameron, R, self-talk, 9
Cardiovascular system
  physical exercise, 110–1, 113, 114
  see also Blood pressure
Catarrh, Öst's applied relaxation,
    67–8
Catecholamines
  hyperventilation syndrome, 120,
    122
  role of, 5–6
Cathartic release, self-awareness,
    129–30
Cerebral cortex
  laterality, 134
  meditation, 162
Chakras, 140–1, 167–8
Childbirth and pregnancy, 183–6
  breathing and antenatal training,
    183–5
  Mitchell method, 83, 185
  muscular relaxation, 185
Cigarette smoking, 23–4
  goal-directed visualization, 147,
    148–50
Circular questions, group discussions,
    17
Cognitive Anxiety Questionnaire, 189
Cognitive strategies
  attention switching, 197, 202
  autogenic training, 72, 155–60, 181,
    195, 196
  hyperventilation, 122
  imagery, 143–53
  on-the-spot use, 181–82
  Öst's applied relaxation method, 62
Cognitive theories, relaxation, 7–8

Cognitive-behavioural theories, relaxation, 9
Colour imagery, 139–41, 153
  chakras, 140–1
  white light, 141, 153
Conditioning
  behaviour theory, 8–9
  cue-controlled relaxation, 62, 65–6, 180
Confidentiality, 13, 17
Consciousness, altered states of, 155–6
  Kokoszka's general theory of relaxation, 195–6
  pitfalls, 173–4
  see also Hypnosis; Meditation
Controlled breathing, in pregnancy and childbirth, 184
Coping skills, stress, 4, 20, 23–4
Coronary heart disease
  personality types, 22
  physical exercise, 110–1, 113, 114
Cortisol, role of, 6
Counting
  with breathing exercises, 118, 164–5
  relaxation through recall, 55, 179
Cramp, muscle relaxation, 50
Creep, spinal joints, 99–100
Cue-controlled relaxation, 62, 65–6, 180

D

Daydreaming, visualization, 152
Decision making
  goal-directed visualization for, 150
  self-awareness, 130
  stress-reduction, 24
Deep relaxation, definition, 11
Depersonalization, grounding for, 164, 173
Depression, 23–4
  Beck Depression Inventory, 189
  cognitive theories, 7–8
  Hospital Anxiety and Depression Scale (HAD), 188–9, 190
  physical exercise, 113
Dermatitis, stress-related, 23
Desensitization, goal-directed visualization, 151
Diaphragmatic (abdominal) breathing, 118–9, 122
  combined relaxation methods, 197
  hyperventilation, 121
  in meditation, 165
  on-the-spot use, 180
Differential relaxation, 95–7
  Bernstein & Borkovec's method, 96
  combined methods, 197
  definition, 95
  evaluation, 97
  Jacobson's method, 35, 95–6
  'mini-relaxation', 72, 97
  on-the-spot methods contrasted, 178

Öst's applied method, 62, 66–7
  use of, 96–7
'Diminishing tensions', progressive relaxation, 33
Distancing
  goal-directed visualization, 146
  in imagery, 139
  stress-reduction, 24
Distraction, behavioural principles, 9
Distress, theories of, 20
Drug dependence, 23–4
  goal-directed visualization, 151

E

Eating disorders, 23–4
  goal-directed visualization, 150–1
Electromyography (EMG)
  progressive relaxation, 29, 30
  visualization, 134
Ellis, A, cognitive theories of anxiety, 7, 8
Emergency (on-the-spot) relaxation, 177–82
  see also Öst's applied relaxation
EMG see Electromyography
Emotional fatigue, trainers, 16
End-gaining, Alexander technique, 87
Endocrine system, 5–6, 7
Endorphins, physical exercise, 113
Environmental markers
  on-the-spot relaxation, 182
  Öst's rapid relaxation, 67
Epilepsy, Öst's applied relaxation, 67–8
Eustress, theory of, 20
Everly, G S, passive neuromuscular relaxation, 54, 55–6
Exercise, physical, 109–13
Eye movements, progressive relaxation, 33–4

F

Facial feedback hypothesis, 69, 198
Facilitators, role of, 16–17
Fear, physiological responses, 4
Ferruci, P
  inner guide, 135
  symbolic imagery, 138
Fight-flight response, 4, 5, 21
Freud, S, the unconscious, 134

G

Gaze meditation, 165–7, 197
General adaptation syndrome, stress, 19–20
General Hospital Questionnaire, 189
Glucocorticoids, 6
Goal setting, stress reduction, 24
Goal-directed visualization, 143–53
  applications, 146–51
  combined methods, 197

method of, 144–6
  pitfalls, 151–3
  relaxation, 146
Goldfried, M R, training in self-control, 61
Graded exposure, behavioural principles, 9
Grounding, for depersonalization, 164, 173
Group training, 16–8
Guided imagery, 141–2, 197

H

HAD (Hospital Anxiety and Depression Scale), 188–9, 190
Handouts, group training, 18
Headaches
  autogenic training, 160
  Öst's applied relaxation, 67–8
Heart disease
  personality types, 22
  physical exercise, 110–1, 113, 114
Homework, relaxation training, 15
Hospital Anxiety and Depression Scale (HAD), 188–9, 190
Human performance curve, stress, 20
Humour therapy, 198
Hypercapnia, relaxing effects, 116, 117
Hypertension
  breathing meditation, 119
  muscle relaxation, 50
  stress-related, 23
Hyperventilation, 23–4, 116, 118, 119–22
  breathing cycle, 181
  in labour, 184
  muscular relaxation, 51
Hypnosis
  autogenic training, 155–6
  fear of, 14, 30, 38–9
  goal-directed visualization, 152–3

I

Ice-breakers, group training, 17
Imagery, 133–42
  colours, 139–41, 153
    chakras, 140–1
    white light, 141, 153
  combined methods, 118, 119, 197
  consciousness, 135
  evaluation, 142, 150
  goal-directed visualization, 143–53
    applications, 146–51
    combined methods, 197
    method of, 144–6
    pitfalls, 151–3
    relaxation, 146
  guided, 141–2, 197
  laterality, 134
  Madders' passive relaxation, 54, 58
  metaphor in, 138–9

on-the-spot use, 181–2
passive relaxation, 54, 55–6
pitfalls, 50, 151–3
in pregnancy and childbirth, 185
procedures, 136
relaxation for, 136
self-awareness, 131–2
single senses explored, 136–7
symbolic, 137–8
therapeutic effects, 135
the unconscious, 134–5
Immediate (on-the-spot) relaxation,
    177–82
see also Öst's applied relaxation
Immune system, cortisol, 6
Inhibition, Alexander technique, 87
Inner guides, imagery, 135
Insomnia, 23–4, 34
Instant (on-the-spot) relaxation,
    177–82
see also Öst's applied relaxation
Instructors
    requirements for, 16
    supervisory back-up, 16
Interviews, assessing relaxation, 188–9
Intuition, self-awareness, 129

J

Jacobson's progressive relaxation, 6–7,
    10, 29–36
    contrasted with progressive
        relaxation training, 38–9
    differential method, 35, 95–6
    passive method, 53, 54
    pitfalls, 50–1, 151–3
    tense–release script, 43–50
Joint changes, Mitchell relaxation
    method, 77–83, 97, 185
Joints
    lotus position for meditation, 174
    physical exercise, 112, 114
    stretching exercises, 99–100
Jung, C G, the unconscious, 134–5

K

Kelly, G A, personal constructs, 8
Kermani, K S, scanning technique, 59,
    180
Key changes, Mitchell method, 82–3,
    97
Kinaesthetic sense, imagery, 137
Kokoszka, A, general theory of
    relaxation, 195–6

L

Labour and pregnancy, relaxation
    techniques for, 182–6
    Mitchell method, 83, 185
Laterality, cerebral cortex, 134, 162
Laughter therapy, 198

Ligaments, physical exercise, 112
Lotus position, meditation, 174

M

Madders' method, passive relaxation,
    54, 57–9
Mandala, meditation, 165–6
Mantras, meditation, 168–9, 197
Massage, in pregnancy and childbirth,
    185
Meditation, 161–9
    benefits of, 162
    breathing type, 119
    combined methods, 72, 197
    evaluation, 169
    focal points, 164–9
        body parts, 167–8
        breaths, 164–5, 174
        mantras, 168–9
        visual objects, 165–7, 197
    Kokoszka's general theory of
        relaxation, 196
    pitfalls, 173–4
        relaxation response, 171–4
    procedure for, 163–4
    similarities with other approaches,
        195
    transcendental (TM), 169
Meichenbaum, D, self-talk, 9
Menopause, bone mineral density,
    111–2
Mental illness, contraindicated
    relaxation methods, 50, 151–2,
    173
Metaphor, in imagery, 138–9
Migraine, Öst's applied relaxation,
    67–8
'Mini-relaxation', 72, 97
Mitchell method, 77–83
    combined methods, 197
    as differential relaxation, 97
    evaluation, 83
    keys and triggers, 82–3
    on-the-spot relaxation, 179
    pitfalls, 50–1
    in pregnancy, 83, 185
    procedure for, 78–82
    rationale of, 77–8
    three-point pull, 83, 179
Monkey position, Alexander technique,
    90, 91, 93
Muscle tone, 30
Muscles, physical exercise, 112, 113
Muscular relaxation
    Alexander technique, 85–93, 179
    applied methods, 61–8
    behavioural principles, 9
    behavioural relaxation training,
        69–75, 180
    Mitchell method, 77–83, 97, 179,
        185, 197
    on-the-spot methods, 178–9

Öst's applied method, 61–8, 177–8,
    180
physical exercise, 109–14
pitfalls, 50–1, 151–3
in pregnancy and childbirth, 185
progressive relaxation, 6–7, 29–36,
    38–9
progressive relaxation training,
    37–41
self-awareness, 130
stretchings, 99–107, 179
tense–release script, 43–51
see also Differential relaxation;
    Passive muscular relaxation
Musculature, skeletal, 6–7
    explanation for trainees, 14
    Jacobson's work on, 29–30
    progressive relaxation, 29–30

N

Neurodermatitis, stress-related, 23
Neuromuscular system
    effects of stress, 6–7
    passive relaxation, 54, 55–6
    progressive relaxation, 29–30, 35–6
Noradrenaline, role of, 5–6

O

Obstetrics, relaxation in, 183–6
    Mitchell method, 83, 185
Oestrogen therapy, bone mineral
    density, 111, 112
On-the-spot relaxation, 177–82
    characteristics, 178
    cognitive, 181–2
    influencing factors, 178
    physical actions, 178–9
    see also Öst's applied relaxation
Osteoarthritis, physical exercise, 112,
    114
Öst's applied relaxation method, 61–8
    anxiety, 62–3, 67
    conditions for and introduction to,
        63–4
    cue-controlled, 62, 65–6, 180
    differential relaxation, 66–7
    evaluation, 67–8
    on-the-spot use, 180
    pitfalls, 50–1
    rapid relaxation, 62, 67, 177–8
    release-only, 64–5
    tense–release, 64
Overbreathing (hyperventilation),
    23–4, 116, 119–22
    in labour, 184
    muscular relaxation, 51

P

Pain
    goal-directed visualization for, 151

Pain (*contd.*)
  Öst's applied relaxation, 67–8
  in pregnancy and childbirth, 183–6
  progressive relaxation, 50–1
Panic disorders, 23–4
  hyperventilation, 121–2
  imagery for, 151, 181–2
  Öst's applied method, 62–3, 67–8
  physical exercise, 113
Parasympathetic nervous system, 4–5, 6
  breathing, 116, 117, 180
  progressive relaxation, 35
Passive attitude, relaxation response, 172, 173
Passive concentration, meditation, 162
Passive muscular relaxation, 53–9
  combined methods, 197
  Kermani's scanning technique, 59, 180
  Madders' method, 54, 57–9
  Öst's applied relaxation, release-only, 64–5
  pitfalls, 50–1, 59, 151–3
  procedure for, 57–9
  relaxation through recall, 37, 54–5, 96, 179
  scanning, 59, 179–80
Passive neuromuscular relaxation, 54, 55–6
Peptic ulcers, stress-related, 23
Personal constructs, cognitive theories, 8
Personality types, stress, 22–3
Physical exercise, 109–14
  bone mineral density, 111–2, 114
  cardiovascular system, 110–1, 113, 114
  muscles, ligaments and joints, 112
  pitfalls, 113–4
  psychological aspects, 112–3
  recommended levels, 109–10
Placebo effects, relaxation training, 192
Poppen, R
  behavioural relaxation training, 69–75, 197
  behavioural relaxation scale (BRS), 72–4, 192
  mini-relaxation, 72, 97
  on-the-spot use, 180
  self-rating scales, 74, 190, 191
Positive self-statements, goal-directed visualization, 145
  on-the-spot use, 181
  smoking, 148
Post-hypnotic suggestion, 152–3
Postural feedback hypothesis, 69, 198
Posture
  Alexander technique, 85–93
  behavioural relaxation training, 69–75, 180
  differential relaxation, 96–7
  Mitchell relaxation method, 77–8, 179

on-the-spot relaxation, 179
Pregnancy and childbirth, 183–6
  breathing and antenatal training, 183–5
  massage, 185
  Mitchell method, 83, 185
  muscular relaxation, 185
  visualization in, 185
Primary control, Alexander technique, 86, 88–9
Problem solving
  goal-directed visualization, 150, 151
  stress reduction, 24
Progesterone therapy, bone mineral density, 112
Programmed visualization, 145–6
  for smoking, 149—80
Progressive relaxation, 6–7, 10, 29–36
  combined methods, 197
  differential method, 35, 66–7, 72, 95–7
  'diminishing tensions', 33
  evaluation, 35–6
  eye movements, 33–4
  Kokoszka's general theory of relaxation, 196
  Öst's applied method, 61–8
  pitfalls, 50–1, 151–3
  procedure for, 30–5
  progressive relaxation training contrasted, 38–9
  self-operations control, 35
  similarities with other approaches, 195
  speech movements, 34–5
  tense–release script, 43–50
  see also Passive muscular relaxation
Progressive relaxation training (PRT), 37–41
  evaluation, 41
  pitfalls, 50–1, 151–3
  procedure, 39–40
  progressive relaxation contrasted, 38–9
  relaxation through recall, 37, 54–5, 96
Psychoanalysis, meditation, 174
Psychoses, contraindicated relaxation methods, 50, 151–2, 173
Psychosomatic illness, 23–4
'Punching position', Mitchell method, 77–8, 79

Q

Questionnaires, assessing relaxation, 188–9, 190
Quick (on-the-spot) relaxation, 177–82
  see also Öst's applied relaxation

R

Rapid relaxation, Öst's applied method, 62, 67, 177–8

Rebreathing, for hyperventilation, 121
Recall, relaxation through, 37, 54–5, 96, 179
Receptive visualization, 145
  for smoking, 148
Reciprocal inhibition, Mitchell method, 77–8
Relaxation
  definitions and aims, 3–4
  Kokoszka's general theory of, 195–6
  physiological theories, 4–7
  psychological theories, 7–9
  'specific effects' hypothesis, 9–10
  techniques for, 10–1
  unitary theories, 10
Relaxation through recall, 37, 54–5, 96, 179
Relaxation response method, 4, 10, 171–4
  combined methods, 197
  evaluation, 173
  features of, 173
  Kokoszka's general theory of relaxation, 196
  origins of, 171–2
  pitfalls, 173–4
  procedure for, 172–3
Relaxation ripple, 56, 180
Relaxation training
  assessment and research, 187–93
  measuring relaxation, 188
  physiological measurement, 191–3
  questionnaires, 188–9, 190
  self-rating, 189–91
  combined approaches, 197–8
  confidentiality, 13
  delivery, 15
  groups, 16–8
  homework, 15
  individual autonomy, 16
  introduction of methods, 14–5
  nature of stress, 23–4
  number of sessions, 16
  pitfalls, 16
  positions for, 13–4
  settings for, 13
  similarities between approaches, 195
  supervisory back-up, 16
  termination, 15
  trainers, 16
Release-only relaxation, 33
  Madders' method, 54, 57–9
  Öst's applied method, 62, 64–5
  passive neuromuscular method, 54, 55–6
  relaxation through recall, 37, 54–5, 96, 179
Research methods, relaxation, 192–3
Respiratory mechanism, 115–6
  see also Breathing
Rheumatoid arthritis, stress-related, 23
Ripple of relaxation, 56, 180
Rosenfeld, R, passive neuromuscular relaxation, 54, 55–6

S

Scanning, passive muscular relaxation, 59, 67, 179–80
Schilling, D J, behavioural relaxation training, 69–75, 197
  behavioural relaxation scale (BRS), 72–4, 192
Self-awareness, 127–32
  benefits and pitfalls, 132
  combined methods, 197
  environment, 130
  feelings (emotions), 129–30
  intuition, 129
  listening to one's body, 130
  relations with others, 130–1
    assertiveness, 9, 131–2
  thinking styles, 128
  through meditation, 162
Self-disclosure, use of, 129
Self-help groups, 17
Self-hypnosis, 156
  see also Autogenic training
Self-operations control, progressive relaxation, 35
Self-rating scales, relaxation training, 74–5, 189–91
Self-statements, goal-directed visualization, 145
  on-the-spot use, 181
  for smoking, 148
Self-talk
  cognitive-behavioural principles, 9
  on-the-spot relaxation, 181
Sleep
  during relaxation sessions, 18
  insomnia, 23–4, 34
Smiling therapy, 182, 198
Smoking, 23–4
  goal-directed visualization, 147, 148–50
Social Readjustment Rating Scale, 21, 22
Social skills
  assertiveness, 9, 131–2
  stress reduction ideas, 24
'Specific effects' hypothesis, 9–10
Speech movements, progressive relaxation, 34–5
Stress
  aims of relaxation, 3–4
  cognitive theories of, 7–8
  measurements, 21
  reduction of, 24
  relaxation training for, 23–4
  sources, 21–3
  symptoms, 21
  theories, 19–20
Stress management, 23–4
  definitions, 10
Stretchings, 99–107
  benefits of, 99–100
  combined methods, 197
  on-the-spot use, 179
  pitfalls, 105–7
  procedures, 100–5
Substance dependency, 23–4
  goal-directed visualization for, 151
Suggestion
  autogenic training, 156
  passive neuromuscular relaxation, 54, 55–6
  progressive relaxation and progressive relaxation training, 30, 38–9
Supervisory back-up, trainers, 16
Symbolic imagery, 137–8
Sympathetic nervous system, 4, 5
  breathing, 116, 120, 121, 180
  progressive relaxation, 30, 35
  transcendental meditation, 171

T

Tapes, use of, 15
Tense–release technique, 6–7, 29–36
  combined methods, 197
  origin of, 29
  Öst's applied relaxation, 62, 64
  pitfalls, 50–1, 151–3
  progressive relaxation training (PRT), 37–41
  script for, 43–50
Termination procedures, relaxation training, 15
Therapists
  requirements for, 16
  supervisory back-up, 16
Thinking styles
  cognitive theories, 8
  self-awareness, 128
Three-point pull, Mitchell method, 83, 179
Thyrotoxicosis, stress-related, 23
Time management, stress reduction, 24

Tinnitus, Öst's applied relaxation, 67–8
TM (transcendental meditation), 169
Tobacco dependency, 23–4
  goal-directed visualization, 147, 148–50
Trainers
  requirements for, 16
  supervisory back-up, 16
Trances, 155–6
  see also Hypnosis
Tranquillizer dependency, 23–4
Transcendental meditation (TM), 169
Transformations, in imagery, 139, 181–2
Triggers of tension, Mitchell method, 82–3

U

Ulcerative colitis, stress-related, 23
Unconscious, the, 134–5
Underbreathing, 116
Unitary theories, relaxation, 10

V

Visualization, 133–42
  combined methods, 197
  goal-directed, 143–53
    applications, 146–51
    method of, 144–6
    pitfalls, 151–3
    relaxation, 146
  Madders' passive relaxation, 54, 58
  on-the-spot use, 181–2
  in pregnancy and childbirth, 185
Voice tone, relaxation procedures, 15

W

Warming up and down, physical exercise, 113
White light, colour imagery, 141, 153
Work environment, stress sources, 21–2

Y

Yantra, meditation, 165–6
Yoga, 167–8